For Ballardians everywhere...

The JG Ballard Book

THE TERMINAL PRESS
2013

The Command Module...

Publisher & Editor Rick McGrath
Cover Painting of JG Ballard Luca Del Baldo
Photography Ana Barrado, Andy Best, Peter Brigg
Book Design & all unattributed Art & Photography Rick McGrath
Proofreader Christy Siegler

The publisher gratefully acknowledges that material by
JG Ballard is used with the kind permission of The Estate of JG Ballard

First Printing

The Terminal Press
135 MacPherson Avenue,
Toronto, Ontario
M5R 1W9 Canada

Set in 12pt Minion Pro

ISBN: 978-0-9918665-0-2

Copyright © 2013 The Terminal Press. All rights reserved.

All Ana Barrado photographs copyright © Ana Barrado. All rights reserved.
All texts copyright © 2013 the writers. All rights reserved.

No part of this book may be reproduced by any means, in any media,
electronic or mechanical, including motion picture film, video, photocopy, recording,
or any other information storage retrieval system, without prior
permission in writing from the publisher.

Reprinted by permission of Farrar, Straus and Giroux, LLC:
Excerpt from *Concrete Island* by JG Ballard. Copyright © 1973 by JG Ballard.
Excerpts from *Crash* by JG Ballard. Copyright © 1973 by JG Ballard.
Excerpts from *The Crystal World* by JG Ballard.
Copyright © 1966, renewed 1994 by JG Ballard.
Excerpt from *The Kindness of Women* by JG Ballard. Copyright © 1991 by JG Ballard.
Excerpts from *War Fever* by JG Ballard. Copyright © 1990 by JG Ballard.

"JG Ballard: Time Out of Mind" by Peter Brigg
was first published in *Extrapolation*, Vol. 35, No. 1, 1994.
"The Impossibility Exhibition" by Paul A Green was written for Jeremy Welsh's
video tribute to JG Ballard, *Terminal Zones*, which was screened at the
London Filmmakers' Co-op in May 1990 as part of the "Apocalypse Culture" series.
"Visualizing the Ballardian Image" by Rick Poynor was first published in two parts on
the *Design Observer* website in February and March 2011.
"Interview with JG Ballard: Psychoanalyst of the Electronic Age" by David Pringle was
first published in *Words: The New Literary Forum*, Vol. 1, No. 4, September 1985.
"Ballardoscope: Some Attempts at Approaching the Writer as a Visionary" by Jordi Costa
was first published in *JG Ballard Autòpsia del nou millenni*, Barcelona, 2008.

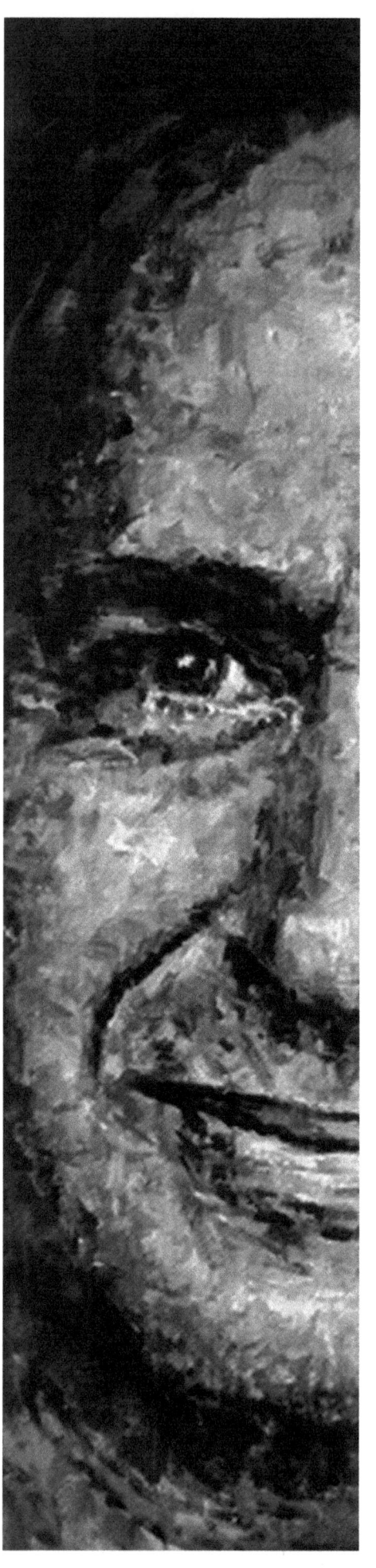

...The Impact Zone

Planes intersect: on one level... billboards...

David Pringle	Interview with JG Ballard: Psychoanalyst of the Electronic Age	8
James Goddard	"Everything is Science Fiction!"	16
Anonymous	The *Repsychling* Interview	32
James Goddard	JG Ballard's Annotations to the 1970 Goddard Bibliography	40
James Goddard	Goddard & Pringle, Interviewers; JG Ballard, Editor	70

Planes intersect: on another level, the immediate personal environment...

Mike Bonsall	JG Ballard in the Dissecting Room	88
James Goddard	JG Ballard's Own Short Story Bibliography	102
Mike Holliday	Desperate Measures: A History of *The Atrocity Exhibition*	104
Rick Poynor	Visualizing the Ballardian Image	116
Peter Brigg	JG Ballard: Time Out of Mind	130
Rick McGrath	JG Ballard's Shanghai	142

Planes intersect: on a third level, the inner world of the psyche...

Jordi Costa	Ballardoscope: Some Attempts at Approaching the Writer as a Visionary	162
Samuel Francis	JG Ballard: A Few Brief Queries	172
Paul A Green	The Impossibility Exhibition	180
Toby Litt	J.G.B. U.X.B.	189

ANA BARRADO
Roman girl statue in front of Caesar's Palace Casino, Las Vegas, 1992

Later, as he sat...

The JG Ballard Book began in the Fall of 2012 when fellow Ballardian James Goddard suggested I jump into the pit and/or pendulum of publishing. He had friends who were seriously involved, and James had even published a little paperback himself. Easy peasy, he said.

Sure, I thought, I could make a book—my background as an adman gave me the technical proficiency—but what about content? Better yet, what about great content? Thinking about it for a moment I had to assume, given the daring and disparate brainpower attracted by Ballard, that finding intelligent yet interesting articles shouldn't be that difficult a problem.

So off the missives went, enigmatic requests for *Interesting Content* to the usual suspects, with vague outlines of not much of an idea of what a book about JG Ballard might actually be, much less include. The general thinking was to do something accessible to the Ballard reader who wants to be entertained as well as informed—and maybe enjoy something unique in all the Ballard literature—in a book that's a sort of an extention of Val Vale's all-bow-to-big-and-bold *Re/Search 8/9*. No theme? Then if nothing else, let the contents be eclectic. No point being specific—let's see what the wind from everywhere blows in.

Almost immediately, much to my surprise and excitement, ideas and articles were on the wing. Toby Litt dropped his little bombshell on the table. Members of the JGB Yahoo Chat Group—David Pringle, Mike Holliday, "Brother" Paul Green, Jordi Costa, Mike Bonsall—all signed on. Bonsall, in fact, had purchased the same edition of the *Cunningham's* anatomy book the young Ballard used at Cambridge. He uses it to more than illuminate JGB's medical prose. Very revealing. In fact, filling this tome to enough pages to be a book proved substantially easier than first imagined, and in hindsight one can only assume the available plethora of prose means there's a B-29 bomb bay full of Ballardania out there, patiently awaiting the opportunity to nuke a new audience of Ballardophiles.

I say let's get it collected and printed for posterity. Which brings me again to James Goddard. The 55-odd pages of what I'm calling "first folio" Ballard will make this collection unique, and it was Goddard's generous offer to contribute these original hand- and type-written pages for publication that really got my adrenalin pumping. Goddard's contributions are absolutely fascinating, as the 1970 interview answers are from the time *The Atrocity Exhibition* was being pulped by Doubleday, *Crash* was in its early violent rewrite stage, and the experimental "Advertiser's Announcements," first revealed in 1967, were still being created, produced and printed in *Ambit*. By the time of the 1975 Goddard/David Pringle interview *Concrete Island* had been in print for a year and *High-Rise* was just in bookstores. Heady times. But wait! (as they say on TV) act now and we'll *double* the offer with JG's handwritten interview responses to Sam Francis, as well as his equally handwritten letters concerning the Brigg 1984 and McGrath 2007 *Shanghai Expeditions*. Yes, a surprisingly large portion of what is printed in this book is right from the Shepperton Source.

Simulacra that.

And while I have this opportunity I'd like to thank Our Man in Shanghai, Andy Best, for all his work and assistance and those exceptional photographs he's contributed over the years. Truly appreciated, Andy, and I've made a career of our day together in the Wicked City. Ditto Professor Peter Brigg, a fellow Torontonian who first introduced me to the concept of Ballard in Shanghai. I've been milking it ever since. Thanks.

And thanks to Fay Ballard, who, for no apparent reason has taken a liking to her father's, ahh, *unique* collection of UK-based fans, and amuses us greatly with her enthisiasm, warm personality and ready wit. And to all the brave contributors—the truly insane. Cheers all round!

Rick McGrath
Toronto, 2013

Interview with JG Ballard: Psychoanalyst of the Electronic Age

by David Pringle

It's 23 September, 1984, and David Pringle is visiting with JG Ballard at his home in Shepperton, Middlesex. Ballard is now 54 years old. His latest novel, *Empire of the Sun*, has been shortlisted for the 1984 Booker Prize, Britain's top literary award. It didn't win, but was subsequently awarded the Guardian Fiction Prize and the James Tait Black Memorial Prize.

The novel is about a boy's traumatic experiences in Shanghai during World War II. The background of the book is autobiographical—between the ages of 11 and 14 Ballard was interned by the Japanese in Lunghua camp near Shanghai—even if the foreground is fictional. Hitherto Ballard had been best known for his science fiction, especially his early short stories, collected in *The Voices of Time*, which had an important impact on British sf and prepared the way for the so-called "New Wave" of the mid 1960s.

Despite being known as a chronicler of disaster and apocalypse, Pringle reports that "Ballard is an ebullient man with a lively sense of humour. He is also surprisingly modest, although sharply opinionated when discussing the work of other writers."

Nineteen-eighty-four has been a great year for Ballard. San Francisco's hip publisher, Val Vale of Re/Search, devoted an entire 180-page issue to his work, reprinting various stories, nonfiction pieces and interviews. An American academic publisher, GK Hall, issued a hardcover edition Pringle's full primary and secondary Ballard bibliography. In France, where he has long been regarded as a major talent, the first issue of the paperback magazine *Science-Fiction* was an homage to him.

"Ballard's hour has come at last, as more and more readers discover the haunting quality of his utterly unique fiction," Pringle wrote in the interview's original preface for the magazine *UK Omni*, which ceased publication after accepting it. This interview was first published in *Words: The New Literary Forum*, Vol. 1, No. 4, September 1985.

David Pringle: You've said in the past that you're proud to be a science-fiction writer. You believe in that label. How do you feel about it now that you're known to a rapidly widening public as the author of the non-sf *Empire of the Sun*?

JG Ballard: I still feel as proud to be a science fiction writer as I ever was. The generous reception that people have given to *Empire of the Sun* doesn't affect my feelings about the sf I've written in the past. It just happens that I have this biographical terrain lying behind me, in my childhood.

I might have spent the war in, say, Berlin or Moscow if my father had been a diplomat and decided to write a novel set there. By pure chance I was brought up and spent the war in Shanghai, and at this late stage, after something like 18 published books, I decided to write a novel about those experiences.

The book doesn't have any obvious connections with my science fiction, though one can never escape the particular cast that a writer's imagination has. But it certainly doesn't affect my high regard for sf as a whole and my feeling of its great importance as the literature of today.

DP: The reviewer in the *Sunday Times*, Nicholas Shrimpton, said something interesting, which in a way links the novel with your sf stories such as "The Terminal Beach." He pointed out that the title has a double meaning, and he said "by the end of the book the 'sun' is also the atom bomb at Hiroshima... In this sense it is about the present and the future, as well as the past, and the empire of the sun is the world in which we all live today."

JGB: I'm glad he said that, because that was entirely my intention in writing the book. Although I never made the point explicitly, the title *Empire of the Sun* does refer both to the empire of Japan with its rising sun flag and to the empire or domain in which we all exist under the sign of the atom bomb: the nuclear age. I absolutely agree with that. To that extent there is a connection with my sf.

DP: Do you read science magazines and do they give you any inspiration?

JGB: I subscribe to *New Scientist* and I read other science magazines occasionally. I'm a great reader of magazines in general. I'm very grateful to a close friend of mine, Dr Martin Bax, who supplies me with interesting scientific material and accounts of his work. He's a research paediatrician (the whole subject of child psychology is one that is interesting to me). Sadly, since the death of another close friend, Dr Christopher Evans—who literally sent me the contents of his waste basket once a week—another major source of information has dried up.

He was a computer scientist at the National Physical Laboratory. Through him I had access to a huge amount of fascinating material on new developments in computers, particularly these interactive programmes which are used in medical diagnosis and the like. I used to visit him at his work frequently and go round the laboratories.

I'd discuss everything that was going on with friends and fellow workers of his, in the pubs around Teddington where we would have lunch. That's come to an end, but I'm still very interested in science. It's a great source of inspiration to me. But there's this crucial problem of gaining access to scientific material, which is more and more difficult for the lay person to do. Years ago I did subscribe to one or two specialist scientific journals, but by the start of the 1970s the subscription costs went right up to the ceiling. Some of the subscriptions were £150, which obviously no private individual pays—the medical practice or the scientific institute pays. I couldn't keep up.

DP: What sort of specialist journals were these?

JGB: One was a journal of psychoneurology, which was very interesting to me. I also subscribed for a while to a psychological abstracts journal —bits of which I incorporated into *The Atrocity Exhibition*. Some of the apparently pseudo-scientific papers in that book were in fact transcriptions of these psychological abstracts (which take the form of a single paragraph summarizing an entire paper). I got that for about three years. That lapsed, but I try to keep abreast of scientific source material because it triggers off so many interesting possibilities. I buy the odd specialized book like *Crash Injuries*, which formed a large part of the underpinning of my novel *Crash*.

DP: That's a serious medical work?

JGB: Yes, it is. It deals with every conceivable aspect of the automobile crash and its effects on the human passenger. Although it is at first glance horrifically explicit in its descriptions of injuries, once you begin to study the text it's no more horrific than *Gray's Anatomy*. It's certainly not a book for the voyeuristic. It's exhaustive in its descriptions of the nightmare interface between the human body and technology at a moment of severe crisis. It's full of comparisons between injuries caused by the rollover of 1955 Pontiacs and 1955 Chevrolets, and it builds up an extraordinary amalgam of deviant technology and a human subject. One can't help but insinuate the element of imagination into that interface. For me, reading that book and the use I made of it was an example of what I feel the sf writer should be doing. He should be looking at reality in its (excuse the pun) sharpest points of contact with ourselves, rather than relying upon endless fantastications of an already well established set of interplanetary conventions.

DP: So how does an sf story come to you? Do you read an article about some scientific concept and think to yourself "can I turn this into a story?"

JGB: That has happened occasionally. Take a story

It seems to me that Sagan, Dyson and O'Neill belong in the territory of flying saucer fanatics, Seventh-Day Adventists, and millennial end of the world religious cults— a bizarre warping of the human imagination around some strange personal obsession like "The Voices of Time." Some of the notions which were current in the late 1950s, stemming from our increased knowledge of genes and chromosomes, led me to the idea that there might be "dormant genes" implanted in our biological past and waiting for the emergence of some transitional zone between Homo sapiens and the next evolutionary phase. I don't say that those ideas came direct from one particular article, but at the time I was writing the story magazines were full of descriptions of research which was advancing our knowledge of the structure of genes, and this was one ingredient that touched my imagination. Or take a story like "The Concentration City," about a giant city infinite in extent—that was inspired by the interest that progressive architects, influenced by Le Corbusier, were showing in vast blocks. Frank Lloyd Wright had come up with the notion of what he called "Mile-high Illinois," a huge Chicago tower. I think he went on to speculate about even larger towers which would incorporate huge city states. That sort of thing, which was popular in scientific and architectural magazines, did directly inspire individual stories. That's happened throughout my career.

I was a medical student, and before that I was familiar with laboratories at school. Later I worked full-time on a scientific journal, *Chemistry and Industry*, for three or four years. I visited a great number of research laboratories, chemical plants and the like, and they played a big part in stimulating my imagination. Most of the inspiration for my sf has come from what I would call scientific *reality* rather than (as I think it's true to say of most sf writers, with the exception of Arthur C Clarke) scientific *fantasy*. That's an important distinction. In our different ways, Clarke and I derive a great deal from Wells, and I would say that the Wellsian strand, of taking inspiration directly from scientific data, has been much stronger in England than it has been in the United States. The American sf writers have not worked in that tradition at all: they've taken their inspiration much more from, at best, the sensationalized popular science of mass magazines, and, at worst, from comic books.

DP: What do you feel about the rather grandiose American scientific speculators, such as Gerard O'Neill, Freeman Dyson or Carl Sagan?

JGB: Dyson is actually British, but now totally Americanized. I regard them as being in a way a new kind of sf writer. Ostensibly they are working within the formal territory of the natural sciences, but in fact (like Desmond Morris over here) they're really working wholly within the realm of science fiction. Their ideas have little grounding in reality and represent over-speculations that obviously satisfy some sort of Messianic need. Freeman Dyson's "Dyson Spheres" and O'Neill's "Cylinders in Space" are bizarre extensions of speculations that even in their most elementary forms are beyond the bounds of credibility. These comic-book ideas, projected through the minds of intelligent and rational men, emerge as vast superfantasies that are given a kind of underpinning of scientific plausibility but are really as preposterous as Von Daniken's fantasies of the "was God an astronaut?" type. It seems to me that Sagan, Dyson and O'Neill belong in the territory of flying saucer fanatics, Seventh-Day Adventists, and millennial end of the world religious cults—a bizarre warping of the human imagination around some strange personal obsession. That's the only way I can describe them: they have nothing to do with realizable projections of the human future. It's like brain transplants—there's a certain sort of imagination that leaps from something like kidney transplants and immediately thinks "let's have brain transplants—we'll have an entire nation in which everybody has a brain transplant and lives for a million years!" Before you know what's happening you've left behind entirely the world of scientific research and organ transplantation and moved into a realm where you're meeting the human obsession with immortality.

I don't think Dyson's spheres, the notion of dismantling an entire planet and reassembling it into a huge radiation shield around the sun, has much to do with reality in any normal way. Likewise, O'Neill's cylinders say something about the psychology of someone who presumably finds living on this planet with his fellow human beings intolerable for whatever personal reasons: he needs to recreate a facsimile of a tranquil garden suburb (which he cannot bear in reality), a segment of Pasadena inside a glass cylinder in orbit around the world! This seems to say something about the psychology of the man itself, and has nothing to do with any feasible scientific projection of present day space exploration—which is still handicapped by the fact that it's impossible to get a large payload into space. All the efforts of the space programmes, since Gagarin's first flight in 1961, show that it is next to impossible to lift a substantial load into space: the costs of doing so are prohibitive.

DP: But they go on trying. The Shuttle flights are becoming more frequent.

JGB: Slightly more frequent. Oh, I'm not denying the fact that it's taking place—but at gigantic cost.

DP: Do you believe in the ultimate desirability of humanity expanding into space and colonizing other planets?

JGB: Yes, of course I do. I'm not opposed to the notion of space travel. One day a method of propulsion will be developed whereby travel to other planets, and the creation of tolerable human environments there, will be feasible. Of course we will move outward to the planets of this solar system and beyond. I've no doubt about that, but I won't be around to see it. I take it for granted that human intelligence will expand to fill the void around it. In all things, in the arts and the sciences, the human imagination is never going to allow itself to become restricted to a minute corner of the universe. That exploratory instinct is enormously important. Human beings are novelty seeking creatures above all else, and I think the enrichment and enlargement of the human imagination that's going to take place in the next thousand years will demand space exploration.

For the past 25 years we've been in the firecracker and bamboo kite stage of astronautics. These preliminary stages have to be gone through, but I'm sure everything will depend on some huge breakthrough in propulsion. At present we put a small capsule on top of a gigantic firework and rely on brute force to propel the thing. No one would think of trying to fly a passenger plane across the Atlantic using the same technique—fortunately we discovered translational flight, the *wing*, which made it unnecessary to rely on pure ballistics. Another breakthrough will take place and then suddenly space flight will become more cost effective and it will probably tap the imagination.

It is extraordinary that the space programmes of the last 30 years have totally failed to touch the human imagination, and it is remarkable how little influence they have had on all other aspects of life. The stupendous achievement of actually landing men on the moon hasn't touched the imagination at all. Why? That is the puzzling thing... I think it's because people perceive that the brute force method by which the Saturn rockets propelled the Apollo astronauts into space are, in imaginative terms, closer to the now antiquated technologies of the 19th century, much closer to the kind of technologies that girdled the earth with railway lines and huge bridges, the technology of giant dams and immense ocean liners, the Brunel era.

People respond much more imaginatively to what I consider to be pure 20th century technology—the world of computers, advanced medical research programmes into, say, the extrauterine foetus, and nuclear technology (which still holds the threat of nuclear war over our heads). People respond with a tremble of horror, fear, excitement or what have you to developments in all those fields rather than to space exploration. It's because brute force technology belongs to the 19th century, with its giant steam engines puffing away like mad, and not to the world of the communications landscape, with its thousands of invisible information channels. People respond much more to that even on the highstreet level of computerized checkout tills, direct debiting and so on. Strangely, the electronics and communications landscape is much more charged with significance than the space programme. In that respect, the reservations I expressed about the space programme years ago have been borne out. It's virtually forgotten.

DP: Let me backtrack. You mentioned HG Wells, which is something that you've rarely done before. In an article you wrote in 1962, "Which Way to Inner Space?," you said: "I'm convinced that Wells has had a disastrous influence on the subsequent course of sf." Have you changed your mind?

JGB: I can't remember what I said in that article that led up to the remark about HG Wells. I've always admired Wells, but I think in many ways he was a bad influence... I think what I was saying in 1962 was that sf had moved excessively in the direction of the physical sciences—in particular, it was too concerned with interplanetary voyages. The space programmes were well under way in 1962 and I felt that the future of sf lay more with the psychological sciences. Wells' extravert scientific confidence was an unfortunate influence on a lot of writers who lacked any sort of interest in psychological space, or inner space, the human domain, if you like.

He seemed to underwrite, and provide the authority for, a lot of third rate speculators to project their own super science fantasies onto outer space. To some extent, Wells provided the authority of a great imaginative writer to these imitators who followed in his footsteps. Of course, the main inspiration lay with books like *The War of the Worlds*...

DP: In which he destroys Shepperton with great glee.

JGB: He does indeed. I've been living here all these years trying to complete the task he began! No, my interest in Wells is much closer to the area he explored in books like *The Time Machine*, *The Invisible Man*, *The Island of Dr Moreau* and the short stories. He is exploring something closer to inner space in those works, but in fact the writers of modern American sf, and people like Dyson and Sagan to some extent, have not taken their inspiration from Moreau but rather from *War of the Worlds*.

DP: And the later works, such as *The Shape of Things to Come*.

JGB: Right. For the most part, the scientific elements in my own fiction are rational projections of known data which depend on the credibility of work done by others, rather than on my own particular obsessions. I've tried in my sf to provide a rational underpinning for the events that take place.

In *The Drought* I offer a reasonable explanation for the worldwide drought. Even in a novel like *The Crystal World* I offer a rational explanation for why this bizarre phenomenon is taking place. I draw my inspiration from that side of Wells—the rational, scientific Wells, whereas modern sf is almost wholly fantasy. I'm not suggesting that we are inheritors of Wells' mantle, but I feel that Wells is an important forerunner of, say, Arthur C Clarke, and in a different way of myself—the rational scientific investigator who is the servant of the imagination, who provides the imaginative writer with his subject matter. That's very different from just using science as a starting point for extravagant fantasies that really belong in the realm of psychological delusion, paranoia, millennial fears, and the like.

The theme of parricide runs through my fiction, like the legend of Oedipus. The Kennedy assassination, for instance

DP: You've been speaking very much in psychological terms. I believe you once wanted to be a psychiatrist?

JGB: Yes, that's true. I was very interested in psychiatry when I was at school, although I was interested in biology at the same time. In the Sixth Form I took physics, chemistry and biology. When I decided to go to university psychiatry, particularly psychoanalysis, had become my chief interest. You needed a medical degree in order to become a psychiatrist, and as I was interested in biology it seemed natural to study medicine. But my need to become a writer supervened.

I could have persisted and become qualified as a doctor, by which time I might have lost the wish to be a psychiatrist and gone into surgery or paediatrics. But I realized, having done two years, that there was no way I could complete a very intensive memory training course of six or seven years and write at the same time. The need to write was just too strong. Also, I think I realized that the wish to become a psychiatrist was part of my attempt to cope with the strangeness of English life (which I'd only known for three or four years). It was an attempt to reestablish contact with my lost self, that in a sense I had left behind in China.

Anyway, by the time I'd done two years of medicine I was pretty certain that I wanted to become a writer. It may be that my wish to be a psychiatrist was a disguised expression of my wish to be a writer. The elements of psychoanalysis that I was interested in were very much those that appeal to the writer. I wasn't interested in a large part of the subject of psychiatry that has nothing to do with the concerns of the novelist. Much of a psychiatrist's time is spent diagnosing complaints that have an organic origin: even someone with hallucinations doesn't necessarily have a psychological illness— he may be suffering from exposure to a large dose of chromium! This doesn't lend itself to the imagination. I was interested in those aspects of psychiatry which are absolutely within the territory of the imaginative novelist. I think I may have been trying to cure myself too, on the basis of "physician, heal thyself." By wanting to be a psychiatrist I was trying to cure whatever adolescent neurosis I had.

DP: Were you a particularly neurotic adolescent?

JGB: No, I don't think I was neurotic at all, any more than I am now. I was aware of, even if I didn't wholly understand, the emergence of a very strong imagination. When you're that age you try to fit yourself into the categories, to step through the doors that you see open around you, and medicine seemed the nearest category or pigeonhole into which I could fit myself. These days I would probably have formed a pop group, or tried to shoot a president...

DP: Why do you say that?

JGB: I'm joking, but the theme of parricide runs through my fiction, like the legend of Oedipus. The Kennedy assassination, for instance.

DP: In 1962 you published a short story called "The Insane Ones." This was prior to Kennedy's assassination and it's about a psychiatrist who unconsciously aids and abets a patient who wants to go out and kill a dictator. This is curiously similar to your recent story, "The Object of the Attack," which appeared in *Interzone* 9 (Autumn 1984).

JGB: Is it? Yes... It didn't occur to me, because they are very different stories. I suppose you're right, it must be a recurring theme. It's also present in *The Atrocity Exhibition*, that theme, running through the stories, and even in *Crash*. Vaughan, the scientist in the novel, is dedicated to the notion of the assassination of famous figures. So that's a very strong theme running through much of my fiction.

DP: Why should this be?

JGB: Is that for me to answer? I think it's tied up with the particular role that public figures play in our highly-charged media landscape. Many people have pointed out the difference between the fame of, say, Gladstone in the 1880s, and the fame of his counterparts today. In a sense, Margaret Thatcher is an intimate friend of ours, but in Gladstone's day most people —if they ever saw Gladstone at all— would see him once in a lifetime addressing a vast public meeting. This difference has been pointed out, but there's a much greater difference in that public figures today are mediated to us through, not merely the domestic television set, but within the terms of a communications landscape which is full of sensation.

As McLuhan said, it's a high-speed information mosaic which passes by, this jostling mass of panel games, sitcoms, political reports and advertising, with everything presented in the most sensational and upbeat way possible. And this charges these figures: it's rather like the flow of ions, charged particles, in a chemical battery. Powerful currents are moved about, electrons and so forth jumping from image to image, charging them in a way that is independent of the fact that we see these images of public figures on our TVs.

This has always interested me; it's the subject matter, really, of *The Atrocity Exhibition*, where our own fantasies interlock with the fantasies projected by the media landscape. Ambivalent feelings are stirred. The theme of parricide, or regicide (they're indistinguishable), taps our need to cope with this colliding mass of sensational fiction. I don't think the parricide theme relates to my own need to dispose of my father, to displace him in my mother's affections. I think it's part and parcel of the attempt by the individual to grapple with this sensory overload that is going on all the time, to cut the colossus down to his clay heels.

DP: To hark back to that article you wrote in 1962: you said you'd like to see in sf "elaboration of concepts such as the time zone, deep time and archaeopsychic time." Where did you come across these concepts?

JGB: I invented them. I think all three phrases occur in *The Drowned World*, which I was writing at the time. The whole notion of states of time, zones of time, existing symbolically like the stations of an underground system, representing stages on our evolutionary journey from the primeval swamp that was obviously what the novel was about. One of the great themes of modern sf is time travel, but it seemed to me that most sf writers were just treating it as a sort of scenic railway. Time travel took place objectively, external to the characters themselves. But there are other ways of travelling in time, through memory, dreams, the imagination, the coded elements of the past and the future one sees in architecture. Something like a World War II bunker on a beach beside Calais seems to beckon, or point the way, to some strange future. The bunkers that the Germans built are like ciphers from a distant future. Likewise, catacombs and Mayan temples enshrine states of time that have come down to us from the past. They evoke powerful resonances. I felt then and still do now that this was a much more fruitful area for finding metaphors for what the world of science, and technology in particular, is doing to us. Much more so than the conventional cliches of sf, where you simply climbed into something resembling a cross between a dentist's chair and a dodgem car and pressed a button and suddenly Ancient Rome appeared through your glass bubble!

It seemed to me that the sort of investigation or imaginative exploration into the psychology of the present day that sf could embark upon had much more in common with, say, Kafka, Sartre, Camus, the surrealists, or the case histories of Jung and Freud, than with the fantasies that most sf writers used.

DP: You also referred in that article to "psycho-literary ideas."

JGB: Don't hold me too tightly to these phrases after twenty years! Often people ask me about sf and the New Wave. They can see that now one is as free in sf to write anything as is the mainstream writer. They don't realize that this was not always the case. "What was all the fuss about?" they ask. "Why did you need to nail your colours to the mast and attack the traditional sf writers?" (as one vigorously did). They don't realize that this freedom that the sf writer has today was not there at all when I began writing in the 1950s. Science fiction was as closed and formalized as the classical ballet—put a foot out of place and you were whipped off the stage and never allowed to perform again. That analogy isn't too fanciful.

I was doing my best to establish the possibility of a different kind of sf. It seemed to me that the sort of investigation or imaginative exploration into the psychology of the present day that sf could embark upon had much more in common with, say, Kafka, Sartre, Camus, the surrealists, or the case histories of Jung and Freud, than with the fantasies that most sf writers used (fictions on which they were building more fictions).

When I talked about "psycho-literary ideas"—not a very nice phrase—I was trying to indicate that sf should move more in the direction of applied psychology and psychoanalysis, which seemed to me a much more fruitful dimension, rather than stay within the confines of these old ideas which were endlessly recirculated. That was what I was aiming at, as I began to demonstrate, for good or bad, in my own science fiction.

1) What is your opinion of World SF today? And what new directions do you forsee it taking during the next 20 or 30 years to ensure survival?

2) In the last ten years or so SF writers have begun to dip into the pool of 'taboo' areas, sex and religion for instance, which until then had remained virtually untouched by the genre. GOOD stories based on sexual and religious themes began to appear, and you were a prime mover in such areas. Why do you think SF was such a late developer in these areas?

3) What do you think the role of a writer should be today? I say this generally, not with any particular reference to SF.

4) In a recent Guardian interview, (Twentieth Century Vox 11.9.70) you said " The impact of science has totally transformed every-body's lives. One would expect that the main literature of the twentieth century would be science fiction." Would you care to enlarge on this?

5) In the same interview you ended by saying "Science fiction celebrates the possibilities of life." Could you also enlarge on this?

6) So much modern fiction is written in what I think you have called "non-linear narrative" that one wonders when and if it will all end. Do you forsee the eventual extinction of "linear narrative" in favour of the non-linear mode of which you are an originator?

7) One reads so many strange things about you views of SF fandom, that one wonders if they are true! What do you really think of the structure of the SF world, as it stands? And what alterations would you feel inclined to make if you could? One remembers that many SF writers seem to serve an "apprenticeship" in fandom before turning proffesional.

8) What do you think of the general standards in SF writing today? And what would you say could be done by writers and publishers, and for that matter fans, to improve these standards?

9) Are you in favour or against the segregation of modern writing into genres such as SF, Western, Historical, Romance, Thriller and so on? Do you think the situation will ever exist where we have "one literature"?

10) Who do you think are the greatest writers working in SF today? And why? (excluding J.G.Ballard of course).

11) Why do you think SF has remained the underdog of literature for so long? And why do you think so many people are still so un--willing to accept it as one of the literary media?

12) At the present time the movement in SF is away from magazines and more toward the original anthologies like John Carnell's New Writings, Damon Knight's Orbit, and Harlan Ellison's Dangerous Visions. Why do you think SF magazines have remained such a minority interest? Why should it be possible for a paperback to sell 30,000 or 40,000 copies, whilst a magazine like Vision of Tomorrow has difficulty in selling 15,000 copies?

13) Do you think SF has any particular brief to fulfill in today's society? Or should it become mere entertainment?

14) Your work has evolved to such an extent since you started writing that one can't really see you finding any new avenue of approach. What direction do you see your work taking in the next ten years?

"Everything is Science Fiction!"
JG Ballard 1970 Interview Answers

by James Goddard

As Goddard reports: "Here's some wit and wisdom from JG Ballard. These are written answers to written questions dating from 1970. This set consists of six 10 x 8 inch sheets, written on both sides."

Q1) Everything is science fiction! I think the future for s-f is tremendously exciting, but there are dangers. At present science fiction is almost the only form of fiction which is thriving — the social novel, for example, is attracting fewer & fewer readers — and for obvious reasons, that social relationships are no longer as important as the individual's relationships with the technological & fictional landscape of the late C20. However, in spite of its increasing readership all over the world, it seems to me that science fiction is in danger of losing its direction & sense of purpose — it may easily become a "closed" fiction similar to the western, with a fixed set of conventions & scope of reference. It is most important that the younger writers continue the good work done in the past 10 years or so. To survive during the next 20 or 30 years? S-f must go on being relevant, making sense of people's lives & imaginations. In practical terms — American s-f of the 1930-60 period is now dead + buried, but it is important to go on stamping the earth down onto the coffin — there are still too many people eager to jerk it out of its grave and dress the corpse in electric flowers.

(Q2) Understandable — basically s-f is a response to science + technology as perceived by the inhabitants of the consumer goods society — it's only recently that science + technology have begun to touch the areas of sex + religion — more + more we can expect to see sex taking a major share of the subject matter of the science fiction writer — I think that sex will play the same role in science fiction that used to be played by outer space, and that the sexual organs will become the starships and the planets of inner space.

(3) I think that the role of the writer today has totally changed — he is now merely one of a huge army of people filling the environment with fictions of every kind — therefore he must become much more analytic, approaching his subject matter far more like a scientist or engineer. Alternatively, if he is to produce fiction, he must out-imagine everyone else, scream louder, whisper more quietly. For the first time in history, it may actually require talent to become a writer — and those writers, both in and outside s-f, who have no talent are being shown up already. They are resented, in particular, for not producing something sufficiently "fictional".

Q4) Self explanatory, I think. My guess is that the human being is ~~naturally~~ a nervous & fearful creature, + nervous + fearful people detest change ~~indeed~~. However, as everyone becomes more confident, so they are prepared to accept change. Ergo, s-f becomes a willingly accepted guide to the greater possibilities of ~~different~~ imagination.

Q6) No — technique matters nothing — the only thing that counts is subject matter — *the idea*. Without a good or original idea no amount of experimental technique can produce anything of worth whatever. New wave, please note!

Q7) I have no news of s-f fandom, apart from some comments I made on the 1957 World Convention which I attended. Perhaps things have changed.

Q8) Most new sf is far inferior to the sf produced during the 1950's & 1960's. The evolution of New Worlds for example, despite its huge achievements, has been a great disappointment. Michael Moorcock, & the people who helped him, such as Charles Platt & Diane Lambert, Langdon Jones, literally gave years of their lives to make that magazine a successful forum for the new. Were their enormous efforts repaid? I doubt it. The writers are to blame.

Q9) I loathe the word "literature".

Q10) Science fiction has always been very much a corporate activity, the writers sharing a common pool of ideas, and the yardsticks of individual achievement don't really measure the worth of the leading s-f writers of the 50's — (6) Sheckley, Matheson, Pohl. Those who seem to stand out as individuals usually tend to be marginal figures — Bradbury, really a writer of C20 fairy tales, the most brilliant talent produced by modern science fiction, Bernard Wolfe, author of Limbo 90, never part of s-f, and William Burroughs. The New Wave has produced no-one yet, but this was little more than a label invented by Michael Moorcock, Judith Merril & myself to wake up a sleeping stupified & stupid audience. However, over the next 10-20 years I think a group of major writers will appear. The one mistake, entirely understandable, of New Worlds, was that about 15 months ago it ceased to be a science fiction magazine.

Q11.

Q12) There are certain to be fluctuations in the publishing of s.f., as of anything else. The 40s & 50's were the great years of magazine s.f., the 60's of the paperback original. I have always disliked original paperback anthologies, which generally are bogus magazines, without the hot blood that runs through a real magazine. Carnell's New Writings is a noble effort by the editor. Knight's Orbit series is workaday (but it's typical that he asked me, in Rio last year, to contribute, "but not anything too original"), while Ellison's Dangerous Visions is a vulgar travesty of the words in its title.

— my own piece "The Assassination of JF Kennedy seen as a Downhill Motor Race" was declined on the grounds "that so many (8 millions of Americans might be offended" — in other words, dangerous, but not too dangerous, visions. I think it a great shame that the news-f cannot support a vital magazine, and I lay the blame for this on the readers + few writers. Michael Moorcock's New Worlds has been one of the most original magazines ever published, and ~~~~~ the history of New Worlds from Ted Carnell's great editorship (when it was without doubt the most important magazine of original fiction in this century) to its present change into a paperback, is the history of original fiction of any kind in this post war period. I am convinced that s-f, whatever forms it takes, will continue to grow + change, and it can only change for the better, but without a magazine, and the commitment of people like Carnell, Moorcock, Platt and others, the task of the young writer will be that much more difficult. Magazines are the best rallying points — they have immediacy + direction, + the passionate involvement of one or 2 people. By contrast, original anthologies are produced within the machinery of a publishing house. As for Visions of Tomorrow — it may have had difficulty in selling 15,000 copies, but it would have had just as much difficulty in giving them away. At least, as a consolation prize, the editor can feel a certain pride in knowing that he produced, for a brief while, the worst science fiction magazine in history.

13) Science Fiction is the most important fiction that has been written for the last 100 years. Its role & importance will increase. It is the most vital & authentic fiction of the C20. Its reading should be compulsory. Fortunately, compulsion will not be necessary, as everyone will read it voluntarily. It is also the fiction of the common man. For the most part,

science fiction has not attracted to it many people of the first rank during the past 30 years, far fewer, certainly, than it deserves. This may be changing. Young people today seem to be very bright. Write! (11

Q14) I hope that my own fiction continues to evolve, & I am certain that it will do so — I have no idea what I shall be writing in 10 years time. I have, at the time of this interview, Nov/2, 1970, almost completed the first draft of a long novel on sex + the ~~scribbled~~ automobile, and I would like to write many new ~~xxxx~~ short stories.

~~[scribbled out]~~. I feel that my own fiction has only just begun, or more truthfully, is on the point of beginning, + that all kinds of interesting things may come up. At the same time, I should very much like to give up writing altogether, and take up painting, my real career, which I have wanted to pursue for many years. All my fiction is really the substitute work of an unfulfilled painter.

"Everything is Science Fiction!"

Q1) James Goddard: What is your opinion of sf today? And what new directions do you foresee it taking during the next 20 years?

JG Ballard: *Everything is science fiction!* I think the future for it is tremendously exciting, but there are dangers. At present science fiction is almost the only form of fiction which is intriguing—the social novel, for example, is attracting fewer & fewer readers—and for the obvious reason that social relationships are no longer as important as the individual's relationship with the technological and fictional landscapes of the late C20. *However*, in spite of its increasing readership all over the world, it seems to me that science fiction is in danger of losing its direction and sense of purpose—it may easily become a "closed" fiction similar to the western, with a fixed set of conventions and scope of reference. It is most important that the younger writers continue the good work done in the past 10 years or so. To survive during the next 20 or 30 years? SF must go on being *relevant*, making sense of people's lives & imaginations. In practical terms —American sf of the 1930-60 period is now dead and buried, but it is important to go on stamping the earth down all over the coffin—there are still too many people eager to jerk it out of its grave and dress the corpse in electronic flowers.

Q2) Goddard: In the last ten years or so sf writers have begun to dip into the pool of 'taboo' areas, sex and religion for instance, which until then had remained virtually untouched by the genre. Good stories based on sexual; and religious themes began to appear, and you were a prime mover in such areas. Why do you think sf was such a late developer in these areas?

Ballard: Understandable—basically sf is a response to science & technology as perceived by the inhabitants of the consumer good society—it's only recently that science & technology have begun to touch the areas of sex & religion—more and more we can expect to see sex taking a major share of the subject matter of the science fiction writer—I think that sex will play the same role in science fiction that used to be played by outer space, and that the sexual organs will become the starships and planets of inner space.

Q3) Goddard: What do you think the role of a writer should be today? I say this generally, not with any particular reference to sf.

Ballard: I think that the role of the writer today is totally changed—he is now merely one of a huge army of people filling the environment with fictions of every kind—therefore he must become much more analytic, approaching his subject matter far more like a scientist or engineer. Alternatively, if he is to produce fiction, he must out-imagine everyone else, scream louder, whisper more quietly. For the first time in history, it may actually requite talent to become a writer—and those writers, both in and outside sf, who have the talent are being shown up already. They are resented, in particular, for not producing something sufficiently "fictional."

Q4) Goddard: In a recent *Guardian* interview, ("Twentieth Century Vox," 11.9.70) you said, "The impact of science has totally transformed everybody's lives. One would expect that the main literature of the twentieth century would be science fiction." Would you care to enlarge on this?

Ballard: Self-explanatory, I think. My guess is that the human being is a nervous and fearful creature, & nervous & fearful people detest change.

Q5) Goddard: In the same interview you end by saying, "Science fiction celebrates the possibilities of life." Could you also enlarge on this?

Ballard: However, as everyone becomes more confident, so they are prepared to accept change. Ergo, sf becomes a willingly accepted guide to the greater possibilities of the imagination.

Q6) Goddard: So much modern fiction is written in what I think you have called "non-linear narrative" that one wonders when and if it will all end. Do you foresee the eventual extinction of "linear narrative" in favour of the non-linear mode of which you are an originator?

Ballard: No—technique matters nothing—the only thing that counts is subject matter—*the idea*. Without a good or original idea no amount of experimental technique can produce anything of interest whatever. *New Wave, please note!*

Q7) Goddard: One reads so many strange things about your views of sf fandom, that one wonders if they are true! What do you really think of the structure of the sf world, as it stands? And what alterations would you feel inclined to make if you could? One remembers that many sf writers seem to serve an "apprenticeship" in fandom before turning professional.

Ballard: I have no news of sf fandom, apart from some comments I made on the 1957 World Convention which I attended. Perhaps things have changed.

Q8) Goddard: What do you think of the general standards in sf writing today? And what would you say could be done by writers and publishers, and for that matter, fans, to improve these standards?

Ballard: Most new sf is far inferior to the sf produced during the 1950s & 1960s. The evolution of *New Worlds*, for example, has been a great disappointment, despite its many achievements. Michael Moorcock, & the people who helped him, such as Charles Platt and Diane Lambert, Langdon Jones, literally gave years of their lives to make that magazine a successful forum of the new. Were these enormous efforts repaid? I doubt it. The writers are to blame.

Q9) Goddard: Are you in favour or against the segregation of modern writing into genres such as sf, western, historical, romance, thriller and so on? Do you think the situation will ever exist where we have "one literature"?

Ballard: I loathe the word "literature."

Q10) Goddard: Who do you think are the greatest writers working in sf today? And why? (excluding JG Ballard, of course)

Ballard: Science fiction has always been very much a corporate activity, the writers sharing a common pool of ideas, and the yardsticks of individual achievement don't really measure the worth of the leading sf writers of the 50s—Sheckley, Matheson, Pohl.

Those who seem to stand out as individuals usually tend to be marginal figures—Bradbury, really a writer of C20 fairy tales, the most brilliant talent produced by modern science fiction. Bernard Wolfe, great author of *Limbo 90*, never part of sf, and William Burroughs.

The New Wave has produced no-one yet, but this was little more than a label invented by Michael Moorcock, Judith Merril & myself to wake up a sleeping, stupefied & stupid audience. However, over the next 10-20 years I think a group of major writers will appear. The one mistake, entirely understandable, of *New Worlds*, was that about 15 months ago it ceased to be a science fiction magazine.

> At the same time, I should very much like to give up writing altogether, and take up painting, my real career, which I have wanted to pursue for many years. All my fiction is really the substitute work of an unfulfilled painter.

Q11) Goddard: Why do you think sf has remained the underdog of literature for so long? And why do you think so many people are still so unwilling to accept it as one of the literary media?

Ballard: (No response)

Q12) Goddard: At the present time the movement in sf is away from magazines and more toward the original anthologies like John Carnell's *New Writings*, Damon Knight's *Orbit*, and Harlan Ellison's *Dangerous Visions*. Why do you think sf magazines have remained such a minority interest? Why should it be possible for a paperback to sell 30,000 or 40,000 copies, whilst a magazine like *Vision of Tomorrow* has difficulty in selling 15,000 copies?

Ballard: There are certain to be fluctuations in the publishing of sf, as of anything else. The 40s and 50s were the great years of magazine sf, the 60s of the paperback original. I have always disliked original anthologies, which generally are bogus magazines without the hot blood that runs through a real magazine.

Cornell's *New Writings* is a noble effort by the editor. Knight's *Orbit* series is workday (but it's typical that he asked me, in Rio last year, to contribute, "but not anything too original"), while Ellison's *Dangerous Visions* is a vulgar travesty of the words in its title—my own piece "The Assassination of John F Kennedy Seen As A Downhill Motor Race" was declined on the grounds "that many millions of Americans might be offended"—in other words, dangerous, but not too dangerous, visions.

I think it a great shame that the new sf cannot support a vital magazine, and I lay the blame for this on the readers and new writers. Michael Moorcock's *New Worlds* has been one of the most original magazines ever published, and the history of *New Worlds* from Ted Carnell's great editorship (when it was without doubt the most important magazine of original fiction in this country) is its present change into a paperback, is *the* history of original fiction of any kind in this post war period.

I am convinced that sf, whatever forms it takes, will continue to grow & change, *and it can only change for the better*, but without a magazine, and the commitment of people like Carnell, Moorcock, Platt and others, the task of the young writer will be that much more difficult. Magazines are the best rallying points—they have immediacy and direction, and the passionate involvement of one or two people. By contrast, original anthologies are produced within the machinery of a publishing house.

As for *Visions of Tomorrow*—it will have had difficulty in selling 15,000 copies, but it would have had just as much difficulty in giving them away. At least, as a consolation prize, the editor can feel a certain pride in knowing that he produced, for a brief while, the worst science fiction magazine in history.

Q13) Goddard: Do you think sf has any particular brief to fulfil in today's society? Or should it become mere entertainment?

Ballard: Science fiction is the most important fiction that has been written for the last 100 years. Its role & importance will increase. It is the most vital and authentic fiction of the C20. Fortunately, compulsion will not be necessary, as everyone will read it voluntarily. It is also the fiction of the common man.

For the most part, science fiction has not attracted to it many people of the first rank during the past 30 years, far fewer, certainly, than it deserves. This may be changing. Young people today seem to be very bright. *Write!*

Q14) Goddard: You work has evolved to such an extent since you started writing that one can't really see you finding any new avenue of approach. What direction do you see your work taking in the next ten years?

Ballard: I hope that my own fiction continues to evolve, & I am certain that it will do so—I have no idea about what I shall be writing in 10 years time.

I have, at the time of this interview, Nov 12, 1970, about completed the first draft of a long novel on sex & the automobile, and I would like to write many new short stories. I feel that my own fiction has only just begun, or more truthfully, is on the point of beginning, & that all kinds of interesting things may come up.

At the same time, I should very much like to give up writing altogether, and take up painting, my real career, which I have wanted to pursue for many years. All my fiction is really the substitute work of an unfulfilled painter.

The JG Ballard
Repsychling Interview

When noted JG Ballard collector, archivist and bibliophile Mike Holliday was told a copy of the elusive publication *Repsychling*, a one-issue wonder that reportedly contained a Ballard interview from the relatively early days of the mid-1970s, had popped up at London's *Beat Books*, he quickly acquired it. Holliday, who had, like all of us, assumed the unknown interview was just a re-tread of an earlier one—"especially given the mag's pun on recycling," happily reported in 2012 that the magazine did indeed contain a previously unknown Ballard interview, which he presumes was transcribed from a tape recorded at Ballard's home in Shepperton. In other words: A Find.

According to the magazine's preamble about the interview: "JG Ballard, the Pope of Atrocity, transvalues supermarkets, fantasizes about TV, flirts with electronics before becoming promiscuous with computers. In his own unique visceral style he speaks frankly about the gut-twisting nightmare metal-tangling adrenal excitement of his own spectacular automobile accident..." And, as you'll read, Ballard certainly does cover those topics. The only publication details for the magazine are a logo on the back saying "Repsychling Anti-copyright 1975," and an address of 209 Archway Road, London.

Andrew Sclanders at *Beat Books* describes the magazine as: *Repsychling 'A Magazine for the Unborn'* #1 (London: 1975). Tabloid newspaper format (16pp.) An anti-copyright, anti-media collection of anonymous, dystopian/Ballardian texts (Ballard himself features in a lengthy exclusive interview in which he discusses his 'Crash' exhibition at the New Arts Lab), informed by an almost unintelligible thesis of transvaluation: "Repsychling is the psychological complement to recycling. The transvaluation is a vagabond roaming the conceptual junk-yard of civilisation sharp-eyed for jagged bits of scrap that a mere mental flourish can transform into tools for growth." Includes texts on cybernetics, suicide, and an interview with Sheila Rowbotham on a feminist riposte to Fontana's Modern Masters series. There may have been no further issues.

(The entire interaction was punctuated by Ballard's gigantic dog "Apollo" performing outrageous fellatio on itself, obviously attempting a massive canine ejaculation all over the carpet, Ballard, and our own reporter. The drowned conversation has reached the widely discussed topic of randomness.)

REPSYCHLING: In your books how do randomness and chance come in?

JG BALLARD: I've tried to do a little of that. I don't know. Maybe it's just my mind. Pop art had a tremendous influence (hey dog—stop sucking yourself...) on me. I'd like to write a novel the way Warhol does a pop painting. I've done one or two pieces which are almost pop paintings—they're in fact accounts of operations in cosmetic surgery. There's one called "Princess Margaret's Facelift." Another I've just done's called "Mae West's Reduction Mamo-plastic" [sic]—the breast thing. And one for an American magazine called "Queen Elizabeth's Rhinoplasty" which is a nose-job. What I've done is to take from a textbook on plastic surgery straightforward accounts of cosmetic operations. Where the text has "the patient" I've inserted "Queen Elizabeth" or "Mae West." That was as close to pop painting as I could get. Now the object of these pieces is not to get a cheap laugh of incongruity. Far from it because they show exactly I think the—I don't take any credit for it myself—radical transformation of something by a small displacement. There's a lot of Chris Evans' computer-generated material—science fiction. And computer-generated detective stories. I think they've published a computer-generated prayer.

RE: Have you thought of using the novel and other things together? For example, like a film of somebody writing a novel? Bringing in more elements and making it more multi-media.

JGB: You mean literally?

RE: Yes.

JGB: Often I've thought of it. Getting out of this terrible constriction of just a lot of words printed between covers. I'd like to do something where the novel consists of a kit. There's a conventional piece of fiction and you come to page 27 then there's a series of instructions which you the reader have to do. You have to ring up certain people. Part of the novel consists of a questionnaire which you have to complete. Track down six left-handed people. Then you have to go out and find a hippy, a millionaire, a streetwalker, you name it. You've got to find these people and integrate them into the novel which continues with you finding that you've got to do other things as well. Why then do I go on writing the same old stuff? Attempts to enlarge the novel don't satisfy the deep need to re-mythologize one.

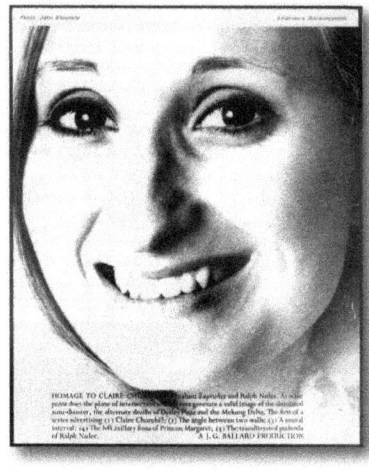

RE: Would you get a lot of shit from your publishers if you tried to do a novel like that, or explode it or take it beyond what it is?

JGB: Publishers on the whole—or at least the ones I've dealt with—are pretty sympathetic to this kind of thing. But what you're up against of course is the terrific conservatism of readers. You're in danger of finding yourself with an audience of one.

RE: But that could be a good thing. Writing novels for just one or two people.

JGB: I like that idea too. If you're a professional painter your paintings are only seen by a very small number of people. I don't see why you shouldn't write a novel in exactly the same way for three people. I mean you'd charge 5,000 pounds. Why not? Right, so they say, "I'd like you to write a novel for me. Not about me but for me. Just a novel for me." And that would be very interesting because I'd have to find out a lot about them. No point in just writing any old novel. A unique fiction which had been created by the person commissioning and myself. Why don't I do it? Writing's extremely difficult. There's no question about it. There's no sort of sensory satisfaction at all. It's just an arid cerebral sort of activity. You have to invent everything. It's a drag. You're working with this very outdated thing—language. So there's experimental activity which I love. In *Ambit* one modest direction was

that I started publishing advertisements. Full page. I thought advertising was an area into which the imaginative writer never moved. There's a huge continent of possibilities totally untapped. Instead of advertising consumer goods or services or whatever, advertise ideas. I think I did five or six of these ads before I ran out of money. They were rather expensive. They looked like something out of *Vogue*. Very glossy with advertising typography. The first person I advertised was my girlfriend. Then I advertised the angle between two walls. That's another one—"A Neural Interval."

RE: What's this one? "Placental Insufficiency"?

JGB: Yes I think Martin Bax dreamed that one up for some reason. It's quite expensive.

RE: I wanted to talk about a strange experience I had with one of your books, *Crash*, which I was reading last November. I got halfway through it one evening and the next day I had to drive up to Stafford to cover an agricultural show. I drove 200 miles and was just going through the gates when I suddenly found myself smashed on to the back window ledge looking at this copy of your book.

JGB: God what happened? You were hit by something?

RE: I was just turning and this other car hit me at about 60mph. I was just left staring at your book while the other guy got out and the radiators were steaming. I just cracked a couple of ribs but no one was hurt. I've never been able to finish the book since then and I wonder if you could suggest a way that I could get over the association?

JGB: Maybe you won't be able to finish it. Maybe you don't need to finish it. I had a rather similar experience myself. After finishing the book and delivering the manuscript to my agent I was driving back from London in the rain about two in the morning and the car skidded and swerved across the central reservation, smashed down a steel sign then rolled on to its back and was carried down the oncoming lane.

It was surprising the amount of traffic around but thank god I didn't hit anything otherwise everyone would have been dead. And I ended up with the roof crushed down upside down in my harness. There was petrol everywhere. People were standing around in the darkness bellowing, "Petrol, petrol." Which was everywhere. They couldn't open the doors because the roof was down.

Of all things, the window winder fell off. I must have knocked it off with my elbow. So I wasn't able to wind down the window. I suppose somebody could've kicked it in. I was lucky the thing didn't ignite. Anyway to cut a long story short, it was a mad evening because I was breathalyzed—well, I refused to be breathalyzed. And I was technically under arrest in this hospital.

I got my head X-rayed and I must have been undergoing euphoria or something because I got into a fierce argument with this girl, the radiographer, about who owned the copyright of these photographs. I was looking at these photographs of my skull—front and side. And the doctor was saying, "Well, there's nothing there but the long-term effects take a long time to show." I thought, "That's great. Who owns the copyright?" "We own the copyright." I was saying, "No. That's my head. I own the copyright. You own the plates, not the copyright. This is an important distinction."

Anyway I got home by taxi. I was ill. I must've had concussion. After about three days the car was over at Richmond held by the police in some pound. I went to the garage here and rented a car for the day and took my camera. I went over to Richmond and photographed the wrecked car. There was a terrible pathos of this machine with which I was so intimately involved.

RE: Did you feel you had to go through that?

JGB: Yes, but not in any self-conscious way. I just wanted to see that car, you see. Because it was such a fierce accident, such a close escape, the car was tremendously important.

RE: What first interested you in cars and the violence of machines juxtaposed to all the visceral gut-wrenching stuff? Did you have car crashes before that?

JGB: No. I'm an idealist in my self which has a fascination with car-crashes—I don't want to go into this thing. I've done it to death. Literally. There's a fascination of people in general. Not just their fascination but their ambivalent attitude with car-crashes that I've been aware of for years. It seems to me that the car and the car-crash as extension of the car was such an important part of the relationship with technology. I really believe we've created a technological landscape which is not just around us but it's actually beginning to enter our minds. I don't want to sound too pretentious but we're getting a sort of marriage between sex and technology. And the car-crash represents the psychopathology of this system. I put on that exhibition at the *New Arts Lab*—an exhibition of crashed cars five or six years ago. It was a kind of experiment because I wanted to see how people would react.

RE: How did they react generally at that time?

JGB: Extraordinary. I hadn't anticipated it. The exhibition was on a month and there was an opening party which I treated exactly as if it was a fine art show. I called it "New Sculpture"—crashed cars. There was this huge Pontiac that had been in a front-end collision. It was from that grand period of the mid-50s, flaring tail fins and all the rest of it, all the rocket engine motifs.

I had a Mini that had been hit from every conceivable direction. It was just a kind of horrible ball of steel mangled together. And then I had one of those Austin family saloons that had gone off the side of a road and obviously landed in a field. In fact there was all this mud and grass on the left hand rain gutter. It hadn't been severely damaged but it had been canted through about fifteen degrees laterally.

The Pontiac was the most impressive thing. I had this opening party and invited all these art critics and people from the demi-monde. I've never seen people get drunk so quickly because they were all excited and disturbed and unsettled by these vehicles. We got a topless girl who was interviewing people on closed circuit TV. They could see themselves being interviewed around the crash so that it was just too much. A psychological overload. Everyone was incredibly drunk. The topless girl nearly got raped in the back of the Pontiac. The party was just mad. People were pouring wine over the cars, breaking everything, smashing glass.

Anyway that show was on a month and the cars were continuously attacked in the gallery. One of the cars was slashed with white paint. The Mini was rolled round the place. The Pontiac had massive front-end damage. Suddenly after about six feet of bonnet the rest of the car was perfect. And it was attacked. The wing mirrors were ripped off.

It was quite obvious to me the image of the crashed car was touching off all sorts of ambiguities and ambivalences. If we had crashed trucks or crashed aircraft that wouldn't have been the same thing. In fact I don't think air crashes have anything of the sort of eroto-whatever-you-like-to-call-it.

RE: You see a direct sexual thing? I have this word—autophilia—which is the direct connexion between people looking on cars as sexual objects, fingering the exhaust and running their fingers over the fenders etc.

JGB: Yes I read about the first congress between a man and a motor car which was regarded as being in very bad taste. But there's a kind of logic. In America automobile designers play on this. I mean you're moving into a kind of organo-metal structure with definite appeal to all sorts of half-conscious identifications between machine and body.

RE: Where do you think this trend's going to go? I agree there's an inextricable link between sex and cars.

JGB: Well, sex and technology. I'm not interested in cars themselves. It's technology that interests me. People of course complain about technology because it's very affectless, this neutral emotionless landscape. The sort of thing you find at a big airport or in the experience of driving a car. Whenever technology appears and begins to mediate between groups of people the first feeling is that this is the emotionless and arid world it's creating.

Everyone deplored the coming into being of modern supermarkets because they seem chill chromium-infested places. But this is not the case of course. Tremendous amount of warmth going on in supermarkets and everyone's much happier and there's this nice intimacy mediated by display lighting.

When Tescos first came to Shepperton all the housewives immediately put on their stretch pants and glammed themselves up so they could spend as much time as possible pushing around among the chromium, racks of packs and the TV spy camera. People don't like somebody saying, "How do you do Mrs Jones. How's the baby today?" That's just a myth. They want more sophisticated relationships with other people, the kind of relationship you get in a supermarket. Not promiscuity exactly. A sort of multi-directional promiscuity. A high-speed mosaic that's moving around the place involving and compounded of glances and glimpses of an attractive man or woman. A whole mosaic of images that are bombarding you—the sensorium, all mediated by the technological ambience of the supermarket, hospital or whatever. It's what TV does.

RE: What about any alienation inherent in that?

JGB: You go beyond the alienation. You get a new kind of rapport. The high-speed mosaic produces its own kind of multi-value flickering. If you go to a supermarket, a department store, a big airport or some huge office building on the open plan—any of these modern structures—you get it. In traffic jams, on a big package holiday.

RE: All mass things?

JGB: Yes, sure. But intimate. It appears to be a very neutral, emotional space loaded with thousands of barely perceived emotional charges. An electronic field of possibility and excitement. We thrive on a new kind of emotion which is based on the cathode tube and all that goes with it. People are never happier than when they are with technology. They love their appliances. It's nice to see people having new relationships with each other in terms of consumer durables. You've only got to watch them drooling over these units in the local shopping precinct. And these are the important things in their lives.

Technology produces a whole vocabulary of ideas, tactile and sexual values. These are very important—aesthetic, sculptural and other values. This is the design. Design is terribly important. Nowadays people are incredibly sophisticated in their tastes. No doubt about that. You can't pull a fast one over them any more. Technology is important. It provides a tremendously rich anthology of techniques. To some extent it's a marriage between science and art. The next big breakthrough will be when the first computer terminals make their appearance on the domestic scene. I'm sorry—the next big breakthrough will be mass-manufactured at reasonable prices TV video systems. Where the home will become basically a TV studio. That's going to be the biggest explosion imaginatively in every conceivable way.

Many of the programmes are just games. Many of these games are obviously going to transform very directly the whole style and content of ordinary life when computers arrive on the domestic scene. Everyone will be able to use the various programmes computers will offer. There may be a computer programme called "Alimony," where you can work out if you get a divorce now, what sort of alimony will I pay? Can I afford to go on holiday this year? Yes. If you divorce your husband. That's not a joke. The computer will now make deductions and the only way you can stop getting these letters from the bank is to divorce your husband. Your whole life will change.

"But I'll be lonely." "No, you won't Mrs So-and-so." Tap tap. The thing will print out a whole mass of games you can play. Because it's all games you see. Perhaps you can link up with friends and devise all sorts of games. The computer. Ultimately it's just a device for maximizing possibilities. With the computer terminal I can play complex games of various kinds involving all aspects of myself.

I can cast myself in a new role. I may decide to be ten years younger. In California people can assume any role they want and be convincing in that role. If you want to be a motor cycle freak buy some black leather gear and a motorbike and everyone accepts you. If you want to be high society you redecorate your dining room with fake Hepplewhite and buy a lot of silver and invite people in dinner jackets. Now the computer will help to approach this from a more cerebral point of view. Plus the home as TV studio. It's marvellous. The playback is terribly important. The whole function of what have to date been called "The Arts" is just playback. Up till now we've always relied on someone to do it for us. But with the home as TV studio and ourself as the star, we'll be our own subject.

RE: I believe people have an inherent need for disaster. When the Moorgate crash happened, the journalists all virtually had orgasms: "a 22-year-old attractive secretary was lying there, twitching with an arm hanging off…" The phenomenon of disaster is like a new kind of addiction.

JGB: I absolutely agree with you. They bring people together and excite people. Stimulate and charge people in a most extraordinary way. There's no question about it. That Trident that came down near Staines a few years ago. The highways were so jammed that they couldn't get the ambulances through. People were writing letters to *The Times* saying, "It's disgusting, these ghouls etc etc." I think in fact it's a very healthy thing to want to get to the scene of a big disaster.

It's a strange paradox that for all the richness of life in every conceivable direction, we're not convinced something is all that obvious. And yet it's only in extreme situations and a disaster is one popular form of extreme situation where you see something. A shop window, let's say, full of washing machines has a strange blankness about it. One brand of new washing machine is identical with another. There's something disturbing about, unsettling, unsatisfactory about all these identical—all this meaningless replication of things. But if you look at a smashed washing machine or let's say a wrecked car, or a broken building, it has a unique identity. It's unlike any other broken car or washing machine or building. This is what people are looking for, I think. Also they're looking for a very complex set of formulae in operation at a big rail disaster or plane disaster, multiple pile-up on a motorway. Visual and conceptual formulae of all kinds.

RE: Whenever there's an accident in the street people are repelled and at the same time attracted and they become neutralized to it almost.

JGB: Absolutely. Our own consciousness somehow isn't enough. Reality isn't wholly convincing. You need that some extra event, extra charge. An increase of electric, of psychological potential that will send a current through the system. Just to be conscious isn't enough. There's something too passive about it. Something's got to happen.

RE: You see it as a whole big spectrum of sensory experience. Supposing the situation arose whereby people found that they were cut off from 90 per cent of technological products.

JGB: But technology actually increases opportunities.

RE: But if technology was withdrawn.

JGB: Everything would go terribly flat. That's why to some extent the cutbacks in growth that have taken place—economic growth—have largely created this exhausted atmosphere in which we find ourselves here, compared with five to ten years ago in the late '60s. There's nothing more exciting than activity, motion, growth.

RE: It was primarily growth of products, and the spinoff from that was the growth people felt, people experience. Is it possible to turn the coin and get this excitement in just personal growth without the products to marry up with it?

JGB: Well, it's not just a ceaseless flow of consumer goods that I'm talking about. It's society as a huge organic structure which is itself moving forward, like some huge revolving space vehicle. It's that sense that carries everybody along and creates limitless new possibilities. It's possibility that people thrive on. Once possibility has become finite, there's a sense of growing entropy that develops and a sense of depression in the physiological sense. I think people thrive in a situation of maximum possibility. They thrive in hazard, in a volatile situation. The technological landscape is the obvious place.

RE: Because it's permanently volatile?

JGB: At its best, when it's growing, yes. Going back to consumer goods, I don't think going out and buying a new pair of tights from the supermarket is an economic action primarily. The cash transfer seems to me irrelevant. It's an extension in a small way of the possibilities in our lives. You have to consider ends rather than beginnings.

RE: So you think there's an actual slump in all possibilities?

JGB: Yes.

RE: What's the driving force behind this decrease in possibilities?

JGB: I think a slight sort of dust-bowl took place in the late '60s. Almost too many possibilities were used up too fast. Art itself suddenly came to town. It was sucked dry of all the interest and excitement and moved out of town fast.

RE: A lot of spastic things have resulted from that.

JGB: Entrepreneurial outfits like the ICA were ripping off left, right and centre. Anything they could lay their hands on. Everybody was having too much. What we need of course is more TV. More channels. There shouldn't just be programmes. The TV tube is the biggest node of possibility that exists at present in our lives. The possibilities aren't really being used. Instead of being a programme structured around news, current affairs and drama, I'd like to see TV operating on a sort of repertory system. You press a button and have any programme you like on any subject whether it's on chess, fishing, opera or any programmes of the kind that the computer companies are generating in their games division. At present TV's in the hands of gigantic units. Thousands of people involved. I'd like to get programmes into the hands of fewer people. More and more individual programmes.

Now why couldn't I have a programme that was say produced by one person? In the home with videotape systems and domestic TV units, every activity would be indulged in. Say I'm playing with my children, having a good time. It's all being recorded without my being aware of it. Then I can play it back. Maybe it can be modulated so I can have it in green or have a random selection of stills from 10 second intervals. These could be printed out off the screen by some sort of xerox system. By some sort of photo-projection technique I could re-wallpaper this room. I could have a continual replay. I could have myself playing with the kids in green multiplied by Mozart. The TV camera, the videotape system and a tube tuned to a whole range of other people's activities. Why shouldn't everyone have access to other people? Everybody's imagination should be plugged into everybody else's. TV is a means of enfranchising everybody's imagination. Locking everybody together in this huge nexus of possibilities. It can be done through electronics. I'm absolutely convinced of that.

It's basically a waste of time driving round the place. If you want to go anywhere, now the TV tube will take you there. The ultimate barrier is the barrier between what's going on inside our brains and the external world. Every person his own TV station. The ultimate brotherhood of man. (Phone rings.)

Dog. Dog. You've got some fleas I think.

I'm not suggesting people spend all their time producing glorified home movies. But I think this may lead to all sorts of other activities. There's a huge range of possibilities. This will come sooner or later.

JG Ballard's Handwritten Annotations to the 1970 Goddard Bibliography

by James Goddard

These are working pages from my early attempt at a JG Ballard bibliography. Ballard was, as usual, very cooperative, and as you can see the carbon copies sent to him for review were returned to me quite heavily annotated. The exterior of the hole punched slide binder I sent to Ballard was quite grubby, but the interior pages are fine. The last two scans are of John Carnell's introduction.

Dear Mr Goddard,

What an effort! I take my hat off to you —

I have filled in all the blanks — particularly in my own list at the end — this is the master list, & you may wish to amplify Section One for it to include non-sf magazines.

Best wishes,

J.G. Ballard

Text lies of J.G.
with
↓

Introduction

I am extremely grateful to Mr James Goddard for the time & effort needed to prepare these inventories — almost as much effort as went into writing the stories. In many cases I had no idea where the stories were originally published, as I have no copies of the original magazines. Throwing away books is a favourite pastime of mine — usually other peoples', I'm happy to say, but often my own. In many ways it makes rather sad reading, seeing the names of all those science fiction magazines which have now vanished, marking the end of modern science fiction as we know it. It is unlikely that anything comparable will ever appear again.

J.G.B.

SECTION ONE
Fiction In / Magazines → Science Fiction

I think you should make this distinction

Have published a good deal of fiction material in Ambit, also in various other magazines — Argosy, Encounter, Transatlantic Review, Circuit, Running Man — though I'm afraid I've no copies & can't say when.

Amazing

Encounter, The	June	1963
Insane Ones, The	Jan.	1962
Passport to Eternity	June	1962
Sherrington Theory, The	March	1963
Thirteen to Centaurus	April	1962
Thousand Dreams of Stellavista, The	March	1962

Fantastic

Question of Re-entry, A	March	1963
Screen Game, The	Oct.	1963
Singing Statues, The	July	1962
Sudden Afternoon, The	Sept.	1963

Fantasy and Science Fiction

Cloud Sculptors of Coral D, The	Dec.	1967
Cry Hope, Cry Fury	Oct.	1967
Garden of Time, The	Feb.	1962
Illuminated Man, The	May	1964
Lost Leonardo, The	March	1964
Now Wakes the Sea	May	1963

Great Science Fiction (reprint)

Insane Ones, The	July	1967	6
Singing Statues, The	April	1968	2
Thousand Dreams of Stellavista, The	Fall	1967	7

Impulse

You and Me and the Continuum	March	1966	1

The Most Thrilling SF Ever Told (reprint)

Passport to Eternity	Spring	1968	9
Sherrington Theory, The	August	1966	2
Thirteen to Centaurus	Winter	1967	7

New Worlds

Title	Month	Year	Issue
Assasination of John Fitzgerald Kennedy Considered as a Downhill Motor Race, The	March	1967	171
Assasination Weapon, The	April	1966	161
Atrocity Exhibition, The	Sept	1966	166
Beach Murders, The	April	1969	189
Billenium	Nov.	1961	112
Build Up	Jan.	1957	55
Cage of Sand, The	June	1962	119
Chronopolis	June	1960	95
Coitus 80	Jan.	1970	197
Day of Forever, The	Jan.	1967	170
Death Module, The	July	1967	173
Deep End	May	1961	106
Dune Limbo	March	1965	148
End Game	June	1963	131
Equinox (2 part serial)	May-Aug.	1964	142-3
Escapement	Dec.	1956	54
Generations of America, The	Oct.	1968	183
Gentle Assasin, The	Dec.	1961	113
How Dr. Christopher Evans Landed on the Moon	Feb.	1969	187
Journey Across a Crater	Feb.	1970	198
Killing Ground, The	March	1969	188
Man on the 99th Floor, The	July	1962	120
Manhole 69	Nov.	1957	65
Overloaded Man, The	July	1961	108
Place and a Time to Die, A	Sept-Oct.	1969	194
Princess Margarets Facelift	March	1970	199
Prisoner of the Coral Deep	May	1965	150
Storm Bird, Storm Dreamer	Nov.	1966	168
Storm Wind (2 part serial)	Sept-Oct.	1961	110-1
Subliminal Man, The	Jan.	1963	126
Summer Cannibals, The	Jan.	1969	186
Terminal Beach, The	March	1964	140
Tomorrow is a Million Years	Dec.	1966	169
Track 12	April	1958	70
Voices of Time, The	Oct.	1960	99
Waiting Grounds, The	Nov.	1959	88
You:Coma:Marilyn Monroe	June	1966	163
Zone of Terror	March	1960	92

New Worlds (American Edition)

Manhole 69	July	N&W.	1960
Waiting Grounds, The		June	1960

Insert PLAYBOY and ROGUE

Science Fantasy

Last World of Mr. Goddard, The	Oct.	1960	43
Minus One	June	1963	59
Mobile	June	1957	23
Mr. F is Mr. F	Aug.	1961	48
Now Zero	Dec.	1959	38
Prima Belladona	Dec.	1956	20
Sound Sweep, The	Feb.	1960	39
Studio 5, The Stars	Feb.	1961	45
Time of Passage	Feb.	1964	63
Watchtowers, The	June	1962	53

Science Fiction Adventures

Drowned World, The	Jan.	1962	24

Worlds of IF

Comsat Angels, The	Dec.	1968
Time Tombs, The	March	1963
Venus Smiles	Sept.	1967

Playboy

Drowned Giant, The (as Souvenir)		1964
The Dead Astronaut		1968

Rogue

Beach Murders, The (as Confetti Royale)	Jan-Feb.	1966

SECTION TWO

Books

Please fill in whatever information you can. If there has not been an edition in any of the categories please put <u>NONE</u>. If a book has been published in the US of A under a different title please put the US name.

The Atrocity Exhibition

  U.K. Hardback   Jonathan Cape 1970
  U.S. Hardback   Doubleday 1970

The Crystal World

  U.K. Hardback   Jonathan Cape 1966
  U.K. Paperback   Panther Books 1968
*U.S. Hardback   Farrar, Straus
*U.S. Paperback   Berkley   year

The Day of Forever

  U.K. Paperback   Panther Books 1967

Containing:

The Day of Forever	New Worlds, January 1967
Prisoner of the Coral Deep	New Worlds, May 1965
Tomorrow is a Million Years	New Worlds, December 1966
The Man on the 99th Floor	New Worlds, July 1962
The Waiting Grounds	New Worlds, November 1959
The Last World of Mr. Goddard	Science Fantasy, October 19
The Gentle Assassin	New Worlds, July 1961
The Sudden Afternoon	Fantastic, September 1963
The Insane Ones	Amazing, January 1962
The Assassination of John Fitzgerald Kennedy Considered as a Downhill Motor Race	New Worlds, February 1967

The Disaster Area

    U.K. Hardback   Jonathan Cape 1967
    U.K. Paperback   Panther Books 1969

Containing:

Storm Bird, Storm Dreamer	New Worlds, November 1966
The Concentration City (BUILD UP)	" " JANUARY 1957
The Subliminal Man	New Worlds, January 1963
Now Wakes the Sea	Fantasy & SF, May 1963
Minus One	Science Fantasy, June 1963
Mr. F. is Mr. F.	Science Fantasy, August 1961
Zone of Terror	New Worlds, March 1960
Manhole 69	New Worlds, November 1957
The Impossible Man	ORIGINAL STORY

The Drought

    U.K. Hardback   Jonathan Cape 1965
    U.K. Paperback   Penguin Books 1968
  *U.S. Hardback   NONE
  *U.S. Paperback   Berkley   1965 year?
    (as The Burning World)

The Drowned World

    U.K. Hardback   Victor Gollancz 1963
    U.K. SFBC Edition   SF Book Club 1964
    U.K. Paperback   Penguin Books 1965
  *U.S. Hardback   Doubleday 1964
  *U.S. Paperback   Berkley   1962   year

The Four Dimensional Nightmare

U.K. Hardback	Victor Gollancz 1963
U.K. Paperback	Penguin Books 1965
U.K. SFBC Edition	SF Book Club 1964
*U.S. Hardback	} None
*U.S. Paperback	

Containing:

The Voices of Time	New Worlds, November 1960
The Sound Sweep	Science Fantasy, February 1960
Prima Belladonna	Science Fantasy, December 1956
Studio 5, The Stars	Science Fantasy, February 1961
The Garden of Time	Fantasy & SF, February 1962
The Cage of Sand	New Worlds, June 1962
The Watchtowers	Science Fantasy, June 1962
Chronopolis	New Worlds, June 1960

The Overloaded Man

U.K. Paperback	Panther Books 1967

Containing:

Now Zero	Science Fantasy, December 1959
The Time Tombs	If, March 1963
Thirteen to Centaurus	Amazing, April 1962
Track 12	New Worlds, April 1958
Passport to Eternity	Amazing, June 1962
Escapement	New Worlds, December 1956
Time of Passage	Science Fantasy, February 1954
The Venus Hunters	
The Coming of the Unconscious	
The Overloaded Man	New Worlds, July 1961

The Terminal Beach

    U.K. Hardback   Victor Gollancz 1964
    U.K. Paperback   Penguin Books 1966
    *U.S. Hardback   None
    *U.S. Paperback   Berkley   year

Containing:

A Question of Re-entry	Fantastic, March 1963
The Drowned Giant	Playboy, 1964
End Game	New Worlds, June 1963
The Illuminated Man	Fantasy & SF, May 1964
The Reptile Enclosure	
The Delta at Sunset	
The Terminal Beach	New Worlds, March 1964
Deep End	New Worlds, May 1961
The Volcano Dances	
Billenium	New Worlds, November 1961
The Gioconda of the Twilight Noon	
The Lost Leonardo	Fantasy & SF, March 1964

The Voices of Time

    U.S. Paperback   Berkley Books 1962

Containing:

The Voices of Time	New Worlds, November 1960
The Sound Sweep	Science Fantasy, February
The Overloaded Man	New Worlds, July 1961
Zone of Terror	New Worlds, March 1960
Manhole 69	New Worlds, November 1957
The Waiting Grounds	New Worlds, November 1959
Deep End	New Worlds, May 1961

The Wind from Nowhere

    U.K. Paperback   Penguin Books 1967
    *U.S. Paperback   Berkley Books 1962 year

Section Three

Anthologised Stories

This section should be scrapped as it is so incomplete —

The Assassination of John Fitzgerald
  Kennedy Considered as a Downhill Motor Race   New Worlds 2/67
    (The Years Best SF 1 - Harrison and Aldiss)
Build Up   New Worlds 1/57
    (Connoiseurs SF - Boardman)
The Cloud Sculptors of Coral F   F & SF   12/67
    (Nebula Award Stories 3 - Zelazny)
The Drowned Giant   Playboy   /64
    (see Souvenir)
The Garden of Time   F & SF   2/62
    (The Best from F & SF 12th Series - Davidson)
The Insane Ones   Amazing   1/62
    (The Best of Sci-Fi 4 - Merrill)
The Lost Leonardo   F & SF   3/64
    (New Worlds of Fantasy - Carr)
Now Wakes the Sea   F & SF   5/63
    (The Best from F & SF 13th Series - Davidson)
Prima Belladona   Science Fantasy 12/56
    (SF:57 Years Greatest SF and Fantasy - Merrill)
    (SF:The Best of the Best - Merrill)
The Recognition   Original Story
    (Dangerous Visions - Ellison)
The Sound Sweep   Science Fantasy 2/60
    (5th Annual of the Years Best SF - Merrill)
    (SF:The Best of the Best - Merrill)
Souvenir   Playboy   /64
    (The Playboy Book of Fantasy and SF - Anon.)
    (as The Drowned Giant in Nebula Award Stories 1 - Knight)
The Terminal Beach   New Worlds 3/64
    (10th Annual SF - Merrill)
    (The Best of New Worlds - Moorcock)
The Time Tombs   If   3/63
    (The 2nd IF Reader - Pohl)
Track 12   New Worlds 4/58
    (Penguin SF - Aldiss)
The Voices of Time   New Worlds 10/60
    (Spectrum 3 - Amis and Conquest)

Section Four

Complete Alphabetical Listing of Published Works

NOTE: Where a story title appears twice this indicates
that it has appeared first in an original publication and then in a re-print issue. Titles in
bold type are book titles, for details of which
see BOOKS section.

Assassination of John Fitzgerald Kennedy Considered as a Downhill Motor Race, The	AMBIT 1966 NW	3/67	171
Assassination Weapon, The	NW	4/66	161
Atrocity Exhibition, The	NW	9/66	166
Atrocity Exhibition, The	E	3/67	
ATROCITY EXHIBITION, THE			
Beach Murders, The (see also Confetti Royale)	NW	4/69	189
Billenium	NW	11/61	112
Bulid Up	NW	1/57	55
Cage of Sand, The	NW	6/62	119
Chronopolis	NW	6/60	95
Cloud Sculptors of Coral D, The	F&SF	12/67	
Coitus 80	NW	1/70	197
*Coming of the Unconscious, The (Not a story) — NW			
Comsat Angels, The	If	12/68	
*Concentration City, The — Build Up			
Confetti Royale (see also The Beach Murders)	R	1-2/66	
*Crash I.C.A. Eventsheet 1969			
Cry Hope, Cry Fury	F&SF	10/67	
CRYSTAL WORLD, THE			
Day of Forever, The	NW	1/67	170
DAY OF FOREVER, THE			
*Dead Astronaut, The Playboy 1968			
Death Module, The	NW	7/67	173
Deep End	NW	5/61	106
*Delta at Sunset, The "The Terminal Beach" Gollancz			

```
DISASTER AREA, THE
DROUGHT, THE
Drowned Giant, The                      P         1/64
Drowned World, The                      SFA       1/62      24
DROWNED WORLD, THE
Dune Limbo                              NW        3/65      148

Encounter, The  (The Venus Hunters)     Amz       6/63
End Game                                NW        6/63      131
Equinox (2 part serial)                 NW        5-8/64    142-3
Escapement                              NW        12/56     54


    FOUR DIMENSIONAL NIGHTMARE, THE


Garden of Time, The                     F&SF      2/62
Generations of America, The             NW        10/68     183
Gentle Assassin, The                    NW        12/61     113
*Gioconda of the Twilight Noon, The     "The Terminal Beach"
*Great American Nude, The               Ambit
Greatest TV Show on Earth, The *(1)

~~How Dr.Christopher Evens Landed on the Moon~~   ~~NW~~  ~~~~   ~~197~~

Illuminated Man, The                    F&SF      5/64
*Impossible Man, The                    The Disaster Area
Insane Ones, The                        Amz       2/62
Insane Ones, The                        GSF       7/67      6

Journey Across A Crater                 NW        2/70      198

Killing Ground, The                     NW        3/69      188

Last World of Mr.Goddard, The           SF        10/60     43
Lost Leonardo, The                      F&SF      3/64
*Love and Napalm                        Circuit 1968
```

Manhole 69	NW	11/57	65
Manhole 69	NWUS	7/60	
Man on the 99th Floor, The	NW	7/62	120
Minus One	SF	6/63	59
Mobile	SF	6/57	23
Mr.F. is Mr.F.	SF	8/61	48
Now Wakes the Sea	F&SF	5/63	
Now : Zero	SF	12/59	38
	NWUS	6/60	
Overloaded Man, The	NW	7/61	108
OVERLOADED MAN, THE			
Passport to Eternity	Amz	2/62	
Passport to Eternity	MTSF	Spr/68	9
Place and a Time to Die, A	NW	9-10/69	194
*Plan For the Assassination of Jackie Kennedy, A	Ambit		
Prima Belladonna	SF	12/56	20
Princess Margarets Facelift	NW	3/70	199
Prisoner of the Coral Deep	NW	5/65	150
	ARGOSY		64
Question of Re-entry, A	Fant	3/63	
Recognition, The	Dangerous Visions		
*Reptile Enclosure, The (The Sherrington Theory)			
Rumour, The *(2)			
Say Goodbye to the Wind *(3)			
Screen Game, The	Fant	10/63	
Sherrington Theory, The	Amz	3/63	
Sherrington, Theory, The	MTSF	8/66	2
Singing Statues, The	Fant	7/62	
Singing Statues, The	GSF	4/67	2
Sound Sweep, The	SF	2/60	39

Storm Bird, Storm Dreamer	NW	11/66	168
Storm Wind	NW	9-10/61	110-1
Studio 5, The Stars	SF	12/61	45
Subliminal Man, The	NW	1/63	126
Sudden Afternoon, The	Fant	9/63	
Summer Cannibals, The	NW	1/69	186
Terminal Beach, The	NW	3/64	140
~~Terminal~~ TERMINAL BEACH, THE			
Thirteen to Centaurus	Amz	4/62	
Thirteen to Centaurus	MTSF	Wint/67	7
Thousand Dreams of Stellavista, The	Amz	3/62	
Thousand Dreams of Stellavista, The	GSF	Fall/67	7
Time of Passage	SF	2/64	63
Time Tombs, The	If	3/63	
Tolerances of the Human Face	E	9/69	
Tomorrow is a Million Years	NW	12/66	169
Track 12	ARGOSY 66 NW	4/58	70
*University of Death, The	Transatlantic Review 1968		
*Venus Hunters, The (The Encounter)			
Venus Smiles	If	9/67	
Voices of Time, The	NW	10/60	99
VOICES OF TIME, THE			
*Volcano Dances, The	"The Terminal Beach"		
Waiting Grounds, The	NW	11/59	88
Waiting Grounds, The	NWUS	6/60	
Watchtowers, The	SF	6/62	53 * 23/5/74
*Why I Want to Fuck Ronald Reagan	International Times 1968		
WIND FROM NOWHERE, THE			

You and Me and the Continuum	Imp	3/66	1
You : Coma : Marilyn Monroe	NW	6/66	163
	Ambit	1966	
Zone of Terror	NW	3/60	92

---

*(1) The Greatest TV Show on Earth - not yet published.
*(2) The Rumour - accepted by Playboy but not yet published.
*(3) Say Goodbye to the Wind - To be published in Amazing.

This is the complete list, though many of the stories are not credited to the first magazine of publication — not that this matters —

SECTION FIVE

Chronological Listing of Stories

(If you want to, you are welcome to use this comment from me ↓)

NOTE: This section is based on the order in which MR. Ballard wrote the stories, which is not necessarily the order in which they were published.

This list contains, in the order in which I wrote them, all the short stories and fictional pieces ~~which~~ I have written since my very first short story in 1956 — Prima Belladonna — and ending with the latest at the time of writing, May 1970 — Princess Margaret's Face Lift. Interested readers will note that despite 15 years of effort not much has changed. The list contains 2 unpublished stories, one which Playboy bought but seems to have declined to publish, and another, which is the only short story of mine I ~~to~~ am happy to say I have been, though I am still trying, unable to place;] As well ←

→ The list reflects the demise of the science fiction magazine, both here + in the U.S.A., and from my point of view, the fortunate appearance on the scene of magazine editors from ~~previous~~ very much outside the field of science fiction — whether of Playboy, Encounter or Ambit — willing and eager to publish experimental science fiction.

Most important of all, this list, like the other inventories here, shows the enormous debt which I owe to New Worlds — above all to its great editor Ted Carnell and his equally courageous successor Michael Moorcock.

J. G. Ballard

Prima Belladonna	SF	12/56	20
Escapement	NW	12/56	54
Bulid Up	NW	1/57	55
Mobile	SF	6/57	23
Manhole 69	NW	11/57	65
	NWUS	7/60	
Track 12	NW	4/58	70
The Waiting Grounds	NW	11/59	88
	NWUS	6/60	
Now Zero	SF	12/59	38
Sound Sweep	SF	2/60	39
Zone of Terror	NW	3/60	92
The Last World of Mr. Goddard	SF	10/60	43
Chronopolis	NW	6/60	95
The Voices of Time	NW	10/60	99
Studio 5, The Stars	SF	2/61	45
Deep End	NW	5/61	106
The Overloaded Man	NW	7/61	108
Mr. F is Mr. F	SF	8/61	48
Billenium	NW	11/61	112
Gentle Assassin	NW	12/61	113
The Thousand Dreams of Stellavista	Amz	3/62	
	GSF	Fall/67	7
The Singing Statues	Fant	7/62	
	GSF	4/67	2
The Man on the 99th Floor	NW	7/62	120
The Insane Ones	Amz	2/62	
	GSF	7/67	6
The Garden of Time	F&SF	2/62	
Thirteen to Centaurus	Amz	4/62	
	MTSF	Wint/67	7
Time of Passage	SF	2/64	63
The Time Tombs	If	3/63	
The Drowned World	SFA	1/62	24
The Subliminal Man	NW	1/63	126
Passport to Eternity	Amz	2/62	
	MTSF	Spri/68	9

The Watchtowers		SF	6/62	53
The Cage of Sand		NW	6/62	119
A Question of Re-entry		Fant	2/63	
The Lost Leonardo		F&SF	3/64	
*The Reptile Enclosure (Sherrington Theory)	AMZ	3/63	
The Screen Game		Fant	10/63	
Now Wakes the Sea		F&SF	5/63	
*The Venus Hunters (The Encounter)	AMZ	6/63	
Minus One		SF	6/63	59
*The Delta at Sunset — *The Terminal Beach*			
End Game		NW	6/63	131
The Illuminated Man		F&SF	5/64	
The Drowned Giant (as Souvenir)		P	/64	
The Sudden Afternoon		Fant	9/63	
Prisoner of the Coral Deep	Argosy 64		5/65	150
The Terminal Beach		NW	3/64	140
*The Volcano Dances — *The Terminal Beach*			
*The Gioconda of the Twilight Noon — *The Terminal Beach*			
Equinox (2 part serial)		NW	5-8/64	142/3
*The Impossible Man — *The Disaster Area*			
Storm Bird, Storm Dreamer		NW	11/66	168
The Recognition		in Dangerous Visions		
The Day of Forever (X) CONFETTI ROYALE		NW	1/67	170
The Assassination of John Fitzgerald Kennedy Considered as a Downhill Motor Race	Ambit 66		3/67	171
You and Me and the Continuum		Imp	3/66	1
The Assassination Weapon		NW	4/66	161
You: Coma: Marilyn Monroe	Ambit 66	NW	6/66	163
The Rumour *(1)				
Tomorrow is a Million Years	Argosy 66	NW	12/66	169
The Atrocity Exhibition		NW	9/66	166
		E	3/67	
The Cloud Sculptors of Coral D		F&SF	12/67	
Cry Hope Cry Fury		F&SF	10/67	
Say Goodbye to the Wind *(2)		AMZ	8/70	

Venus Smiles	If	9/67	
The Greatest TV Show on Earth *(3)			
The Dead Astronaut	*Playboy 1968*		
Plan for the Assassination of Jackie Kennedy	*Ambit*		
The Death Module	NW	7/67	173
Why I Want to Fuck Ronald Reagan	*International Times 1968*		
The Killing Ground	NW	3/69	188
The Comsat Angels	If	12/68	
Love and Napalm: EXPORT U.S.A.	*Circuit 1968*		
University of Death	*Transatlantic Review 1968*		
The Great American Nude	*Ambit 1968*		
The Generations of America	NW	10/68	183
The Summer Cannibals	NW	1/69	186
Crash	*ICA Eventsheet 1968*		
Tolerances of the Human Face	E	9/69	
The Beach Murders	R	1-2/66	
(as Confetti Royale)			
(as The Beach Murders)	NW	4/69	189
A Place and a Time to Die	NW	9-10/69	194
Journey Across a Crater	NW	2/70	198
Coitus 80	NW	1/70	197
Princess Margaret's Facelift	NW	3/70	199

---

*(1) The Rumour - accepted by Playboy but not yet published.
*(2) Say Goodbye to the Wind - to be published in Amazing.
*(3) The Greatest TV Show on Earth - not yet published.

TRANSFER TO POINT (X)

A. J.G. Ballard Bibliography

INTRODUCTION by John Carnell

Now that science fiction is so well established, bibliographies of the works of prominent authors are an essential part of every collector's life -- and even more essential to anthologising editors. In endorsing James Goddard's presentation of the published works of Mr. Ballard, my pleasure is manifold; as a reader, a collector, an editor, an anthologist but above all as the 'discoverer' of Jim Ballard. Actually this is a misnomer because editors do not 'discover' authors, they 'find' each other by a mutual symbiosis which seems to stem from some hidden literary chemical formula invisible to the reader's eye.

Jim Ballard sent me a story, "Escapement," in the summer of 1956, when I was editing <u>New Worlds Science Fiction</u> and <u>Science Fantasy</u>, which I liked and offered to buy. He then followed it up with a personal visit to my office, bringing with him a fantasy story titled "Prima Belladonna," which I liked even better. The chemicals had begun to catalyse. In a very short time, stories were flowing steadily from the versatile mind of Jim Ballard -- in five years I published forty in the two magazines, all of which I enjoyed but some more than others. They covered a wide range of thought-provoking ideas, from the musical plants in "Prima Belladonna" and the fascinating background to "The Soundsweep," to the hard science fiction of "The Voices Of Time" and "The Waiting Grounds."

Throughout all these stories one can see the gradual expansion of the author's experimental thinking and exploration into what he himself eventually termed "inner space," until he finally burst out of the restricting bonds of the then accepted framework of story writing in the early 1960's. Fragments of this later development can be seen in his two early novels, "The Wind From Nowhere" and "The Drowned World," both of which I was fortunate enough to be able to publish in magazine form, the former under the title of "Storm Wind."

cont/2

J.G. Ballard Bibliography

cont/2

Jim Ballard's literary qualities were evident from the beginning; it only remained for him to experiment and expand to find his true metier in the literary scheme of things. Personal preference always play a large part in a reader's enjoyment of a writer's works and these must be left to the individual. My own personal favourites are all the 'Vermilion Sands' stories, "The Sound Sweep," "Now Wakes The Sea," "Chronopolis," and the incomparable "Billenium." Too short a list really; I could list dozens more but those came immediately to mind.

May 1970 <u>John Carnell</u>

ANA BARRADO
South River Drive, Miami, Florida, 1996

ANA BARRADO
DC-10 over Miami International Airport, 1996

ANA BARRADO
Agenas A & B, Cape Canaveral, 1995

Goddard & Pringle, Interviewers
JG Ballard, Editor

Contributed by James Goddard

On 4 January 1975 David Pringle and James Goddard sat down with JG Ballard at his home in Shepperton and had an extended chat. The interview that followed was published in full in *Vector* and later in the book, *JG Ballard: The First 20 Years*; but Goddard also had the opportunity to publish another version of it in *Science Fiction Monthly*. This magazine's more mainstream audience prompted Goddard to send a transcript of the interview to Ballard for checking/approval before publication, and what follows are scans of the pages Ballard returned. All additions, deletions and comments are Ballard's. The edited interview was published as "JG Ballard's Science Fiction for Today."

~~THE DRAMATISED LANDSCAPES OF J.G. BALLARD~~

An Interview

Goddard: I'd like to start off if I may by asking you to tell us something about your origins and background?

Ballard: I was born in Shanghai in China in 1930; my father was a businessman there. We returned to England in 1946 after three years of internment by the Japanese. I went to school, and then to Cambridge University where I started off by reading medicine. After two years I gave that up and began writing. In 1956 I had my first short story published in New Worlds. After working on a scientific journal for a while I became a full-time writer, that was about fifteen years ago, and I've been at it ever since.

Goddard: Do you think the period of internment under the Japanese had any effect on the kind of fiction you produce?

Ballard: I would guess it had. The landscapes of the Far East had a tremendously powerful influence on me - as did the whole war experience. All the abandoned cities and towns and beach resorts that I keep returning to in my fiction were there in that huge landscape, the area just around our camp, which was about eight miles from Shanghai out in the paddy fields near the mouth of the Yangtse River. There was a period when we didn't know if the war had ended, when the Japanese had more or less left, and the Americans had yet to come in. All the empty airfields and the bits of advanced technology that had been totally abandoned, houses, must have touched something in my mind. It was a very interesting zone, and obviously had a big influence; as did the semi-tropical nature of the place, lush vegetation, a totally water-logged world, huge rivers, canals, paddies, great sheets of water everywhere. It was a very dramatized landscape thanks to the war and to the collapse of all the irrigation systems, a landscape dramatized in a way that is difficult to find in, say, Western Europe. Don't forget, too, that I was about 500 miles from the Nagasaki and Hiroshima A-bombs about the distance from here to Aberdeen — that sort of closeness produces very ambiguous attitudes to violence in particular.

Goddard: One of the most popular areas of your work is the series of <u>Vermilion Sands</u> stories. A critical reading of these shows that they are all, to some extent, variations on the same theme. Could you tell us something about why you wrote these stories? What you were trying to achieve?

Ballard: I've never really analysed them myself. I suppose I was just interested in inventing an imaginary Palm Springs, a kind of world I imagined all the suburbs of North America and Northern Europe might be like in about 200 years time. Everyone will be permanently on vacation, or doing about one day's work a year. People will give in to any whim that occurs to them – like taking up cloud sculpture – leisure and work will merge. I think everybody will be very relaxed, almost too relaxed. It will also be a landscape of not so much <u>suburbia</u> but <u>exurbia</u>, a kind of country-club belt, which will be largely the product of advanced technologies devoted entirely to leisure. I think the future will be like <u>Vermilion Sands</u>, if I have to make a guess, it isn't going to be like <u>Brave New World</u> or <u>1984</u>. It's going to be like a country-club paradise.

Pringle: It's not the impression of the future people would get from your books as a whole, where you write about disaster and doom.

Ballard: I think that's a false reading, I don't see my fiction as being disaster orientated, certainly not most of my SF,

People sometimes think that these are books with unhappy endings, but the reverse is true, they're books with happy endings, stoires of psychic fulfillment. The geophysical changes that take place in the novels The Drought, The Drowned World and The Crystal World, are all positive and good changes, they are what the books are about. The changes lead us to our real psychological goals; so they are not disaster stories at all. When The Drowned World was accepted by my American publisher about twelve years ago, he said: 'Yes, great, but why don't we have a happy ending? Have the hero going North, instead of South into the jungle and sun'. He thought I'd made a slight technical mistake by a slip of the pen, and had the hero going in the wrong direction. I said no, this is a happy ending. I don't understand the use of the word 'disaster'. I'm trying to show a new kind of logic emerging, and this is to be embraced.

Goddard: Why have you never produced a work with a sympathetic male/female relationship?

Ballard: That's an interesting question.

Pringle: It's in the great tradition of the English novel!

Ballard: Being serious, of the twentieth century writers which would you say do this?

Goddard: Some of Hemingway......

Ballard: Now that's interesting, really! What? Which? Where? You're thinking of the film version of For Whom the Bell Tolls presumably?

Goddard: No, I've never seen that......

Ballard: I suppose the relationship in To Have and Have Not, between the tough guy and his wife, is happy in a way. What I'm really saying is that sypathetic male/female relationships - and your question is quite

My fiction is about one person, coming to terms with various forms of isolation; the sense of isolation in the vastness of the universe that the hero of "The Voices of Time" feels, or the psychological isolation in the face of the limitless destructiveness of the H-Bomb that the hero of "The Terminal Beach" feels. That tends to exclude the possibility of a warm fruitful relationship with anybody, let alone anyone as potentially close as a woman. I don't think this has anything to do with any quirks of my own. I've got three children with whom I'm extremely close, and yet I've never introduced a child into any of my stories.

Pringle: There have been one or two dead children.

Ballard: That's true, but there are no living children in my fiction, yet all the people who know me closely know that I'm a very fond father.

Goddard: Why are the female characters in Vermilion Sands all of movie-queen types?

Ballard: Well, these stories are frolics of a kind. I've never been to Palm Springs, but I dare say if you go there in season, or to St. Moritz in season, you'll find a lot of movie-queens and pink Cadilacs. If you wander round Shepperton on a Saturday in Summer, Shepperton being the Malibu of the Thames Valley, you'll find that sort of atmosphere.

Goddard: Could you tell us something about your four disaster novels, which you insist aren't disaster novels? The Wind from Nowhere, The Drowned World, The Drought and The Crystal World, which all have disasters in them, in the classic British SF form.

Ballard: You're right when you say that it's a classic English SF form, but that's the reason why I used the formula of the disaster story.

Usually these cataclysms are treated as though they are disasters, they're treated straight, everyone's running for the hills — if it's going to be cold they're all putting on their overcoats, if it's going to be hot they're taking them off. I deliberately want to invert all this. That's the whole point of my novels — the heroes' psychological compulsions embrace the particular upheaval. These are really stories of huge psychic transformations, and I use the external transformation of the landscape to reflect the internal transformation, the psychological transformation, of the characters. They're transformation stories rather than disaster stories. If you take that classic English disaster story, The Day of the Triffids, I think it's fair to say that there's absolutely no psychological dimension. The characters react to the changes that are taking place, but they are not in any psychological way involved with the proliferating vegetation, or whatever else is going on. They cope with the situation in the same way as the inhabitants of Shepperton might cope with, say, a local reservoir bursting. In the classic English disaster story there's no involvement on a psychological level with whatever is taking place. My novels are completely different.

Goddard: Why did you stop writing them, when plot permutations seem endless?

Ballard: I don't think I did. Crash is a disaster novel, an urban disaster story, so is Concrete Island, so is the one I've just finished, High-Rise, about a high-rise apartment block.

Even the stories in The Atrocity Exhibition are disaster stories of a kind. The book is written about the communications explosion of the sixties. From my point of view the sixties started in 1963 with the assassination of President Kennedy, his death and Vietnam presided over the whole of the sixties. Those two events, transmitted through television and mass communications, overshadowed the whole decade — a sort of institutionalised disaster area.

there are limitless possibilities, well, what are they? You've got to have a convincing and interesting transformation of the physical landscape.

Goddard: For a few years in the mid-sixties your work had a sort of Jekyll and Hyde nature about it; you were producing both lineal SF stories, and the so-called experimental stories. Were you testing the water before taking the plunge, gauging public reaction?

Ballard: They weren't called experimental by me, I dislike that term. It implies a test procedure of uncertain outcome. The trouble with most British experimental writing is that it proves one thing, and that is that the experiment has not worked. I wasn't influenced by market consiserations at all. In fact, all through the sixties I was writing eonventional short stories at the same time, there weren't very many of them, but I was still writing them. I've started writing some more now. ~~In a review that Peter Linnett wrote he said something about my giving up writing those Atrocity Exhibition pieces for financial reasons, I don't know where he got~~ that idea from. The simple fact is that the ideas that went into that book, good or bad, took years to generate; I'd like to write a follow up to it, but it will take me ten years, probably, to accumalate the material inside my own head, also, the climate is wrong now.

Pringle: There may have been no financial reasons for you to stop writing them, but were you at all influenced by adverse criticism, because there was a lot of it in this country?

Ballard: Criticism by whom? By the SF readership? The literary critics or reviewers? I don't know. Obviously a book like that is not going to be as popular as a conventionally written book, there's no doubt about that. ~~Just as a book like Crash is not going to be popular.~~ All the same, I found ~~that stories in~~ The Atrocity Exhibition produced more response from people than anything else I've ever written; people whom I'd never had any contact with, from all over the world, took the trouble to get in touch with me, which is a sure test of something. I felt the response to that book was better and larger than anything else I've ever had. ~~In fact, I was encouraged to go on, because as I wrote the stories over a period of four or five years, the response grew.~~

~~Pringle: Your have written some stories in this mode since the book was published?~~

Goddard: Could you tell us something about what it was like to work for *New Worlds* during the time of its change from an SF magazine to a literary magazine in a wider context?

Ballard: I've been tremendously lucky, that was a most exciting time. The late sixties were a period of totally unprecedented excitement in almost every field. I think by the time that *New Worlds* changed from a paperback to a large format magazine this was really the final break with the American-dominated SF of the forties and fifties, is shown. The battle had been won. The group of writers Moorcock published in *New Worlds*, myself included, had proved their point, and the old guard had run of gas. By the late sixties *New Worlds* was not just the most exciting SF magazine in the world — it made all the American mags like *Analog* look terribly old-fashioned — it was one of the most exciting magazines of *any* kind in this country, and we were to some extent lucky to have Mike Moorcock running it. It ceased to be an SF magazine at all, even within my elastic definition of the term, and became something much closer to avant garde experimental writing; perhaps that was inevitable.

Goddard: Why did it change from an SF magazine to an avant garde magazine?

Was it a matter of editorial policy, or did the writers orchestrate it?

Ballard: I think the writers themselves lost touch with SF. A group of writers came along who weren't really interested in SF. Many of them are close friends of mine, and they won't mind me saying this, but writers like Sladek, Disch, Spinrad, Pam Zoline, even Mike Moorcock himself, none of them are really science fiction writers.

~~cause that I am a science fiction writer. These~~ ~~recent New Worlds~~ ~~writers~~ began ~~writing~~ outside the genre, I think the ~~magazine~~ suffered from that, ~~but~~ ~~~~. I'm not knocking New Worlds, I'm extremely grateful to Mike Moorcock, and before him to Ted Carnell, without those two it's hard to see how I would have published any of my fiction at all over the years. It was a very exciting period and it's a pity there's no magazine like it now.

Goddard: You have credited Ted Carnell with sowing the seeds of change as far as you personally were concerned. How much of an influence was he on your development as a writer?

Ballard: He was an influence in the sense that, but for New Worlds, I would have been in a bit of a spot; he had three magazines for which I was encouraged to produce a continuous stream of short stories over a period of ~~getting on for~~ ten years. ~~He gave me every freedom, I don't think he ever rejected a story of mine.~~ He gave me complete freedom to write anything I wanted ~~at a time when, and you will r~~Remember that I began writing in '56 – '57, round about the time of the first flight of Sputnik 1, which seemed to confirm everything that the old-guard SF fans, writers and publishers in America believed in. This was their millenium, ~~it had arrived,~~ and it ~~would have~~ seemed ~~superficially~~ the worst time for moving away from ~~things~~ science-fiction ~~sort~~ based on space, interplanetary travel, the far future. However, Ted Carnell encouraged me to make the break with this kind of SF. ~~and what have you, it would have seemed the worst time to stop writing that kind of thing, and yet he encouraged me, said go ahead.~~ One tends to forget how resistant to change and experiment of any kind SF is, that's the paradox. It ought to be dedicated to change and novelty and experiment, but in fact it's deeply conservative. ~~You found in the 50s and 60s in the States an absolute resistance to any kind of novelty.~~ Ted Carnell was unique in giving me this freedom to write anything I wanted ~~to, and I dealt with the American editors and publishers. I don't know whether Ted would have published the stories in The Atrocity Exhibition, possibly not, though he did publish "The Terminal Beach"; I remember some of the rejection slips I got from American editors when that story came back. Ted established the possibility of change; he recognised that SF, by the mid fifties, had used all its material, it had built its world, the last brick, as it were, was slotted into place, there was no way out, there was no possibility of change; he recognised that. He used to caution other young writers who modelled their fiction on the kind of stories that appeared in Galaxy in the early and mid fifties; and he would caution them very much against the kind of SF~~

[struck through:] that required an intense familiarity with science fiction before you even began to understand it. The kind of stories that Galaxy and Astounding, in their different ways, were publishing made very little sense to an outsider, because they didn't know what the narrative and plot and subject matterconventions were, and without that knowledge you were lost. Ted, even before I arrived on the scene, felt that the time had come for a change of direction. [end struck through] English SF has always been much more open to change and novelty. It always depresses me when I meet Americans who really believe that they invented SF [struck through: round about Gernsback's first mag, 1926, and the ten years after.] In fact, what they did was to limit its range, conventionalise it, and fossilize it. [struck through: English writers, who've been writing the stuff for 150 years or more have always had a much more open approach to the SF they've written, so English SF has always been much less homogeneous than American SF.]

[struck through:]
Goddard: Did Carnell ever suggest ways in which your work could take new directions?

Ballard: I think there were one or two stories where he suggested I could enlarge a particular aspect, but he never suggested any idea, or particular directions I should take. Most of the stuff I wrote then is pretty conventional, at least outside the narrow little world of SF, half of the stories aren't even SF within the popular definition of the term.
[end struck through]

Goddard: You have none of the science-fictional background that was almost regarded as obligatory for success as an SF writer at one time; and yet you've achieved an enviable reputation as one of the leading exponents of the field. Any comments?

Ballard: Was it obligatory? I did it [struck through: I don't] know.

Goddard: Well, we read of people like Bradbury and Pohl and Asimov growing up reading the stuff, writing letters to magazines, joining clubs, doing their own fanzines and so on, yet you have none of this background.

Ballard: In America, yes, that's true. But there have always been people outside that. Bradbury apart, I think the best American SF novel I've ever read is Bernard Wolfe's Limbo 90, he's never struck me as having anything to do with SF fandom. [struck through: You're really talking about fandom aren't you, which is an entirely different kettle of fish!]

Goddard: I'm thinking of the writers who have come out of fandom.

Ballard: There are some, I suppose. It's a very peculiar thing. Modern American SF was virtually invented by a single generation of writers. They lived in an intense closed world with each other, intermarrying, everyone seemed to be married to someone else's second wife or third husband. The anthologist Judith Merril once described to me the American SF writers in the fifties, moving around the States like something out of On the Road, living together in little enclaves; there were all these collaborations going on, and they surfaced now and then at an SF convention, and then took off again on their endless car rides, a strange sort of Bonnie and Clyde existence. They never seemed to meet anyone outside that little world. The tremendous homogeneity of American SF, and the rigid conventions that sprang up concerning what was or wasn't the correct way to write a story, were all part of the self-protective ghetto they built. That's something that's never taken place over here. Americans are always surprised when they come over here and realise that for the most part English SF writers don't meet each other, there's no more homogeneity here among SF writers than there is among writers in general.

Pringle: You mentioned collaborations. Would writing in collaboration with someone else be entirely unthinkable to you?

Ballard: I'd love to collaborate, and I talked it over once or twice with Mike Moorcock. The Americans collaborated very easily, partly because they all produced this very standardised fiction. It's not all that easy to tell if you're given a paragraph of Pohl that it's not by Sheckley or Matheson or Kuttner, particularly with all the pseudonyms they used. There are very few writers you can identify stylistically. Here the opposite is true, collaborations would be difficult because the writers have been free to evolve in their own seperate directions; they've not been, for the most part, constrained by a set of house rules.

Pringle: Talking about style, to what extent are you aware that you evolved your style deliberately? I suppose it just happened with most writers, but your style is very distinctive, and most readers who know your work don't confuse it with that of other writers. How conscious was this?

Ballard: Totally unconscious, I've never given it a thought. I've written certain stories and novels in a particular style, the style that seemed natural to the subject, but I've never consciously tried to evolve a literary style that is unique to myself. One writes the way one feels.

Pringle: One of the very notable things about your style is a certain repetitiousness of words and phrases, particularly in The Atrocity Exhibition, and to some extent in Crash. ~~You repeat words, and this is something people have criticised. It was Martin Amis, I think, in his review of Crash, who went through and counted how many times you use the word "metalized", and one or two others, and came up with a figure of fifty or sixty.~~

Ballard: That's very true, ~~but I was using language~~ I use certain words and phrases for deliberate reasons. ~~to a certain fixed and obvious end.~~ The medical and scientific terminology ~~language pseudo-medical jargon~~ that I use ~~, is all deliberate, these are particular notes that I can strike, which, I hope, signify something to the reader. It~~ is all part of a second language, ~~if you like, that is~~ carried along by the surface of the narrative, a series of signposts with codes, or whatever you like to call them. There's a lot of jargon, too — ~~These are jokes on myself, in a way~~ I suppose.

Pringle: Apart from the medical language you mentioned, there's also use of emotional, picturesque, rather poetic language, ~~about flowers and things,~~ which reminds me of the French surrealists. Did they influence you?

Ballard: Yes, they certainly did. ~~Genet, not a surrealist, but Genet certainly, Genet, their sort of language was a big influence, there's no question about it.~~ But not many English writers.

Pringle: Conrad?

Ballard: It's a funny thing ~~really~~, but when The Drowned World was published people said it was heavily influenced by Conrad; oddly enough, at that time, though I was 31 or 32, I'd never read a word of Conrad. I remember Victor Gollancz, the publisher, taking me out to lunch after ~~the~~ he'd bought The Drowned World, and turning to me jokingly and saying: "Well, you stole the whole thing from Conrad." I thought, oh, what's this? I went away and actually read some Conrad, which I found rather heavy going, though obviously he's a great writer with a unique evocative style. I could see a resemblance; but that's partly because if you're going to try and build up the atmosphere of steaming jungles, there's only one way of doing it.

Pringle: I think it was Graham Greene who compared Heart of Darkness with your Crystal World; was there any influence there?

Ballard: I don't know whether I'd read Heart of Darkness at the time I wrote Crystal World. I honestly don't think I was influenced by Conrad. I don't mind being influenced, after all, we're all influenced to some extent, but if you're talking about conscious imitation - certainly not.

Pringle: Were you influenced by Graham Greene?

Ballard: Probably, yes. There's something about Greene's handling of solitary characters, his ways of externalizing a character's mind in terms of the situation in which he finds himself. He does this so brilliantly. He can have a solitary figure standing by a jetty in the Far East looking at some sampans, and he brings in a few things like the local police chief scratching his neck and so on, and within a paragraph one has a marvellous evocation of the psychology of the hero and of what the book is about. Yes, I probably was influenced by Greene, but I never consciously imitated him.

Pringle: Were you attracted to Greene because of your Far East background?

Ballard: What I like about Greene, and still do, is that although he's a brilliant writer, he has not, from my point of view, been ensnared by the English literary scene. He's very much a twentieth century man, and his fiction is generated by his experience of the world outside England. He couldn't be further apart from someone like Kingsley Amis or Anthony Powell, whose fiction is entirely generated by the closed world, not just of England, but of a very small part of England. In Greene's fiction one can breathe the smells, and see the sights, and hear the sounds of the whole world. Not having spent my childhood and adolescence in England, I received a very big shock when I got here in 1946 and found it was a closed little island containing a whole lot of lesser islands. The world of professional middle-class life in those days was incredibly narrow, I just couldn't breathe in it. That's one of the reasons why I started writing SF, one could get away from all this sort of thing. I certainly admire Graham Greene a great deal.

Goddard: How do you view your books since <u>The Atrocity Exhibition</u> in the greater science fiction context, in which you maintain they still have a niche?

Ballard: I was tremendously exhilarated when I started reading American science fiction when I was 18 or 19, the excitement, the enormous power of imagination. But I felt that the writers weren't really making the most of their own subject matter. Right from the start what I wanted to do was write a type of science fiction that got away from spaceships, interplanetary novel and the far future, which I felt were basically rather juvenile, to writing an adult science fiction based upon the present. Why couldn't one harness this freedom and vitality? Science fiction is a form, above all else, that puts a tremendous premium upon the imagination, and that's something that seems to have left the English novel in the last 150 years. Imagination is enormously important, and I felt that if one could only harness this capacity to think imaginatively in an adult SF, one would have achieved something. Right from the begining I tried to write a science fiction about the present day, which is more difficult to do than one realises, because the natural tendency when writing in a basically allegorical mode is to set something at a distance because it makes the separateness of the allegory that much more obvious. I wanted to write about the present day, and I think <u>Crash</u>, <u>Concrete Island</u> and the book I've just finished, High-Rise, which are a kind of trilogy, represent the conclusion of the particular logic I've been trying to unfold ever since I began writing. Are they SF? I don't know; maybe the science fiction of the present day <u>will</u> be something like <u>Crash</u>. They come into the category of works of imaginative fiction, with a strong moralistic, cautionary and exploratory note. But I don't know whether they're SF or not.

Pringle: What do you mean by 'moralistic'?

Ballard: Trying to say something about the quality of one's moral direction

Pringle: There's one thing that people who dislike your work often talk about, and that's a lack of moral standards, lack of some sort of touchstone, where you stand......

Ballard: I would have thought there was too much moralising in my stuff.

Pringle: ......this disturbed a lot of people who reviewed Crash!

Ballard: They were supposed to be disturbed. When I set out to write Crash, I wanted to write a book in which there was nowhere to hide. I wanted the reader, once I'd got him inside the book, never to loose sight of the subject matter. It would have been very easy to write a conventional book about car-crashes in which it was quite clear that the author was on the side of sanity, justice, and against injuring small children, deaths on the road, bad driving etc. What could be easier? I chose to completely accept the demands of the subject matter, which was to provoke the reader by appearing to say that car-crashes are good for you, you thoroughly enjoy them, they make your sex-life richer, they represent part of the marriage between sex - the human organism - and technology. I say all these things in order to provoke the reader and also to test him. There may be truth in some of these sentiments, disagreeable though they are to consider. Nobody likes that, they'll think, God, the man's mad, but any other way of writing that book would have been a cop-out.

Goddard: Was Crash in any way an experiment in self-exorcism? I believe you did experience a serious car-crash once.

Ballard: Yes, but that was after I'd finished the book. Ones attitudes and feelings to a whole range of human activities are ambiguous, aren't they? This is the whole problem, what one's real motives are. There are elements of self-exorcism, I suppose. I'm an introverted person, my real life is going on inside my head; obviously I can see that in writing Concrete Island and describing a man who resembles me to some extent, I am playing on my awareness of my own reclusiveness. I probably wouldn't mind being marooned on a desert island, or put in solitary confinement as much as a lot of other people; there's an element of that, but the books are not, in any way, biographical pieces.

Goddard: Why do you call the protagonist of Crash 'Ballard'?

Ballard: I was trying to be as honest as I could. I wanted a first-person narrator to stand between Vaughan and the reader, the honest thing to do was give him my own name. Also, I wanted to anchor the book more in reality; I had a named film-star, Elizabeth Taylor. The constant striving of the writer over the last few years has been to lower the threshold of fiction in what he writes, to reduce the amount of fiction. One's seen this in the theatre over the last fifteen years, and in the visual arts it started a long long time ago. overlap reality as much as possible,

Goddard: How do you react to criticism of your books? I'm thinking particularly of inane criticisms; going back to Martin Amis and his review of Crash, he said something like: 'he uses the word penis 147 times'.

Ballard: I didn't read that, I didn't read any reviews of Crash in this country, there didn't seem any point after the reviews of The Atrocity Exhibition, nobody read the book. Having been a reviewer myself, I can always tell at once when somebody has stopped reading the book he's reviewing. As for criticism in general, well, science fiction writers have always been handicapped by a lack of intelligent critical response, maybe that's a good thing, that's why it's so encouraging to find intelligent magazines like Cypher around now, and intelligent critics like David Pringle here, they didn't exist ten years ago. On the other hand, in America particularly, the critical response to SF has got totally out of hand. Now and then someone shows me a copy of The New York Review of Books, and I recently saw an ad for some of the most extraordinary stuff, either a series of lectures someone was giving, or a series of publications, sort of Levi-Strauss and Heinlein's such and such, all of them sounding like self-parodies, the application of serious literary criticism to popular SF authors.

Goddard: In Billion Year Spree, Brian Aldiss said of your early work that you had never resolved the problem of writing a narrative in which the central character pursues no purposeful course of action. That seemed rather harsh!

Ballard: old-fashioned ~~It ties in with what I was saying earlier~~. I think Brian is at heart an SF fan, and he approaches my stuff, about which he's very generous, ~~and has always been,~~ like an SF fan. ~~He judges what he sees.~~ To him, these books have a ~~sort of~~ vacuum at their centre. The characters' behaviour, superficially, seems to be either passive or meaningless in the context of the events. Why don't they just run for the hills? Why don't they head North? There won't be a problem, then there won't be a novel either, of course! ~~Therefore,~~ I think he fails to realise that, in a novel like The Drowned World, and this applies to all my fiction, the hero is the only one who is pursuing a meaningful course of action. In The Drowned World, Kerans' ~~is the only one to do nothing ~~ decision to stay, to come to terms with the changes taking place within himself, to understand the logic of his relationship with the shifting biological kingdom, and his decision finally, to go South and greet the sun, is a totally meaningful course of action. The behaviour of the other people, which superficially appears to be meaningful, getting the hell out, or draining the lagoons, is totally meaningless. The book is about the discovery by the hero, of his true compass bearings, both mentally and literally. It's the same in the others; in The Crystal World the hero decides to go back and immolate himself in a timeless world. In "The Terminal Beach", why does the man stagger ashore on an abandoned island, what is he doing there? I can well understand that to the old-fashioned SF fan his behaviour is meaningless or lacks purpose, ~~this, I think, means that~~ perhaps Brian has read too much SF.

Goddard: He goes on to say, in the same book, that the stories of your "Terminal Beach" period will probably be best remembered.

Ballard: Which stories does he mean?

Goddard: Well he says your "Terminal Beach" period, that came about '62 or '63, so I suppose he means the stories you were writing around the late fifties and early sixties.

Ballard: What he means, I think, is that the traditionally constructed stories will last the longest. A lot of American and British SF is extremely well written, well constructed, really very old fashioned in construction. They're all based on the authors' early reading of Maupasant or Somerset Maughan. All SF is really constructed in the classical mould;

stories like that do tend to survive, not because they're particularly important or anything like that, but because they're well told.

Goddard: Would you care to tell us something about what your future plans are?

Ballard: I finished my latest novel, High-Rise, about three weeks ago, and since then I've written a couple of short-stories, and am writing a third now, and just catching my breath a bit.

Goddard: You've no plans for another trilogy of books on the lines of the last three?

Ballard: I write whatever comes mentally to hand, and what I find interetsing at a particular time; these decisions as to what one's going to write tend to be made somewhere at the back of one's mind, so one can't consciously say: "that's what I'm going to write", it doesn't work out like that!

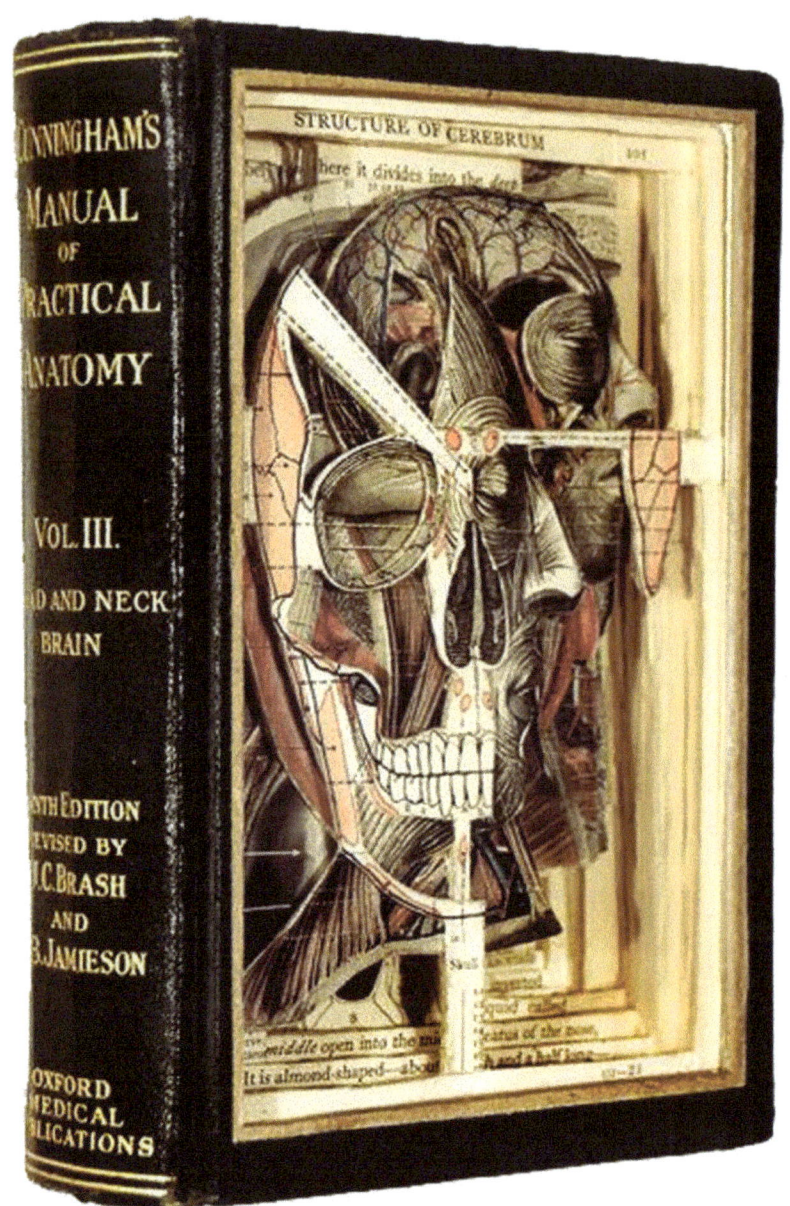

JG Ballard in the Dissecting Room

by Mike Bonsall

Illustration: *Cunningham's Manual of Practical Anatomy Volume III. Head, Neck and Brain* by Brian Dettmer

"Nearly sixty years later, I still think that my two years of anatomy were among the most important of my life, and helped to frame a large part of my imagination."

Miracles of Life

JG Ballard studied medicine at Cambridge from October 1949 to 1951, studying anatomy, physiology and biochemistry before he would be allowed to touch a living patient.

I had a similar experience of medical school—from October 1986 to 1988 I studied medicine at Charing Cross and Westminster medical school.

> Several students in my group dropped out, unable to cope with the sight of their first dead bodies, but in many ways the experience of dissection was just as overwhelming for me.
> *Miracles of Life*

My own first visit to the dissecting room felt unreal. The rows of corpses not just unmoving but somehow unhuman. Completely unnerved by this exhibition of death, I screamed soundlessly at my legs to walk to the exit, never to come back. But I was frozen by fear, knowing it wasn't possible to go back. Ballard's dissecting room seems to have been in some kind of cellar, while mine was the 'penthouse' of the *High-Rise* that is Charing Cross Hospital, with magnificent views over the Thames—but mostly we were turned inwards.

Like Ballard I had a female cadaver to dissect, tied into a muslin tube, a label attached to her big toe like in a cheap gangster film. The name on that label I can still remember thirty years later. We six students firstly had to extract her from this cloth pupa so we could start her lengthy journey to flayed butterfly. It was sobering to realise our dissection guides were practical documents rather than science fiction.

I used my clumsy scalpel to make that first cut into the hardened skin below her shrunken breasts and eventually removed them completely to allow access to her chest wall. Later—a dark dissecting room joke—I would say to my male colleagues; "Wouldn't it be horrible, if the first time we saw a naked woman, we had to cut her tits off?" From their reactions I could tell this *had* to have been the first time they had seen a naked woman.

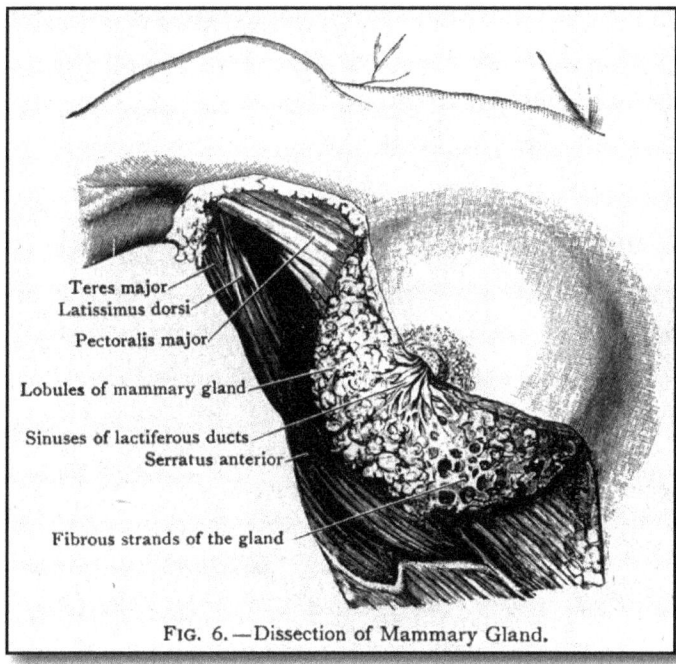

Fig. 6.—Dissection of Mammary Gland.

It is typical of Ballard's sublime imagination that he was able to transform the grisly process of dissection into an apotheosis. Beyond our student pranks and black humour of the dissection room, we also had a passionate care for our cadavers.

I clearly remember the tortuous process of opening our Mrs A's skull and the feeling of awe at holding her brain in my hands. Perhaps the last time Mrs. A. was cared for as a human being, a plaster was placed in the crook of her left arm, possibly after a last blood sample was taken. Despite all our other decrements, we found ourselves unable to simply rip that plaster off, or even touch it. Eventually we defused this talisman of our own death by cutting the skin around it and removing the whole block of skin from under it. As we gradually examined and cut away each part of our body, the discarded parts were placed into a large steel bin, one bin per cadaver—it was a matter of honour always to put your body parts in the right bin.

> If nothing else was going on
> we would go to the DR, put
> on our white coats, take our
> particular body part... and start
> work alongside our *Cunningham*
> dissection manuals (never *Gray's*),
> whose pages would soon be
> stained with human fat.
> *Miracles of Life*

At the end of our ministrations, these scraps would be bundled together and buried. We students were encouraged to attend the end-of-year church service where our cadavers were finally laid to rest, though I managed to avoid that ritual. Like Ballard I had a dissection manual, a minutely detailed guide to the two-year process of dismantling the human form. Like his, mine was soon stained with human fat and formalin preservative. The acrid smell of formaldehyde became a central part of my life, leaching deep into the skin of my hands. The wearing of gloves was frowned on; "You have to be able to feel your way about inside the body..." The smell was with me as I ate a sandwich for lunch, and with me at night, stronger than the scent of my partner. After a while I no longer cared if there were parts of Mrs. A. under my fingernails.

Several times Ballard mentions that his dissection guide was *Cunningham's*. Ballard would have used the eleventh edition of *Cunningham's Manual of Practical Anatomy* which was published from 1948 to 1952. I obtained copies of all three volumes of this edition. With its precise, matter-of-fact technical language, partnered with the most extraordinary images of human dismemberment—drawn with unflinching accuracy from cadavers in the dissecting room—it gives some insight into Ballard's experiences at the time.

> My years in the dissection room
> were important because they taught
> me that though death was the end,
> the human imagination and the hu-
> man spirit could triumph over our
> own dissolution. In many ways my
> entire fiction is the dissection of a
> deep pathology that I had witnessed
> in Shanghai and later in the post-
> war world... Or it may be that my
> two years in the dissecting room
> were an unconscious way of keeping
> Shanghai alive by other means.
> *Miracles of Life*

Ballard's work is indeed suffused with the language and terminology of the dissecting room, sometimes obviously, as in *Crash*, but sometimes the very landscape is described in anatomical terms, external reality quantified in terms of internal spaces.

What follows are some examples of the way Ballard reworked his early anatomical experience into a new kind of fiction, together with some of the words and images from the *Cunningham's Manual* that might have settled into his uniquely fertile teenage mind.

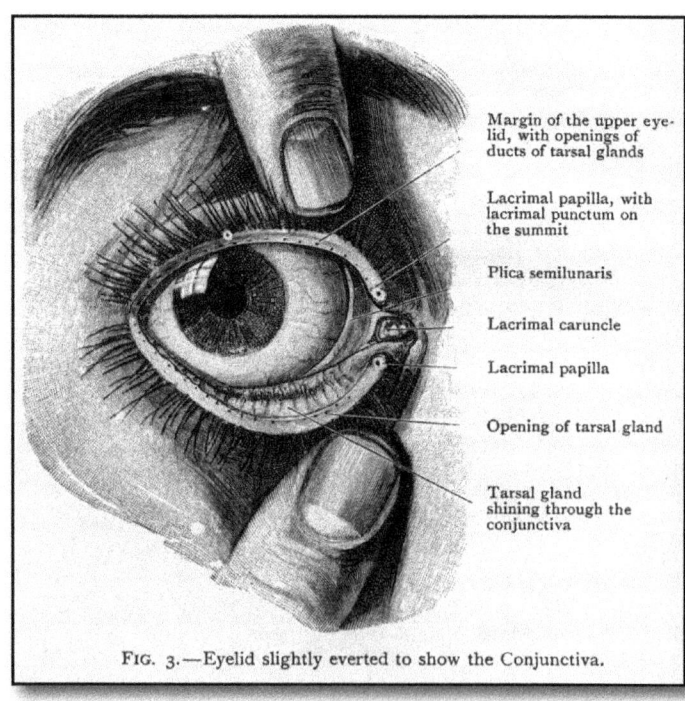

FIG. 3.—Eyelid slightly everted to show the Conjunctiva.

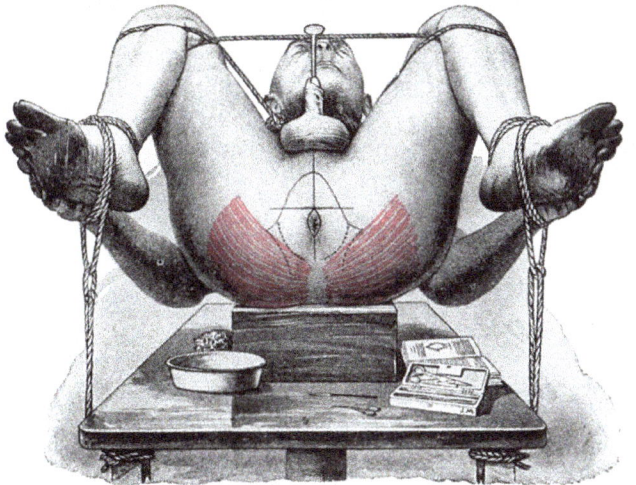

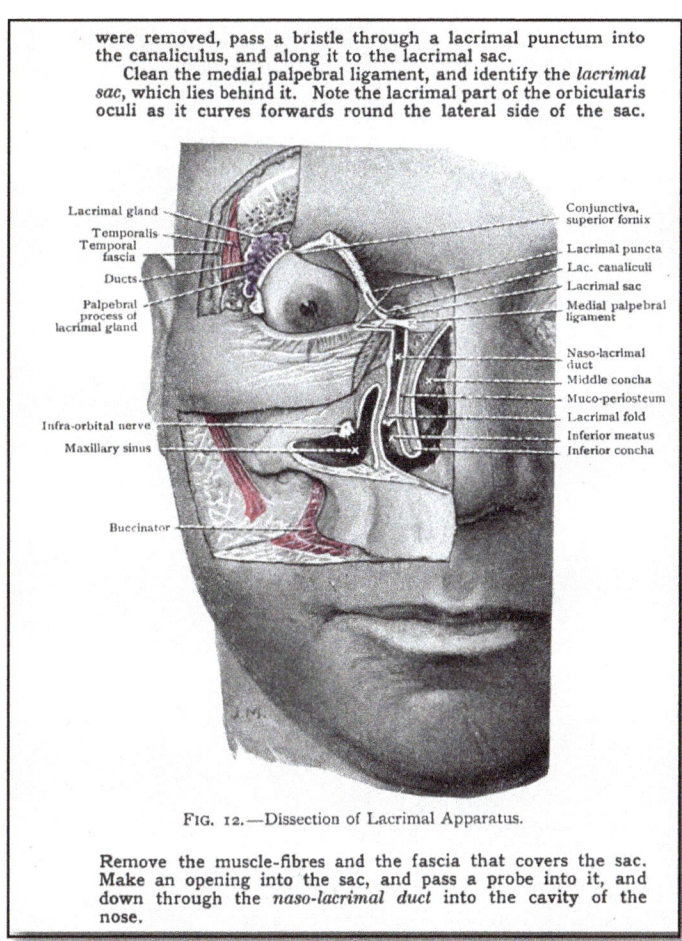

I felt the warm vinyl of the seat beside me, and then stroked the damp aisle of Helen's perineum. Her hand pressed against my right testicle. The plastic laminates around me, the colour of washed anthracite, were the same tones as her pubic hairs parted at the vestibule of her vulva. (*Crash*, 1973)

Tasting blood in his mouth, he stopped and sat down. Squatting on the powdery slope, he took the handkerchief from his pocket and touched his tongue and lips. The red stain formed the imprint of his shaky mouth, like an illicit kiss. Maitland felt the tender skin of his right temple and cheekbone. The bruise ran from the ear as far as his right nostril. Pressing a finger into the nasal cleft, he could feel the injured sinus and gums, a loosened eye-tooth. (*Concrete Island*, 1974)

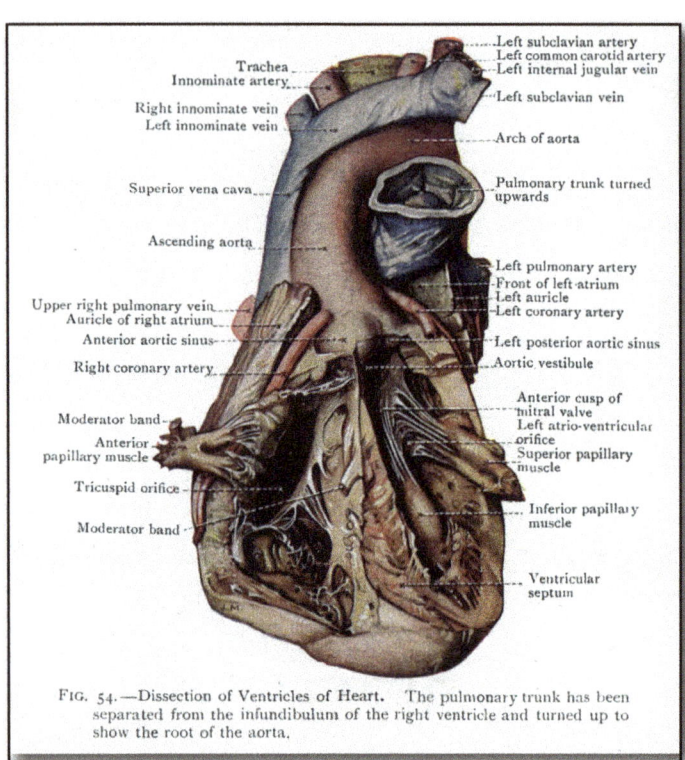

FIG. 54.—Dissection of Ventricles of Heart. The pulmonary trunk has been separated from the infundibulum of the right ventricle and turned up to show the root of the aorta.

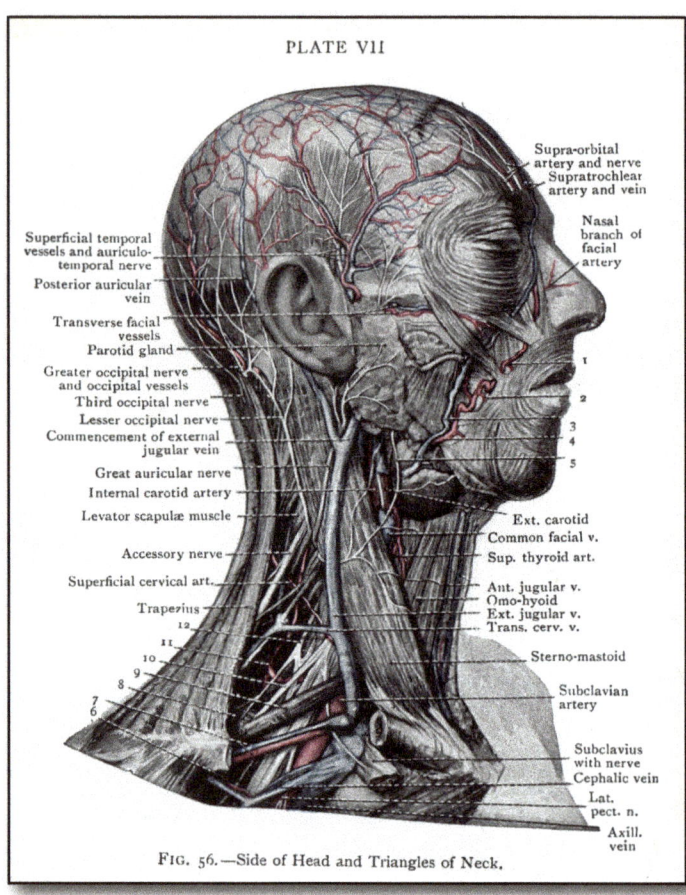

FIG. 56.—Side of Head and Triangles of Neck.

'Of course.' Jim reflected on all this as he walked to the hospital. He often watched the eyes of the patients as they died, trying to detect a flash of light when the soul left. Once he had helped Dr Ransome as he massaged the naked chest of a young Belgian woman wasted by dysentery. Dr Bowen had said that she was dead, but Dr Ransome squeezed her heart under her ribs and suddenly her eyes swivelled and looked at Jim. At first Jim thought that her soul had returned to her, but she was still dead. Mrs Philips and Mrs Gilmour took her away and buried her an hour later. Dr Ransome explained that for a few seconds he had pumped the blood back into her brain. (*Empire of the Sun*, 1984)

He looked down at the translucent skin over the anterior triangle of her neck, barely hiding its scenarios of nerve and blood-vessel. Marker lines sped past them, dividing and turning. ("The Great American Nude," 1967)

Even that morning's swim in the lagoon had failed to clear his head. Neil gripped his thighs, trying to steady the sweating muscles that still jumped in a fever of their own. The effort of spear-fishing in the lagoon each day had leached all the fat from his skin, and the strings of his muscles reminded him of the anatomical plates in his father's textbooks, the skin flayed back to expose the knotted cords and straps. (*Rushing to Paradise*, 1994)

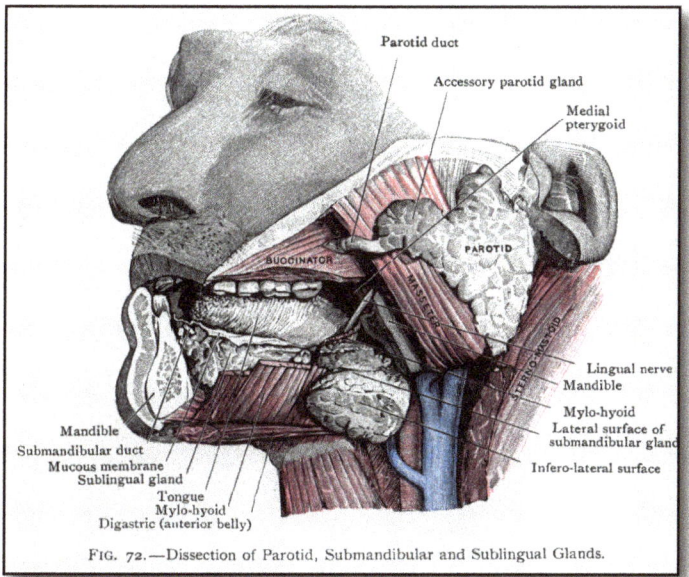

FIG. 72.—Dissection of Parotid, Submandibular and Sublingual Glands.

Looking at the contents of the cabin as he sipped his drink, Ransom debated which of his possessions to take with him. The cabin had become, unintentionally, a repository of all the talismans of his life. On the bookshelf were the anatomy texts he had used in the dissecting room as a student, the pages stained with the formalin that leaked from the corpses on the tables, somewhere among them the unknown face of his surgeon father. (*The Drought*, 1965)

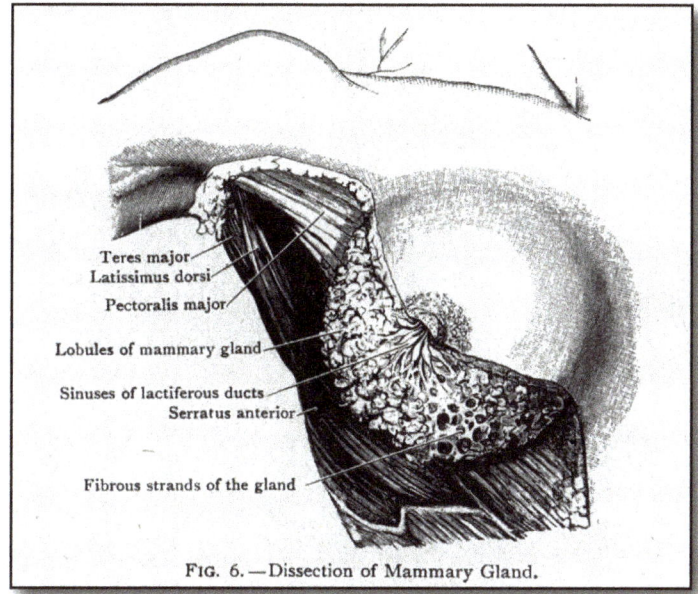

FIG. 6.—Dissection of Mammary Gland.

These deaths preoccupied Travers... Jayne Mansfield: the death of the erotic junction, the polite section of the lower mammary curvature by the glass guillotine of the windshield assembly. ("Tolerances of the Human Face," 1969)

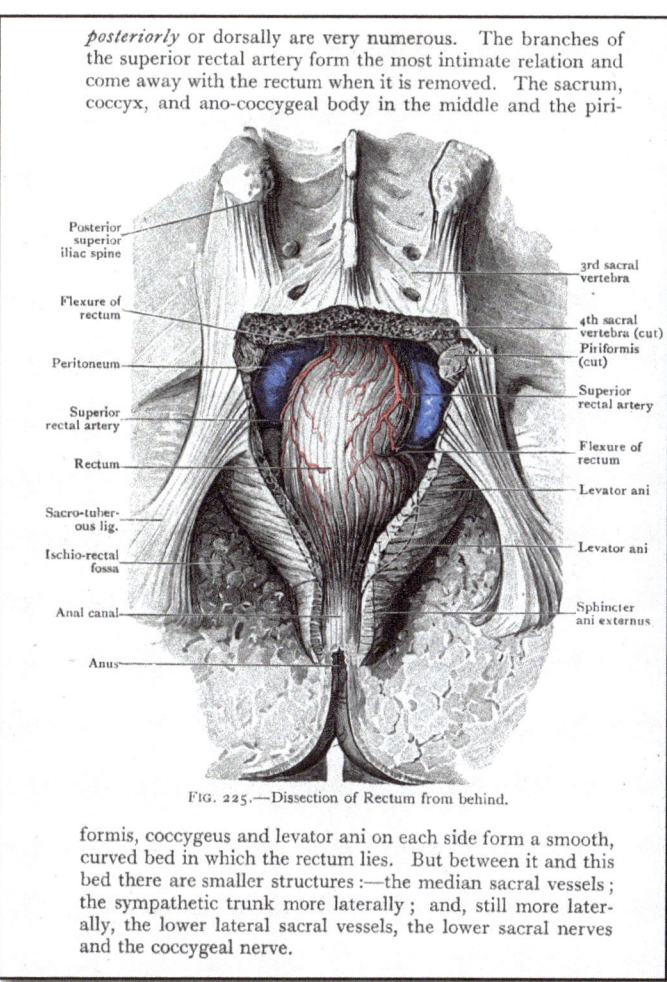

posteriorly or dorsally are very numerous. The branches of the superior rectal artery form the most intimate relation and come away with the rectum when it is removed. The sacrum, coccyx, and ano-coccygeal body in the middle and the piri-

FIG. 225.—Dissection of Rectum from behind.

formis, coccygeus and levator ani on each side form a smooth, curved bed in which the rectum lies. But between it and this bed there are smaller structures:—the median sacral vessels; the sympathetic trunk more laterally; and, still more laterally, the lower lateral sacral vessels, the lower sacral nerves and the coccygeal nerve.

She knelt on the carpet, her chest and shoulders across the cushions. Spitting on her fingers, she pushed the saliva into her anus with one hand, testing my penis with the other. I hesitated to enter her, nervous of tearing her scarred anus, but she pressed my penis into her, adding more spit between the gasps of pain. When I was fully inside her she at last relaxed, and her rectum was as soft as the vagina of a child-bearing woman. She buried her face among the teddy bears and brought her wrists behind her back, inviting me to force them to her shoulder blades. I moved carefully, trying to control her prolapsing rectum, gently forcing her arms as she wanted, picking the hairs from her mouth as she shouted to me, an eager, desperate child.

"Bugger me, daddy! Beat me! Pixie wants to be buggered!" (*The Kindness of Women*, 1991)

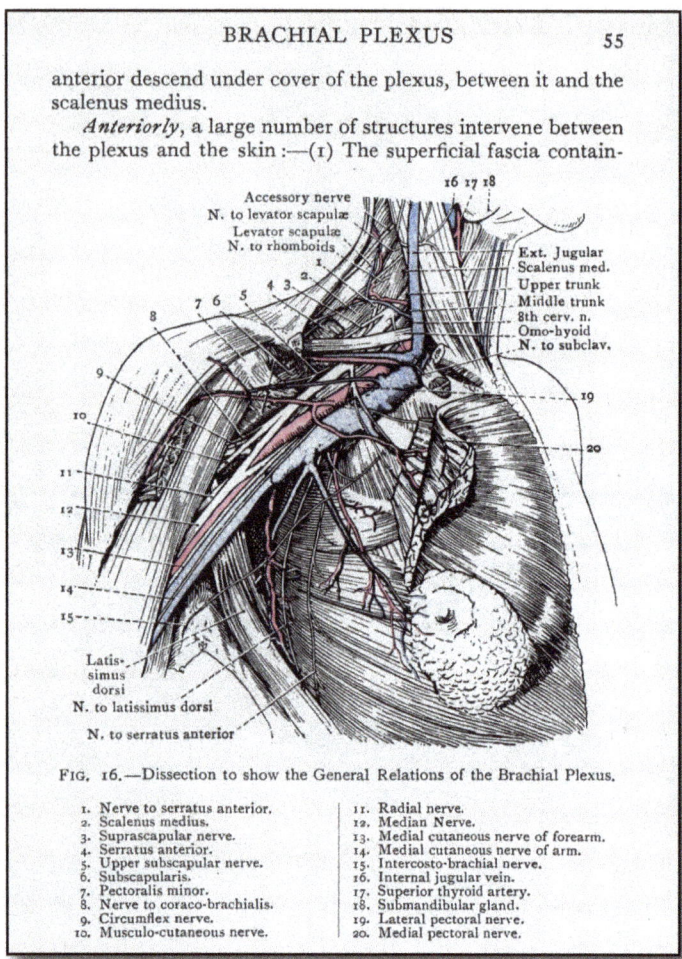

"Not in our minds, Robert. These are the oldest memories on Earth, the time-codes carried in every chromosome and gene. Every step we've taken in our evolution is a milestone inscribed with organic memories—from the enzymes controlling the carbon dioxide cycle to the organisation of the brachial plexus and the nerve pathways of the Pyramid cells in the mid-brain, each is a record of a thousand decisions taken in the face of a sudden physico-chemical crisis. Just as psychoanalysis reconstructs the original traumatic situation in order to release the repressed material, so we are now being plunged back into the archaeopsychic past, uncovering the ancient taboos and drives that have been dormant for epochs…" (*The Drowned World*, 1962)

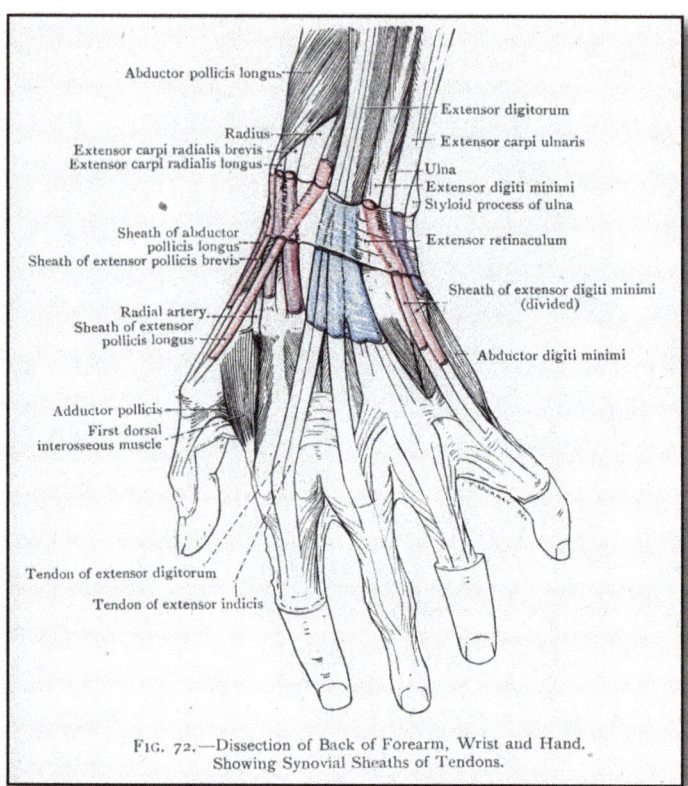

"Doctor…" Kagwa's strong hand gripped my right elbow, his fingers deliberately bruising the ulna nerve. He closed the cell door on the soldier, who had placed the mess-tin on the floor beside the European and was about to remove the slops bucket. "Your duties now are complete. You may return to your clinic and finish your packing." (*The Day of Creation*, 1987)

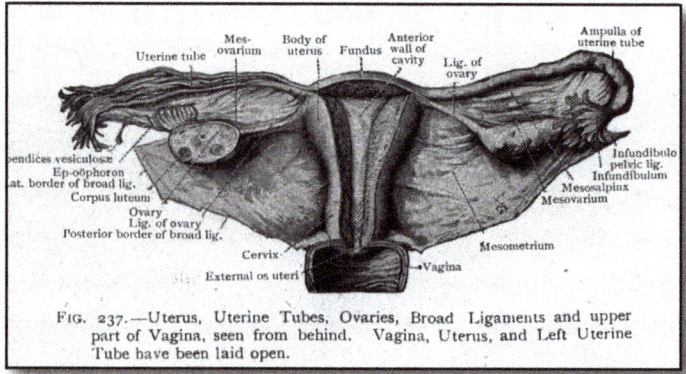

On the bedside table was the intra-uterine coil, with the draw-string he had felt at the neck of her womb. On some confused impulse she had decided to remove it, as if determined to preserve at least one set of his wild genes within the safekeeping of her placental vault. ("Zodiac 2000," 1978)

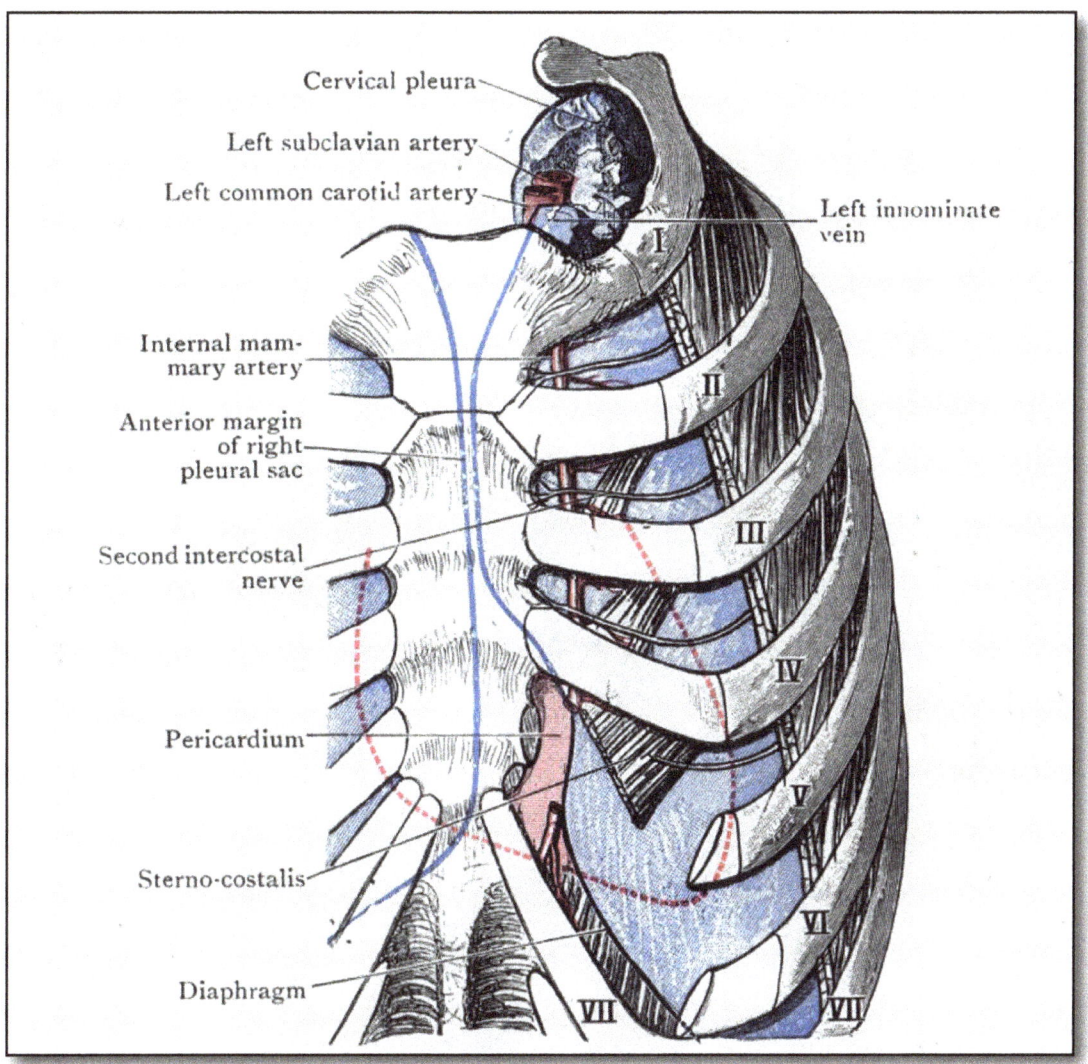

Mallory sat down and placed his hands on her diaphragm, gently respiring her. Every morning he feared that time would run out for Anne while she slept, leaving her forever in the middle of a last uneasy dream. (*Memories of the Space Age*, 1982)

I freed his tongue and windpipe, massaged his diaphragm until his breath was even, and placed a choir cushion below his shoulders. On the floor beside him were the barrel, receiver, breech and magazine of a stockless rifle whose parts he had been oiling in the moments before his attack, and which I knew he would reassemble the instant he awoke. ("The Object of the Attack," 1984)

Jim squatted beside Mr Maxted, working his diaphragm like a bellows. He had seen Dr Ransome bring his patients back from the dead, and it was important for Mr Maxted to be well enough to join the march. Around them the prisoners were sitting upright, and a few men stood beside their huddled wives and children. Several of the older internees had died in the night—ten feet away Mrs Wentworth, who had played the part of Lady Bracknell, lay in her faded cotton dress, staring at the sky. Others were surrounded by shallow pools of water formed by the pressure of their bodies on the soft grass. (*Empire of the Sun*, 1984)

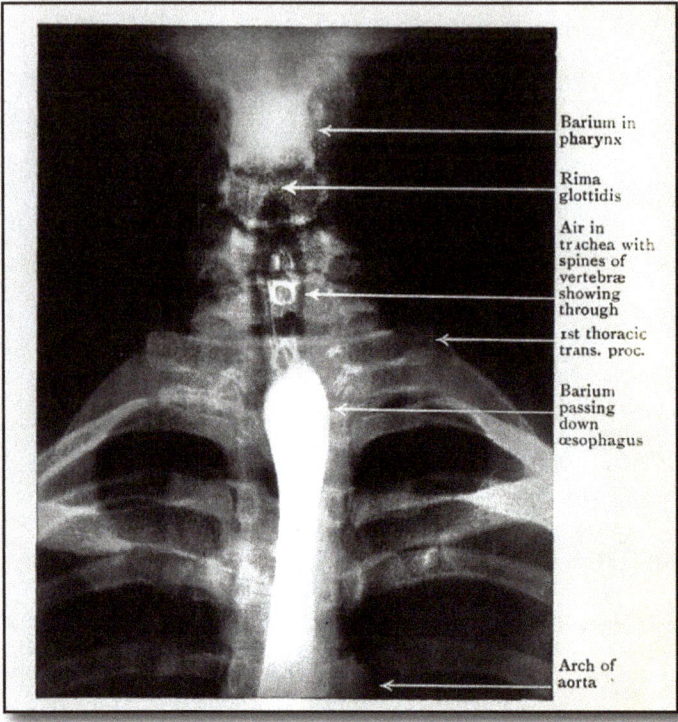

(2) a transverse section through the spinal level T-12... (5) an antero-posterior radiograph of a skull, estimated capacity 1500 cc. ("You and Me and the Continuum," 1966)

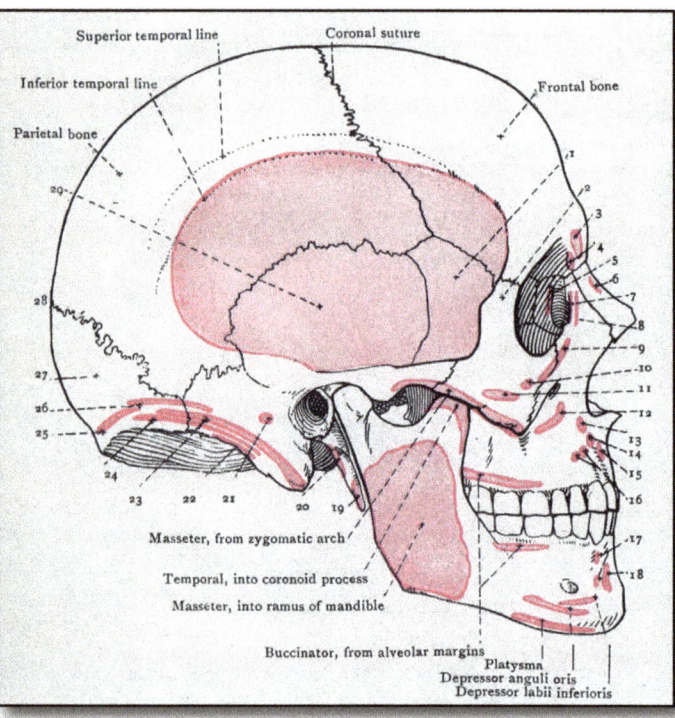

Waking: the concrete embankment of a motorway extension. Roadworks, cars drumming two hundred yards below. In the sunlight the seams between the sections are illuminated like the sutures of an exposed skull. ("The Assassination Weapon", 1966)

A faded agency picture of the car in which Albert Camus had died was elaborately re-worked, the dashboard and windshield marked with the words "nasal bridge," "soft palate," "left zygomatic arch." ("You: Coma: Marilyn Monroe," 1966)

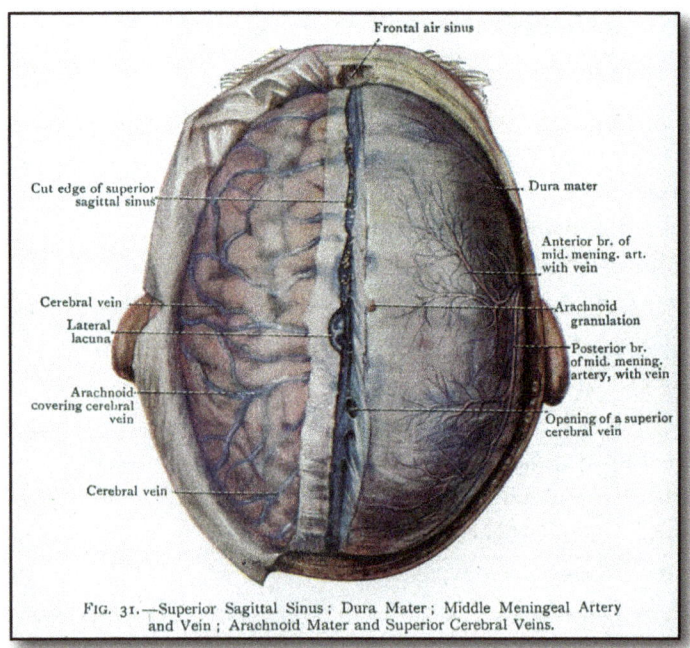

Precisely. The stream of retinal images reaching the optic lobe is nothing more than a film strip. Every image is stored away, thousands of reels, a hundred thousand hours of running time. ("Zone of Terror," 1960)

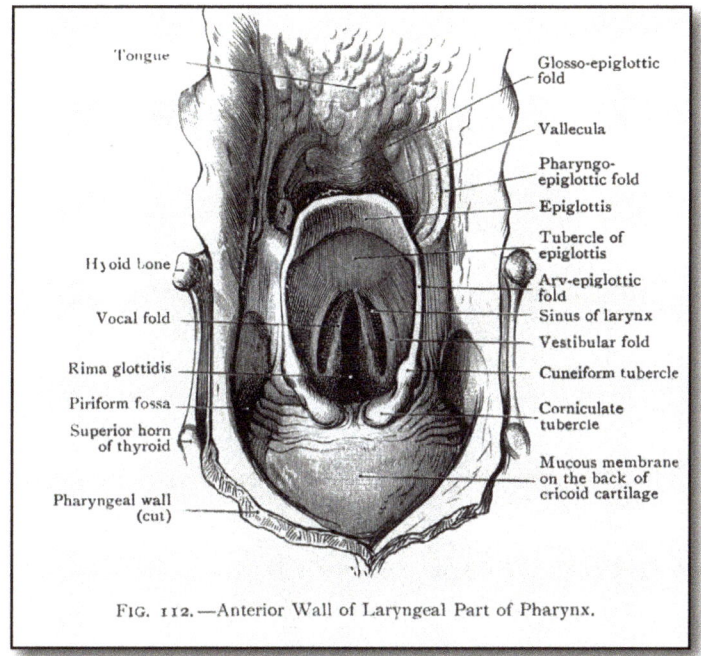

FIG. 112.—Anterior Wall of Laryngeal Part of Pharynx.

"A professional killer? It's remarkable that you can talk at all. Dr Hamilton says your throat isn't damaged."

"It's hard to explain, Inspector." Lips pursed, Paula pointed to the bruises on my neck left by the assailant's fingertips. The attack had shocked her. Usually so quick-witted, and never at a loss for a word, she was almost silent. By leaving me alone in the apartment she had made herself partly responsible for my injuries. Yet she seemed unsurprised by the assault, as if expecting it to take place. Speaking in her flat, lecture-room voice, she said: "In cases of strangulation the voice-box is almost always crushed. In fact, it's difficult to strangle someone to the point of unconsciousness without doing serious structural damage to the nerves and blood vessels. You were lucky, Charles. If you blacked out that was probably because you hit your head on the floor." (*Cocaine Nights*, 1996)

Lang was lying in his cot, body motionless under the canvas sheet. His lips were parted slightly. No sound came from them but Morley, bending over next to Neill, could see his hyoid bone vibrating in spasms. ("Manhole 69," 1957)

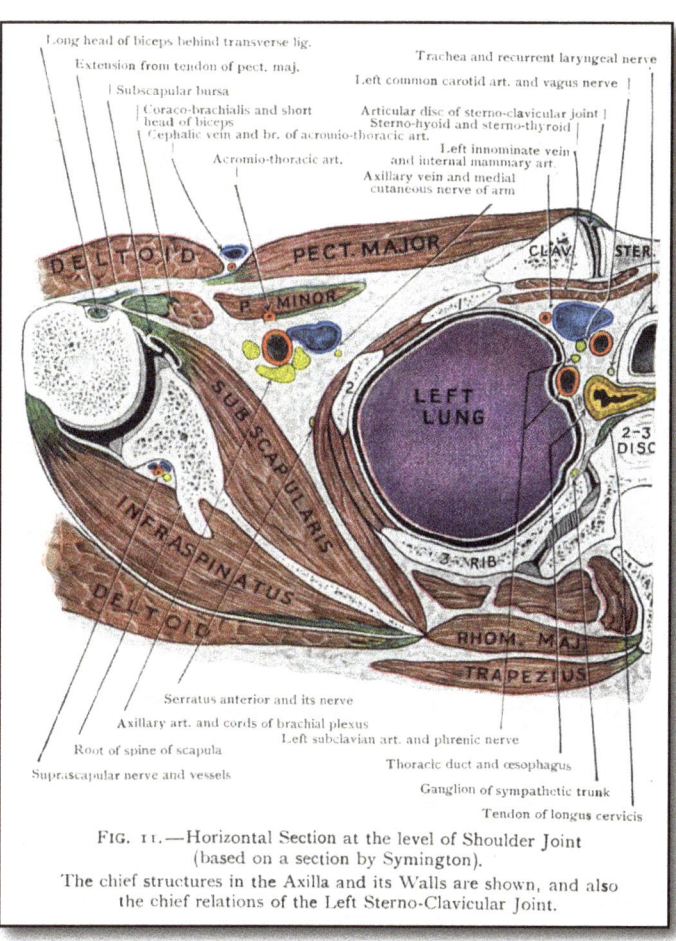

FIG. 11.—Horizontal Section at the level of Shoulder Joint (based on a section by Symington).
The chief structures in the Axilla and its Walls are shown, and also the chief relations of the Left Sterno-Clavicular Joint.

He walked among the displaced contours of her pectoral girdle. What time could be read off the slopes and inclines of this inorganic musculature, the drifting planes of its face? ("You: Coma: Marilyn Monroe," 1966)

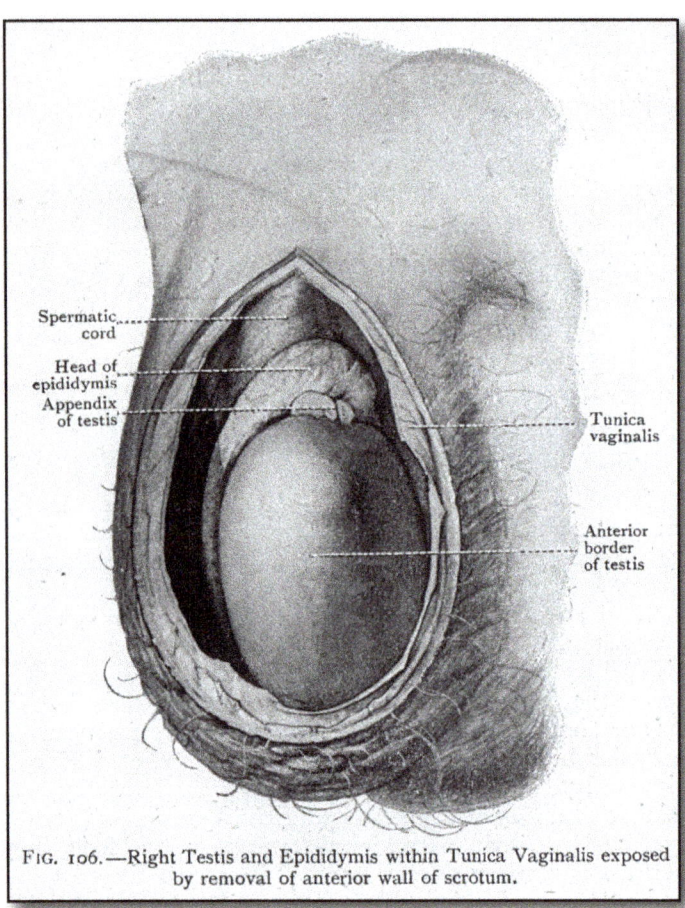

FIG. 106.—Right Testis and Epididymis within Tunica Vaginalis exposed by removal of anterior wall of scrotum.

Other correspondences or respiratory and urinogenital function came to mind, enshrined both in popular mythology (the supposed equivalence in size of nose and penis) and psychoanalytic symbolism (the "eyes" are a common code for the testicles). (*The Atrocity Exhibition*, 1966)

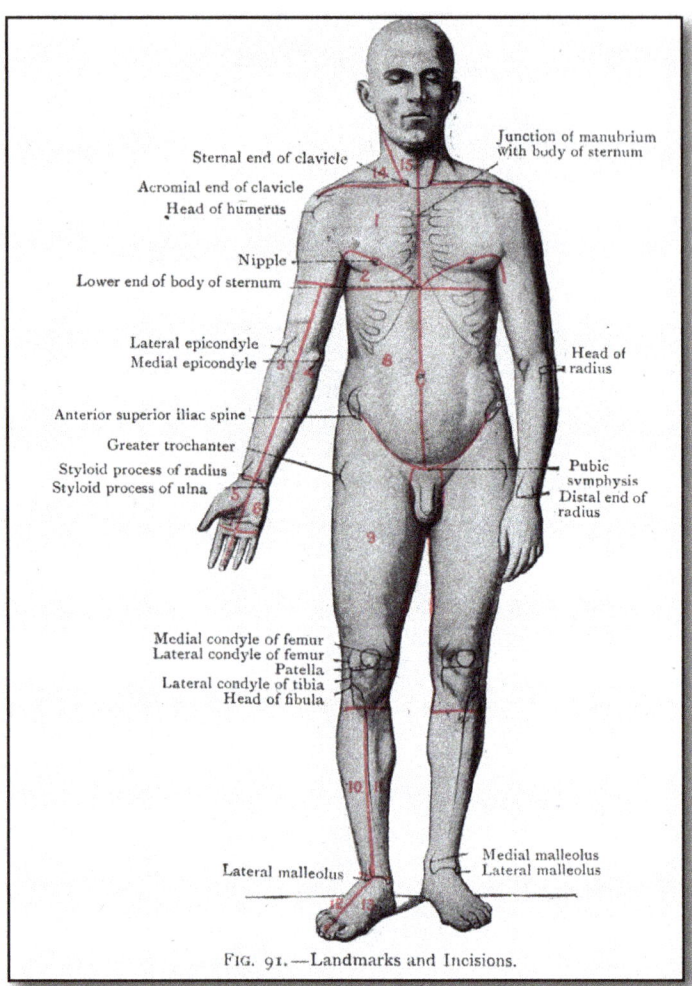

FIG. 91.—Landmarks and Incisions.

After a year at London University I was thrown out of the medical school—while dissecting a thorax in the anatomy laboratory one afternoon I suddenly became convinced that the cadaver was still alive. I terrorized a weak fellow student into helping me to frogmarch the corpse up and down the laboratory in an attempt to revive it. I am still half-certain that we would have succeeded. (*The Unlimited Dream Company*, 1979)

(2) mean intra-patellar distances (estimated during funeral services) of Coretta King and Ethel M. Kennedy; (3) close-up of the perineum of a six-year-old girl ("Tolerances of the Human Face," 1969)

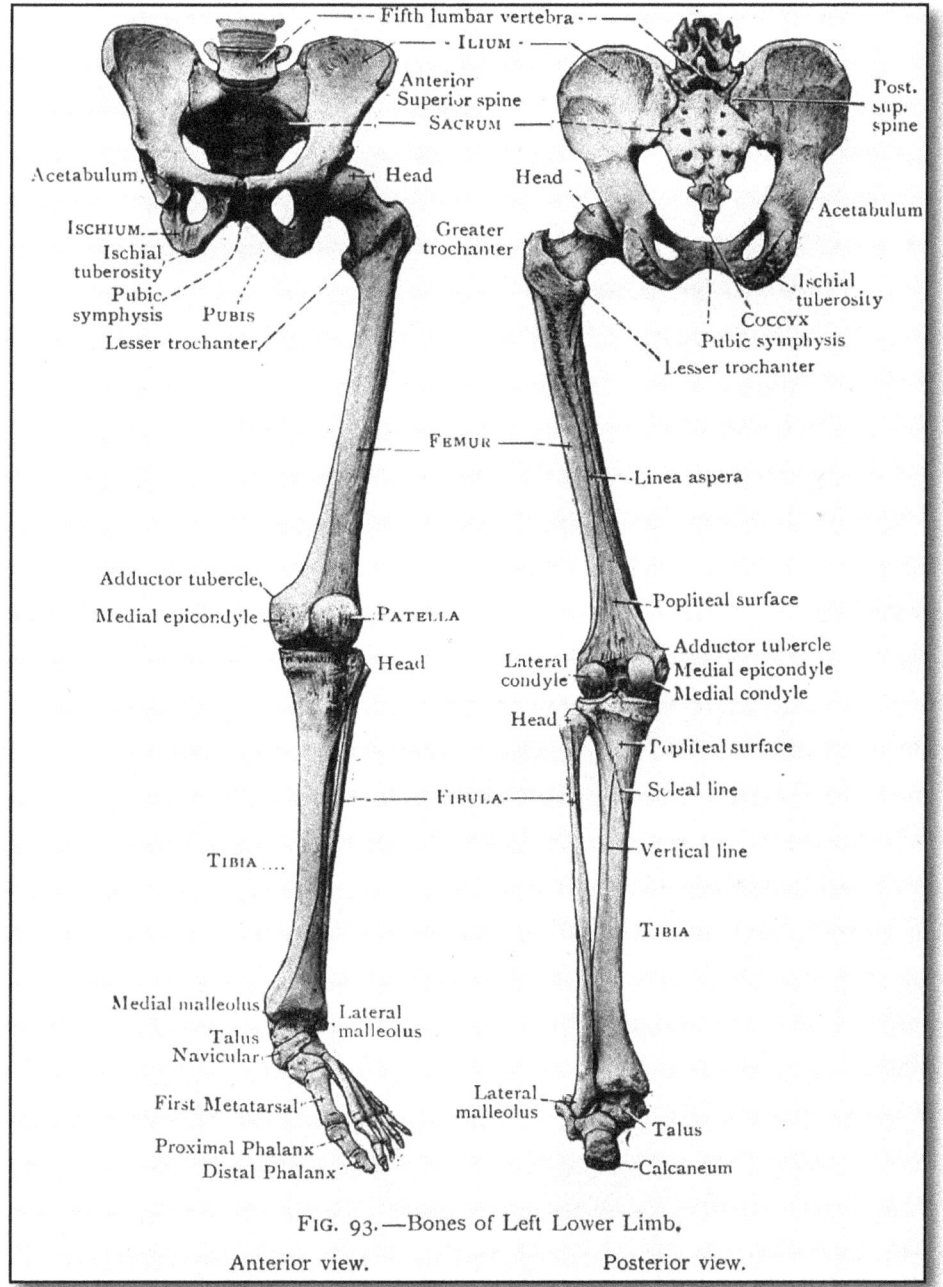

FIG. 93.—Bones of Left Lower Limb.
Anterior view. Posterior view.

The contractor's hut, the crane and the scaffolding have been removed, and the sand being driven into the bay along the coast has buried the pelvis and backbone. In the winter the high curved bones are deserted, battered by the breaking waves, but in the summer they provide an excellent perch for the sea-wearying gulls. ("The Drowned Giant," 1964)

She pumped her buttocks rapidly, forcing her pubic bone against mine, then leaned back against the dashboard as a Land-Rover thudded past along the track, sending a cloud of dust against the windows. (*Crash*, 1973)

Lumbering about to the rhythm of the bongos, he selected a skull and femur from the pile of bones around the throne, began to beat out a tattoo for Kerans, tapping the varying thicknesses of the temporal and occipital lobes to pick out a crude cranial octave. Several others joined in, and with a rattle of femur and tibia, radius and ulna, a mad dance of the bones ensued. (*Drowned World*, 1962)

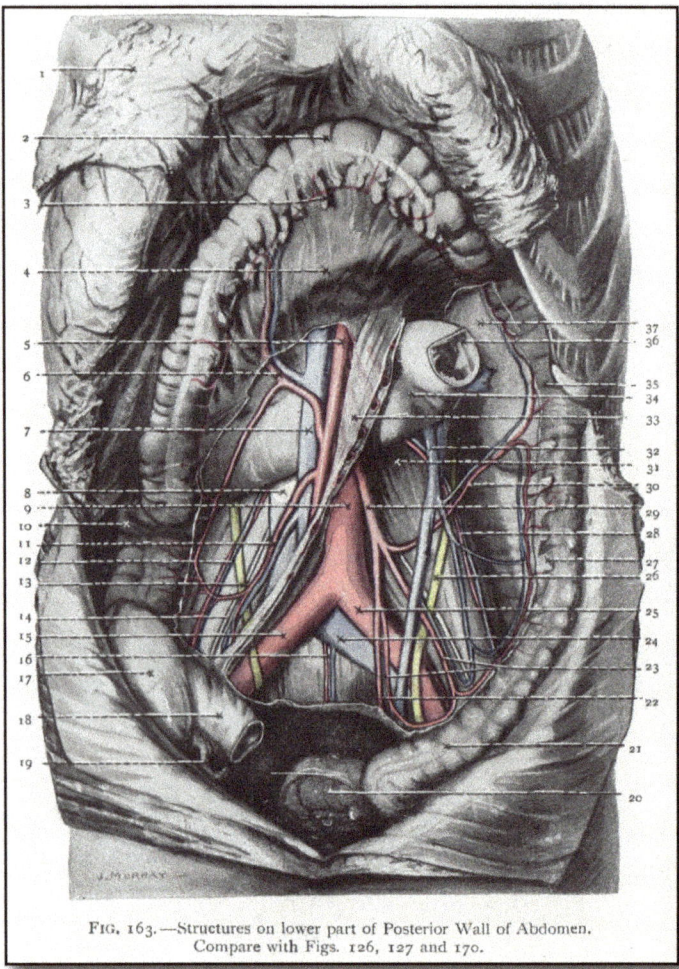

FIG. 163.—Structures on lower part of Posterior Wall of Abdomen. Compare with Figs. 126, 127 and 170.

I looked down at my calves and arms, at the balls of muscles that hunted beneath the thinning skin. I had lost at least twenty pounds in weight, and my hip bones jutted above my shorts like the rim of our empty rice basin. I imagined my once plump mesentery as a fraying clothes line, on which was strung an ever-more hungry intestine. Nonetheless, I felt stronger than at any time since leaving Port-la-Nouvelle, and eager to cope with the exhausting task of steering the ferry and moving the oil drums to the fuel manifold. (*The Day of Creation*, 1987)

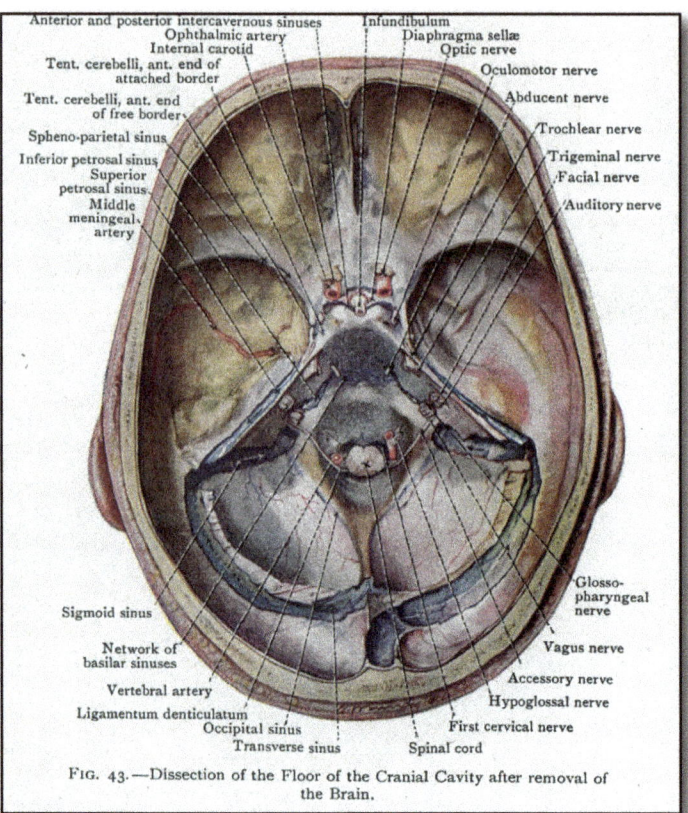

FIG. 43.—Dissection of the Floor of the Cranial Cavity after removal of the Brain.

Surgery is necessary but be careful. Too much cortical damage and the archetypes may get restive. (Passport to Eternity," 1962)

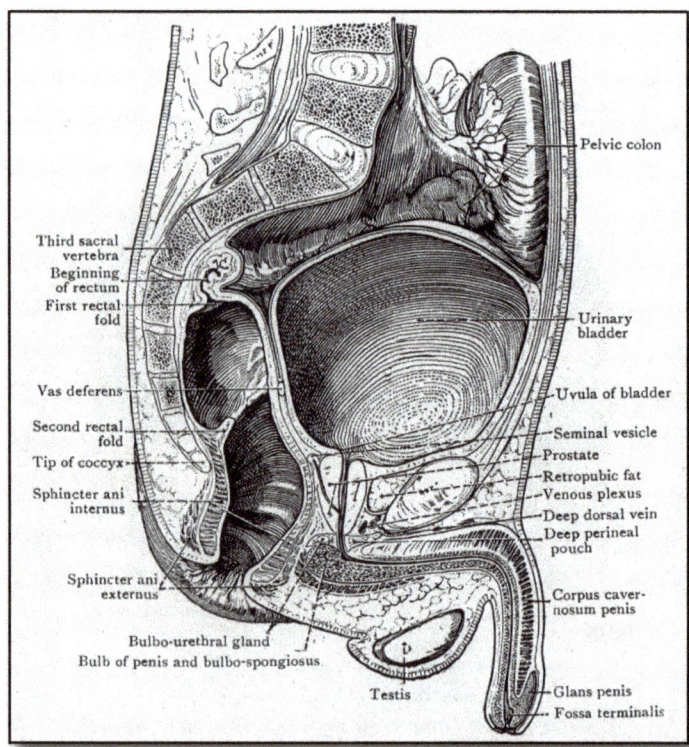

I looked down. She was holding my limp penis between thumb and forefinger, waiting for me to decide whether I wanted it to lie to right or left of the central bandage. (*Crash*, 1973)

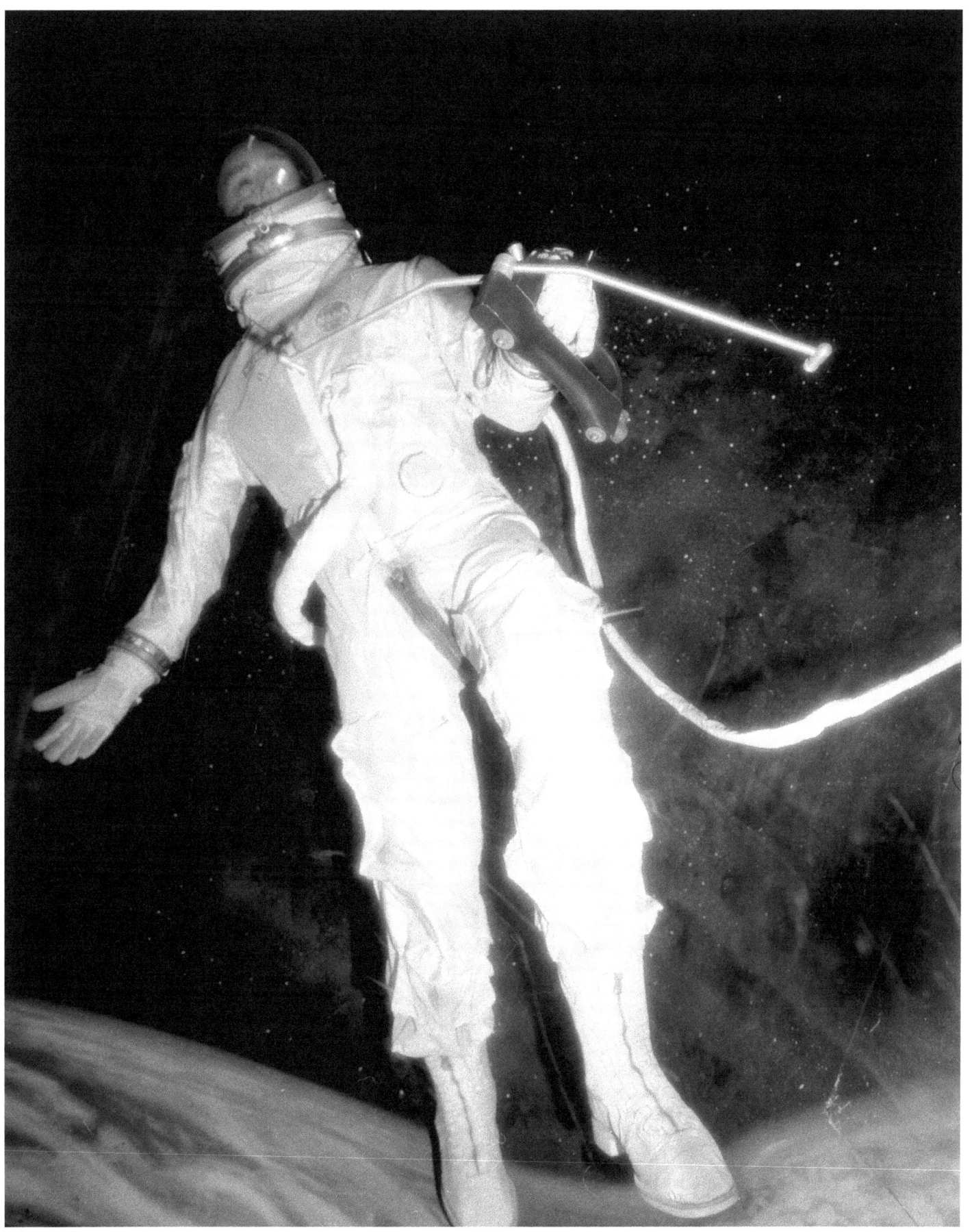

ANA BARRADO
Spacewalker Astronaut, Kennedy Space Center Museum, 1995

1. Prima Belladonna
2. Escapement
3. Build-Up
4. Mobile
5. Manhole 69
6. Track 12
7. The Waiting Grounds
8. Now Zero
9. Sound Sweep
10. Zone of Terror
11. Last World of Mr Goddard
12. Chronopolis
13. Voices of Time
14. Studio 5 the Stars
15. Deep End
16. Overloaded Man
17. Mr F is Mr F
18. Billennium
19. Gentle Assassin
20. 1000 Dreams of Stellavista
21. Singing Statues
22. Man on the 99th Floor
23. The Insane Ones
24. Garden of Time
25. 13 to Centaurus
26. Time of Passage
27. Time Tombs
28. Drowned World (short version)
29. Subliminal Man
30. Passport to Eternity
31. Watch Towers
32. Cage of Sand
33. Question of Re-entry
34. Lord Leonardo
35. Reptile Enclosure
36. The Screen Game
37. Now Wakes the Sea
38. Venus Hunters
39. Minus One
40. Delta at Sunset
41. End Game
42. Illuminated Man

JG Ballard's Own 1970 Short Story Bibliography

Contributed by James Goddard

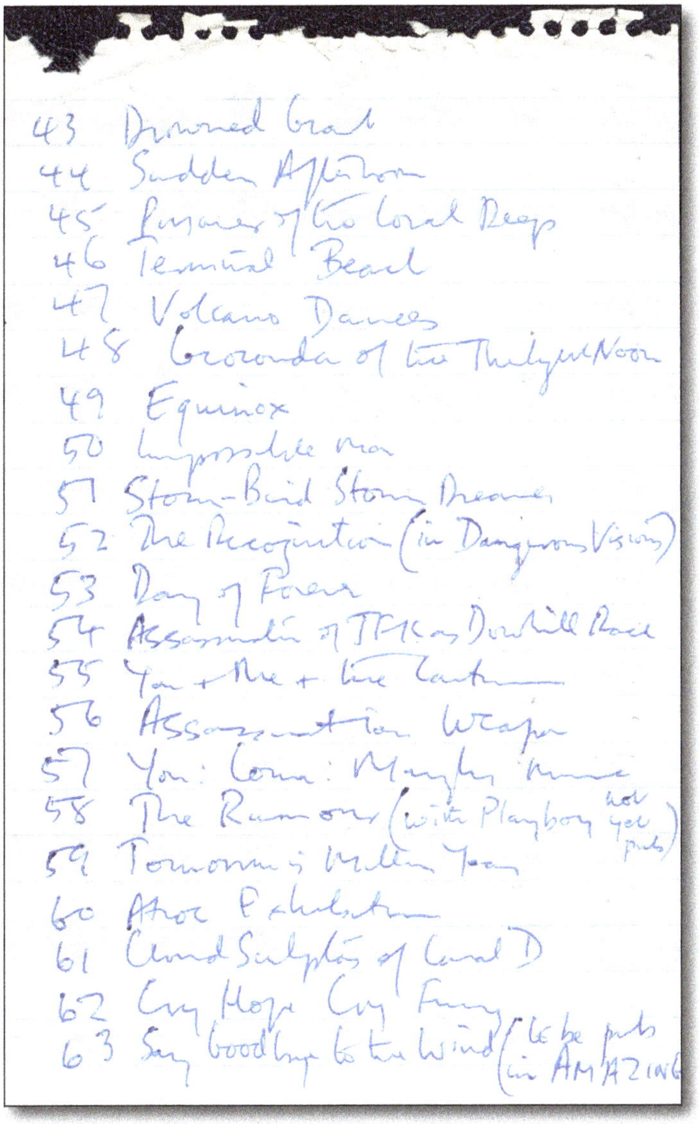

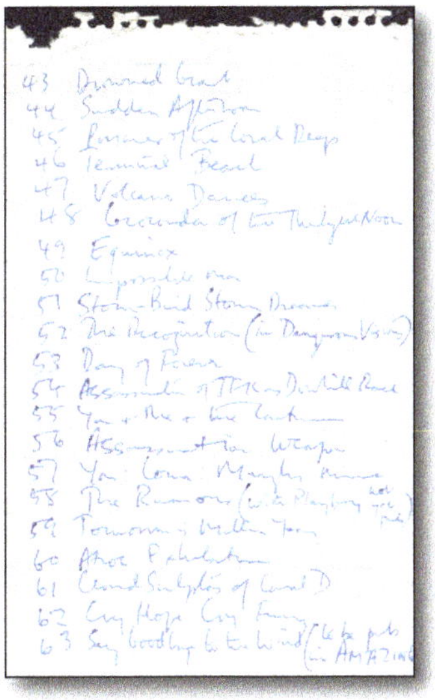

43 Drowned Giant
44 Sudden Afternoon
45 Prisoner of the Coral Deep
46 Terminal Beach
47 Volcano Dances
48 Gioconda of the Twilight Noon
49 Equinox
50 Impossible Man
51 Storm-Bird Storm Dreamer
52 The Recognition (in Dangerous Visions)
53 Day of Forever
54 Assassination of JFK as Downhill Race
55 You + Me + the Continuum
56 Assassination Weapon
57 You: Coma: Marilyn Monroe
58 The Rumours (with Playboy not yet pub)
59 Tomorrow's Million Years
60 Atoe Pakistan
61 Cloud Sculptors of Coral D
62 Cry Hope Cry Fury
63 Say Goodbye to the Wind (to be pub in AMAZING)

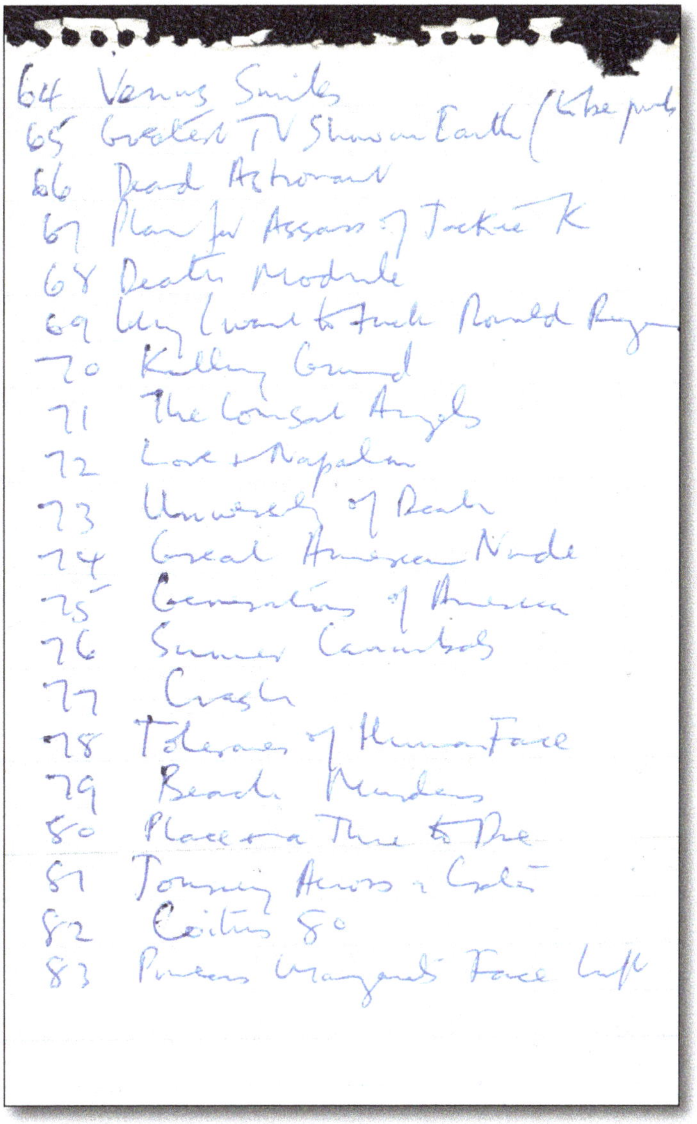

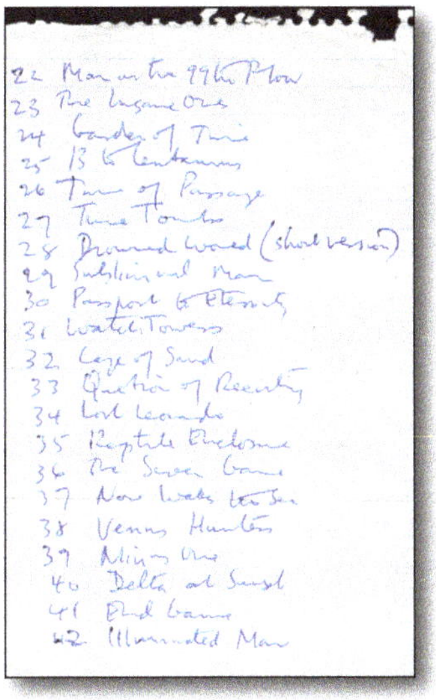

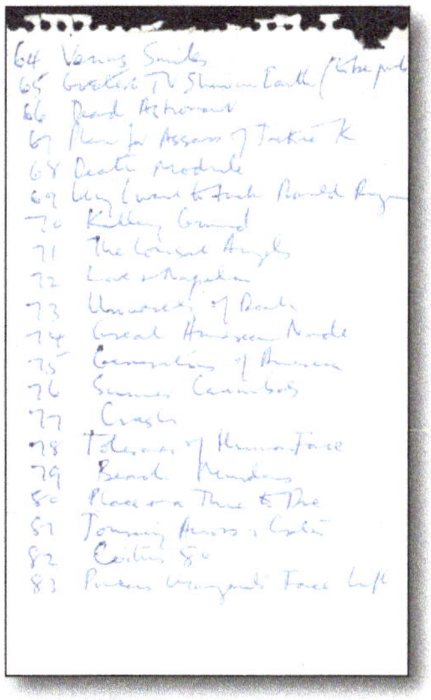

64 Venus Smiles
65 Greatest TV Show on Earth (to be pub)
66 Dead Astronaut
67 Plan for Assass of Jackie K
68 Death Module
69 Why I want to Fuck Ronald Reagan
70 Killing Ground
71 The Consul Angels
72 Love + Napalm
73 University of Death
74 Great American Nude
75 Generations of America
76 Summer Cannibals
77 Crash
78 Tolerances of Human Face
79 Beach Murders
80 Place + a Time to Die
81 Journey Across a Crater
82 Coitus 80
83 Princess Margaret's Face Lift

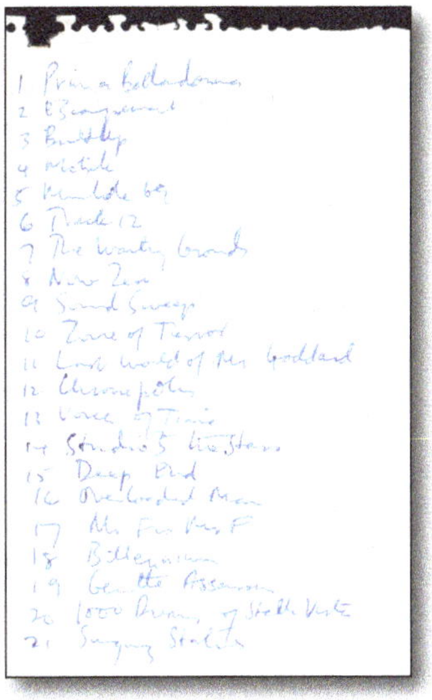

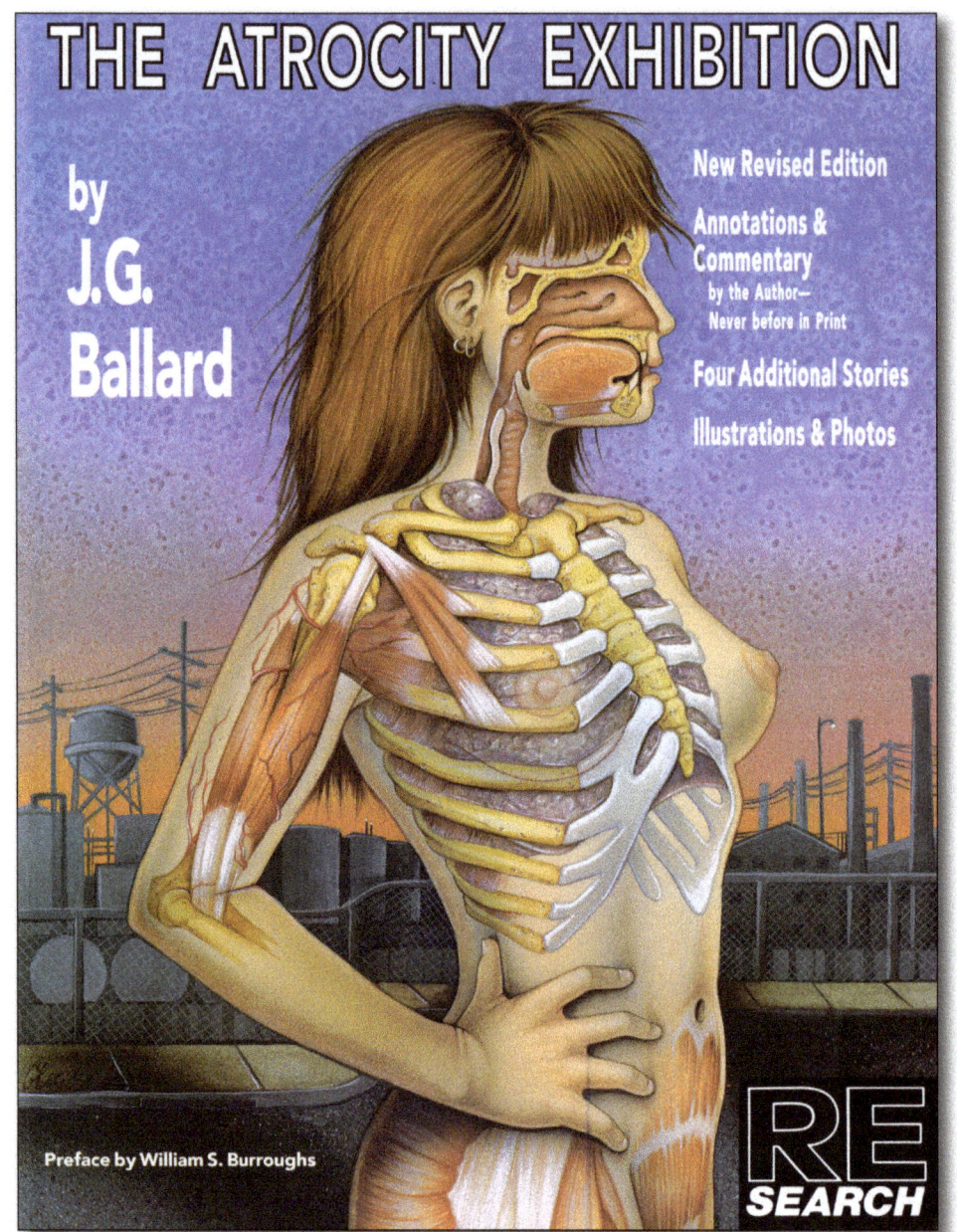

Desperate Measures:
A History of *The Atrocity Exhibition*

by Mike Holliday

Empire of the Sun is probably JG Ballard's best-known book, and *Crash* his most notorious, even more so after David Cronenberg's 1996 film adaptation. Today's readers are also likely to be familiar with recent novels such as *Cocaine Nights* and *Super-Cannes*. However, *The Atrocity Exhibition* is perhaps Ballard's masterpiece. Described by the *New York Times* as "a high-water mark in English experimental fiction," and chosen by Michael Moorcock as "book of the century," it was written just as the cultural and political frenzy of the 1960s reached its height, and at a point of significant change in Ballard's personal life.

The concerns that exercised Ballard in writing *The Atrocity Exhibition*, especially the media-driven confusion of reality and fiction, are even more apparent today, as a glance at the latest car commercials, politicians' sound-bites, and reality TV shows will indicate. So the original magazine appearances of these stories are an opportunity to view them in the context in which they were written, a time when the world we live in today was being born.

Ballard was drawn to write the stories that comprise *The Atrocity Exhibition* through a conjunction of private and public events. His wife had died unexpectedly of pneumonia whilst on holiday in the summer of 1964. He had now to make sense of what felt like a meaningless crime against a young woman, and her death became linked in his mind with the violence that he saw daily in magazines and on his television screen: "I was writing against a background of a sensation-hungry media landscape that seized on all the violent imagery emerging from Vietnam, from the Kennedy assassination, from civil wars in Africa. I was writing about the way in which sensation had usurped the place previously occupied by some kind of sympathetic engagement with the subject. I mean, one saw blowups of the Kennedy motorcade used as backdrops in fashion magazines. Images that should have elicited pity and concern were drained of any kind of human response." (JG Ballard, interview in *Artforum*, 1997)

To do justice to this subject matter, Ballard believed, would require an appropriate narrative style. Sequential narration, with its straightforward ordering of events and emphasis on what has already happened, seemed unsuited to material that concentrated on a complex, interconnected world and an open and unknown future.

In fact, Ballard was no stranger to stylistic exploration. Inspired principally by Joyce and Kafka, he had tried his hand at writing experimental fiction even before his first published story in 1956. Some time later, towards the end of the 1950s, he had put together what he referred to as "Project for a New Novel," a series of spreads using magazine-style layout and headlines, accompanied by largely meaningless text. The intention was for the titles and layout to provide the imaginative content, as is the case with an advertising hoarding. This technique

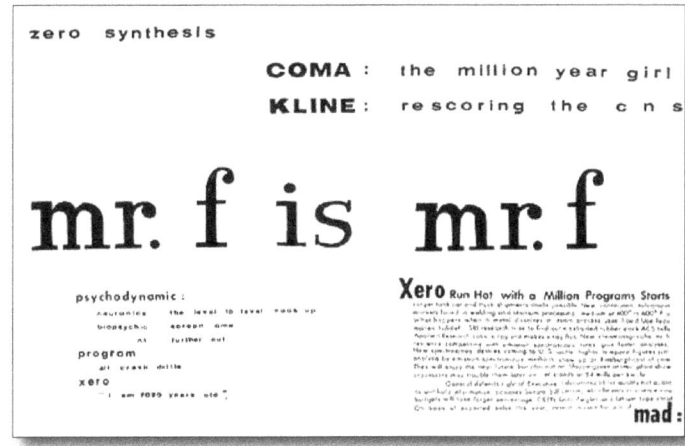

Kline, Coma, Xero: these three avatars of the unconscious from *The Atrocity Exhibition* first manifested themselves in "Project for a New Novel" (late-1950s).

of leaving the reader free to establish connections between the various elements of the 'story' would be utilised by Ballard when he came to write *The Atrocity Exhibition*, in which some of the names and phrases from "Project for a New Novel" would also re-emerge. These textual collages were finally published in *New Worlds* #213 in 1978.

Ballard had also written "The Terminal Beach" (1964), a short story concerning an ex-bomber pilot named Traven, who deliberately maroons himself on the atoll of Eniwetok, a U.S. hydrogen-bomb test site. The story was divided into a number of short, headlined sections, each of which contained its own narrative, leaving the overall account of what happens to Traven at Eniwetok largely implicit. The story contains the same mirroring of exterior landscape and subjective state of mind that Ballard had used in his novel *The Drowned World* (1962), but here the descriptions are overtly interiorized, such that Traven's 'terminal beach' is his own mind, rather than Eniwetok.

Another story from the same year explicitly recognizes the change in emphasis; in "The Delta at Sunset," the sick archaeologist Gifford asks "How else is nature meaningful, unless she illustrates some inner experience? The only real landscapes are the internal ones, or the external projections of them," thereby setting out one of the key themes of *The Atrocity Exhibition*.

"The Terminal Beach" was sufficiently beyond the parameters of what was commercially acceptable that Ballard's New York agent refused to handle it. In London, even EJ Carnell, who had published every story Ballard had sent him, had his doubts.

But Gollancz wanted another book to follow the success of *The Drowned World* and the collection *The Four-Dimensional Nightmare*, and as Ballard didn't have another novel ready, they decided on a second volume of short stories. Possibly to produce a striking collection, and to widen Ballard's appeal, they opted to make its contents more varied than its predecessor, considering for inclusion several as yet unpublished stories, including "The Terminal Beach." Given that it was acceptable to Gollancz, Carnell published the story in *New Worlds* #140 (March, 1964). Ironically, it went on to become one of Ballard's most anthologized pieces of fiction.

After his wife's death in mid-1964, the flow of stories ceased for around eighteen months. During that period, Cape published *The Drought* (1965), a novel which had been completed before the death of Ballard's wife, and which is set in the desert environment of a world where the rains have ceased. Ballard subsequently felt dissatisfied with the book, believing that the aridity of the landscapes overwhelmed the story. Nevertheless, it contained some of the concepts that he was to subsequently utilise in *The Atrocity Exhibition*: "*The Drought* was my second novel, written after *The Drowned World*. I didn't like it very much at the time. There was something rather too arid—something of the aridity of the landscape spilled over into the novel, and it didn't take off for me. I still don't care for it very much, but it contains so many of the ideas—quantified image, isolated object, and emotion detached from any human context—that I began to develop in *The Atrocity Exhibition* and in *Crash*. They were all implicit in that book." (JG Ballard, interview with Jim Goddard & David Pringle, 1975).

When a short story did eventually appear, it was not in a science fiction magazine but a US men's periodical. "Confetti Royale" (*Rogue*, February/March 1966) was a light-hearted story concerning the machinations of CIA agents and Russian spies, laid out in a series of loosely connected paragraphs, each with a heading and arranged in alphabetical order, the whole comprising a presumably insoluble mystery. This odd piece had been inspired by "The Ski Murders," written by one of Ballard's friends, the poet and BBC radio producer George MacBeth—on its next appearance, in *New Worlds* #189 (April 1969), it was re-titled "The Beach Murders: An Entertainment for George MacBeth."

The format of "Confetti Royale" was retained for Ballard's next story, "You and Me and the Continuum," which owed its origin to a suggestion by Kyril Bonfiglioli, the editor of *Science Fantasy*, that Ballard and other writers submit stories based on the notion of 'sacrifice': "The theme of sacrifice led me to think of the Messiah or, more exactly, the idea of the second coming and how this might take place in the twentieth century. In my version, which I would describe as a botched second coming, the Messiah never quite managing to come to terms with the twentieth century, I have used a fragmentary and non-sequential technique... and have tried to invoke some of the images that a twentieth-century Messiah might see." (JG Ballard, introduction to "You and Me and the Continuum," 1966)

Here is the theme of *The Atrocity Exhibition* as

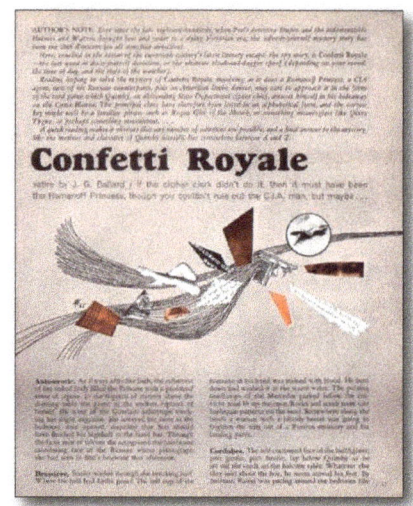

First appearance of Ballard's entertainment for his friend George MacBeth, as "Confetti Royale" in *Rogue* (1966).

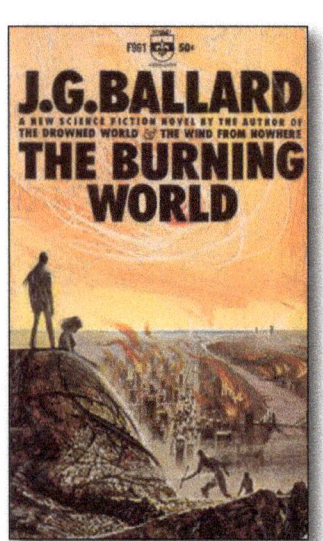 

The Drought was originally published as a US paperback under the title *The Burning World* (1964); artwork by Richard Powers. Cape published it in the UK as a hardcover in 1965; artwork by David Fawcett.

a whole—the protagonist tries to make sense of the modern world and of his place in it. But although "You and Me and the Continuum" would find its way into *The Atrocity Exhibition*, it was not written with the later stories in mind—many of the key themes of the book are either absent or referred to only in passing; the protagonist is not, as in most of the stories, a disturbed psychiatrist, but an unnamed Christ-like figure who is making an abortive return to Earth; and the story retains some of the humour of "Confetti Royale," It does, however, feature two characters who would fill important roles in later stories: Karen Novotny, a young woman who usually dies violently near the end of each story, almost as if she recapitulates the death of Ballard's wife, and Dr Nathan, whose pseudo-scientific explanations are contrasted with the main figure's reliance on the powers of his imagination and subconscious mind.

Science Fantasy was relaunched as *Impulse* in March 1966, and the first issue contained the themed stories that Bonfiglioli had commissioned, including "You and Me and the Continuum." The following month, "The Assassination Weapon" was published in *New Worlds* #161.

Ballard again used headed paragraphs but dropped the alphabetical order, a format that he was to retain for the stories that followed. This time the main character is Traven, an H-bomber pilot who has suffered a psychological dislocation after a plane crash—almost a replay of the pilot featured in "The Terminal Beach." Some of the key themes of *The Atrocity Exhibition* appear here for the first time, notably an attempt to re-enact, "but in a way that makes sense," the assassination of President Kennedy. However, "The Assassination Weapon" is still a restrained piece compared to some of the later stories, with their films of war atrocities and exhibitions of fatal car crashes. "You: Coma: Marilyn Monroe" followed quickly, being published in *Ambit* #27 in the spring of 1966. *Ambit* had been started by London paediatrician Martin Bax in 1959 and mixed poetry, fiction, and art. Ballard had met Bax in 1965, and the following year he started appearing on its masthead as prose editor. "You: Coma: Marilyn Monroe," in which "Tallis" and Karen Novotny are marooned in a near-deserted resort, is a muted but complex story, a classic example of how Ballard's condensed stories can open up like a series of Russian dolls. By the fourth of the stories, "The

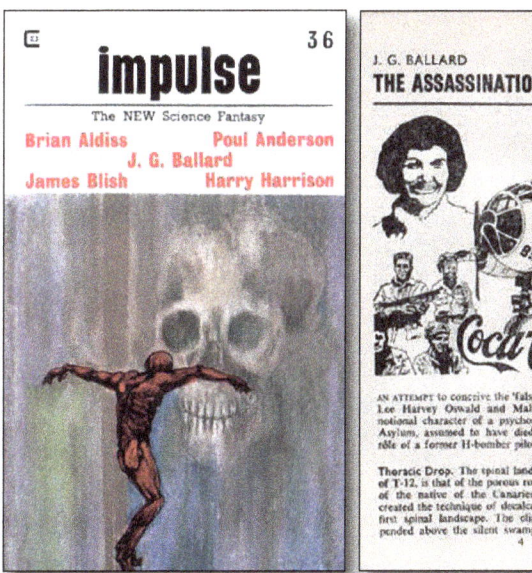

(Left) "You and Me and the Continuum" appeared in *Impulse* (March 1966) (Right) The second *Atrocity Exhibition* story in *New Worlds* (April 1966); artwork by Harry Douthwaite.

Atrocity Exhibition," the mood is darker, and all of the key themes of the book are now in place—death and violence, an overbearing media landscape, a mythology constituted by twentieth-century icons, and an obsession with the geometry of time and space—all experienced by a psychiatrist undergoing some form of mental breakdown, who falls back on the resources of his unconscious in order to resolve his difficulties. "The Atrocity Exhibition" was first published in *New Worlds* #166 (September 1966), now under the editorship of Ballard's friend and fellow-writer, Michael Moorcock. This number was a classic issue of the magazine, as it also contained Moorcock's award-winning novella "Behold the Man," as well as stories by Brian W. Aldiss and Thomas M. Disch, and an appreciation of Philip K. Dick written by John Brunner. "The Assassination of John Fitzgerald Kennedy Considered as a Downhill Motor Race" was published in *Ambit* #29 in the autumn of 1966. This satire was explicitly based on Alfred Jarry's "The Crucifixion Considered As An Uphill Bicycle

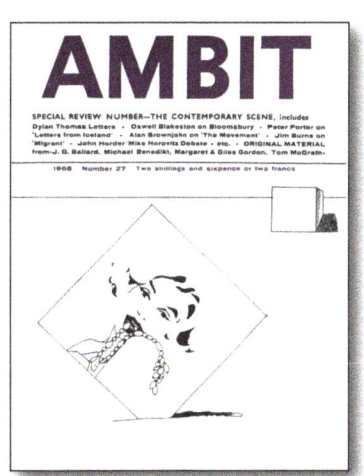

Ambit (Spring 1966) contained "You: Coma: Marilyn Monroe."

Race," which the French absurdist had published in 1894. Although it is only thematically linked to the rest of *The Atrocity Exhibition*, it was included as the final chapter on the book's publication.

By now, Ballard had realised that he was definitely on to something, and he published an article in *New Worlds* ("Notes from Nowhere," October 1966) which attempted to explain this dramatic turn that his work had taken: "In 'The Terminal Beach' the elements of sequential narrative had been almost completely eliminated. It occurred to me that one could carry this to its logical conclusion, and a recent group of stories—'You and Me and the Continuum,' 'The Assassination Weapon,' 'You: Coma: Marilyn Monroe' and 'The Atrocity Exhibition'—show some of the results. Apart from anything else, this new narrative technique seems to show a tremendous gain in the density of ideas and images. In fact, I regard each of them as a complete novel." (JG Ballard, "Notes from Nowhere," 1966)

The next section to be published, in early 1967, once again showed up in *Ambit*. "Plan for the Assassination of Jacqueline Kennedy" differed in form from the earlier stories; this was a satire, a mock report on a series of psychological tests designed to study the effect on the general public of media displays of violence and sex.

Meanwhile, over at BBC Radio, George MacBeth was sufficiently impressed by the new stories that he devoted an interview with Ballard to their discussion: "The great bulk of fiction still being written is retrospective in character; it's concerned with the origins of experience, behaviour, development of character over a great span of years; it interprets the present in terms of the past, and it uses a narrative technique, by and large the linear narrative, in which events are shown in more-or-less chronological sequence, which is suited to it. But when you turn to the present—and what I feel

This issue of *New Worlds* (September 1966) included both "The Atrocity Exhibition" and Michael Moorcock's "Behold the Man."

JGB's "non-Freudian assassination plan" for Jackie Kennedy in *Ambit*'s Anti-Sex issue (Spring 1967).

I've done in these pieces of mine is to rediscover the present for myself—I feel that one needs a non-linear technique, simply because our lives today are not conducted in linear terms. They are much more quantified; a whole stream of random events is taking place." (JG Ballard, BBC Radio interview, 1967) In "Notes from Nowhere," Ballard had referred to a story he was working on concerning a disaster in space and how it might be reflected in our inner and outer environments: "No one in science fiction has ever written about outer space... At present I am working on a story about a disaster in space which, however badly, makes a first attempt to describe what space means. So far, science fiction's idea of outer space has resembled a fish's image of life on land as a goldfish bowl. The surrealist painter, Matta: 'Why must we await, and fear, a disaster in space in order to understand our own times?'" (JG Ballard, "Notes from Nowhere," 1966)

Whatever this story may have been, it was overtaken by events in the real world when the three Apollo 1 astronauts died in a launch-pad fire in January 1967. "The Death Module," which appeared six months later in *New Worlds* #173, featured a re-enactment of these deaths by Trabert, another version of the disturbed psychiatrist. The story was re-titled for inclusion in *The Atrocity Exhibition*, appearing there as "Notes Towards a Mental Breakdown."

Ballard seems to have worked on other material during the second half of 1967, but returned to the fray dramatically early the following year with a second mock psychological study, this time aimed at what he referred to elsewhere as "politics conducted as a branch of advertising." This was the provocatively titled "Why I Want To Fuck Ronald Reagan," first published as a pamphlet by Brighton's

Unicorn Bookshop, which was run by the American poet, Bill Butler.

On the day that it was published in January 1968, the police raided Butler's shop for obscene publications, seizing thousands of magazines and books, including three copies of the "Reagan" booklet, which featured in Butler's trial in August 1968. In the meantime, *International Times* had reprinted the Reagan piece to accompany an article on why the forthcoming US election was too important to leave to the Americans alone. *International Times* erred on the side of caution by using asterisks in the four-letter word in the title, and by printing the piece over photographs of Reagan, partially masking its legibility.

It was likely that "Why I Want To…" was originally intended for the eccentrically titled *Ronald Reagan: The Magazine of Poetry*, edited by *New Worlds* authors John Sladek and Pamela Zoline, but that magazine did not appear until the second half of 1968.

Yet another satire followed in the summer of 1968, with "Love and Napalm: Export USA" appearing in *Circuit* #6 (June 1968). This was a short-lived magazine published by a group of students at Cambridge University, which ran between 1966 and 1969. The contents were largely about contemporary art and politics, with the aim of "enabling the student mind to escape from the imprisonment of the narrow compass of academic degree requirements." "Love and Napalm" had a second publication in *The Running Man* #2 (July/August 1968), a literary and arts magazine published in London by Christopher Kypreos, which seems to have lasted only five issues before folding. "The University of Death" (in which the psychiatrist is named Talbot) and "The Great American Nude" (on this occasion, he is Talbert) were published during the summer of 1968 in *Transatlantic Review* #29 and *Ambit* #36, respectively. These were followed by "The Generations of America," which starts off, "These are the generations of America. Sirhan Sirhan shot Robert F Kennedy. And Ethel M Kennedy shot Judith Birnbaum. And Judith Birnbaum shot Elizabeth Bochnak. And Elizabeth Bochnak shot Andrew Witwer," and continues in like vein for a further twelve-hundred words. This one-trick piece appeared in *New Worlds* #183 in October 1968; by now, the magazine was suffering from distribution problems following the reluctance of the wholesalers to handle the magazine due to concerns about obscenity and libel.

"The Death Module" appeared in *New Worlds* (July 1967). This was the first large-format issue, which allowed the inclusion of artwork and photography.

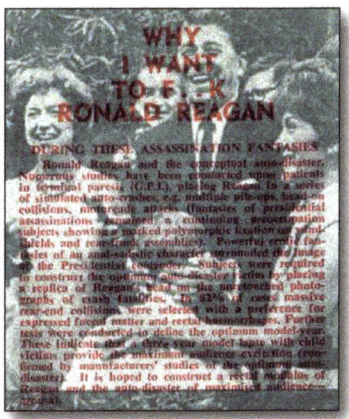

Ballard's Reagan satire in *International Times* (February 1968); notice the curious position of the young boy's head.

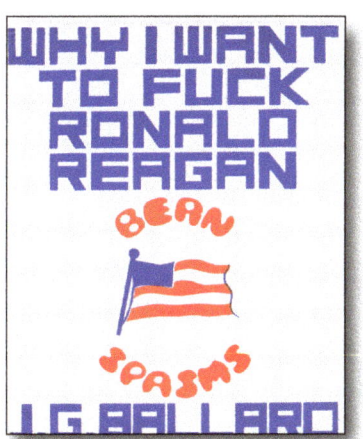

The booklet published by Bill Butler of the Unicorn Bookshop, Brighton (January 1968).

"Love and Napalm: Export U.S.A." appeared in *Circuit* (1968), and in *The Running Man* (1968).

The next section to appear was "The Summer Cannibals" (*New Worlds* #186, January 1969), which was set in an off-season holiday village and was markedly more subdued. The protagonist is not named, but is clearly another version of the psychiatrist from the earlier stories. This was another classic issue of *New Worlds*, since it also contained work by Michael Moorcock (a Jerry Cornelius story) and Brian Aldiss (an episode from his "Acid Head Wars" series).

New Worlds #186, featuring Ballard, Moorcock, and Aldiss.

The layout for "The Summer Cannibals" was put together by Charles Platt, fellow *New Worlds* author and associate editor of the magazine: "Initially JG Ballard embedded his crash obsession in the 'condensed novels' that we published in *New Worlds*. My father had been a director of the British company Vauxhall Motors, which was owned by General Motors. This gave me ready access to color pictures of American cars, which I used in my layouts for Ballard's stories, much to his pleasure. I also supplied him with American car brochures which, as he later put it, he 'plundered' for his stories." (Charles Platt, in *The New York Review of Science Fiction*, 2008)

A final mock psychological study, "Crash!," appeared in the *Eventsheet* of London's Institute of Contemporary Arts for February 1969, being printed over what appears to be a screenshot from

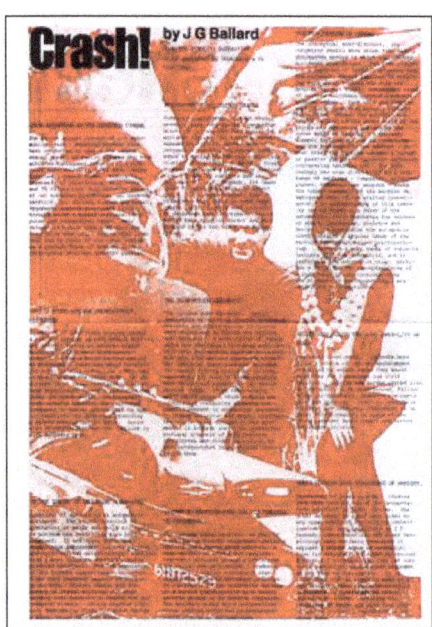

"Crash!" as it appeared in the *ICA Eventsheet* (1969).

Layout for "The Summer Cannibals" by Charles Platt.

Jean-Luc Godard's *Week-end*. The later sections of *The Atrocity Exhibition* had displayed Ballard's interest in what would become the subject matter of his next novel—our fascination with the automobile, a dangerous piece of machinery that plays to some of our deepest fears and desires. An exhibition of crashed cars had featured in "The University of Death," and the theme had become explicit in "Crash!"

It seems that at one point Ballard was thinking of putting on a play at the ICA involving a reconstruction of a car crash, which would feature dummy figures produced by Eduardo Paolozzi and a narration by Ballard's friend, the psychologist Dr. Christopher Evans. The play was heralded in advance in the *Sunday Mirror*, where Ballard explained that car crashes had the effect of: "liberating sexual libido, radiating the sexuality and energy of the victim who died in an intensity impossible in any other form. Crash victims like Jayne Mansfield, James Dean, Aly Khan, Jim Clark and President Kennedy (the first man to be murdered in a motorcade) act out the Crucifixion for us. Their deaths heighten our vitality in a blinding flash. The death of Kennedy was a sacrificial murder, connived at by the millions of people who watched it endlessly recapitulated on television. If Christ came again, he would be killed in a car crash." (JG Ballard, *The Sunday Mirror*, 1968)

There is no evidence that this proposed collaboration between Ballard, Paolozzi, and Evans ever took place. However, Ballard did go on to stage his own exhibition of three crashed automobiles at London's New Arts Lab in April 1970, as an experiment to confirm his intuitions before proceeding to write his new novel. He also attempted to explore the theme using the condensed style of *The Atrocity Exhibition*. The result was published as "Journey Across a Crater" (*New Worlds* #198, February 1970), but Ballard felt that it had not been a success. For the novel *Crash*, he therefore returned to a straightforward narrative style, explaining that "the ideas themselves… are so unexpected, incomprehensible to some people, challenging, if you like. The best way of expressing them is in a straightforward way." (interview for the Canadian Broadcasting Corporation, 1973).

The publication of "Crash!" in early 1969 had been accompanied by a brief statement that *The Atrocity Exhibition* would be forthcoming from Doubleday later that year. However, Ballard had still to write the final section, and "Tolerances of the

The very first publication of *The Atrocity Exhibition*, in Danish (1969).

(Left) *New Worlds* for February 1970 featured "Journey Across a Crater," an attempt to explore the themes of *Crash* using the narrative style of *The Atrocity Exhibition*. (Right) "Tolerances of the Human Face" appeared in *Encounter*, a magazine founded by neoconservative author Irving Kristol and a recipient of CIA funding.

Human Face" did not appear until September 1969, when it was published in *Encounter*. Although the subject matter remains the same, and the paragraphs are still accompanied by headings, the story reads rather more like a traditional narrative, almost as if the psychiatrist, Travers, is on the way to making a recovery. "Tolerances of the Human Face" also introduced a new character, Vaughan, who was to become the "hoodlum scientist" of *Crash*. By now, Cape had accepted *The Atrocity Exhibition* for publication in the U.K. However, its first appearance in book form was actually a Danish translation by Jannick Storm, with the title *Grusomhedsudstillingen* (Rhodos, 1969). Storm had visited England and met Ballard in the late-1960s, and translated the individual pieces after they had appeared in the magazines.

Ballard's original intention was for *The Atrocity Exhibition* to be an illustrated book, possibly along the lines of Charles Platt's layout for "The Summer Cannibals," but his UK publishers balked at the prospect: "My original idea for *The Atrocity Exhibition* was that I would do collage illustrations. I put that up to Cape. I originally wanted a large-format book, printed by photo-offset, in which I could prepare the artwork—a lot of collages, material taken from medical documents and medical photographs, crashing cars and all that sort of iconography. It wouldn't have been any more expensive for them to photograph the pages of collages than the pages of text. But to them illustrated books meant six pages of line drawings by some distinguished artist, Felix Topolski or somebody. So that fell through." (JG Ballard, "From Shanghai to Shepperton," 1982)

Cape published *The Atrocity Exhibition* in July 1970, with a jacket featuring Dali's *City of Drawers*, but the proposed US edition from Doubleday never appeared. The entire edition, with the exception of a few review and file copies, was destroyed just prior to publication after senior management at Doubleday had become aware of the contents and had taken exception. It isn't clear exactly how many copies still survive (perhaps around a dozen or so), but this is certainly the rarest of Ballard's books. In addition to the 15 stories that comprised the Cape edition, Doubleday had included drawings by Michael Foreman, and a transcription of George MacBeth's 1967 radio interview with Ballard.

Following the pulping by Doubleday, EP Dutton took up *The Atrocity Exhibition*, but eventually decided against publication after advice from their lawyers. The first US publication was therefore not until 1972 when Grove Press published the book under the revised title *Love and Napalm: Export USA*.

This edition went out of print fairly quickly, and the book did not reappear in the US until 1990 when Re/Search Publications brought out a large format, extensively illustrated, paperback edition. This reverted to the original title and added sidebar annotations by Ballard, as well as four additional pieces—three of Ballard's "surgical fictions" from

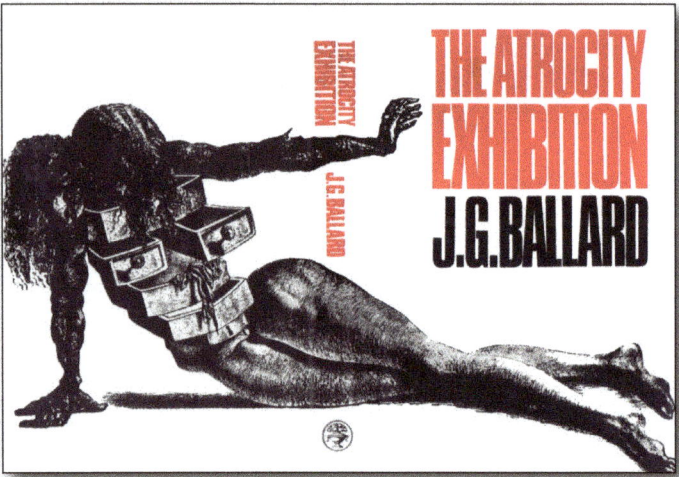

The first UK edition of *The Atrocity Exhibition*, Jonathan Cape (1970).

The suppressed US edition from Doubleday (1970).

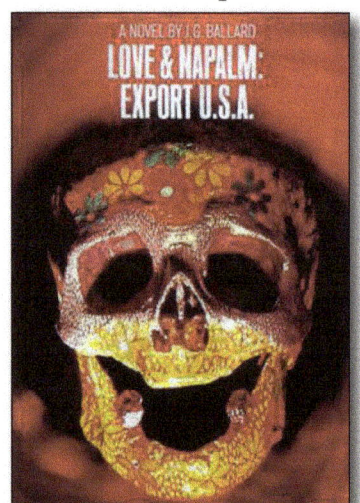

The first U.S. edition, retitled *Love & Napalm: Export USA*, features an introduction by William S Burroughs.

the 1970s and a story from the late-1980s that once again featured Ronald Reagan. Simultaneously, Re/Search brought out a signed hardback edition, limited to 400 un-numbered copies; at the time of writing, a few copies are still available.

The surgical fictions that were incorporated into the Re/Search edition had been intended by Ballard as another illustration of the effect that the media has on how we perceive the world. He had taken actual descriptions of surgical procedures and replaced references to 'the patient' with the name of a famous personality: "I've just published a piece in *New Worlds* called 'Princess Margaret's Facelift,' in which I've taken the text of a classic description of a plastic surgery operation, a facelift, and where the original says "the patient," I've inserted "Princess Margaret." So I've done precisely what the pop painters did, using images from everyday life—Coca-Cola bottles, Marilyn Monroe—and manipulated them. The great thing about pop painters is their honesty. They've turned their backs on the traditional subject matter of the fine arts—which had hardly changed since the Renaissance— and looked at their own environment and decided: yes, the shine on domestic hardware, like the refrigerator or the washing machine, the particular gleam on the mouldings of a cabinet, the moulding of doorhandles, are of importance to people, because these are the visual landscapes of people's lives, and if we're going to be honest we're going to use reality material instead of fiction. I want to do the same." (JG Ballard, interview in *Penthouse*, 1970)

"Coitus 80: A Description of the Sexual Act in 1980" had been something of an early prototype, leading to "Princess Margaret's Facelift" and "Mae West's Reduction Mammoplasty," all published in 1970. "Queen Elizabeth's Rhinoplasty" was a later piece, appearing in 1976. A final surgical piece, "Jane Fonda's Augmentation Mammoplasty," was written for *Semiotext(e) SF*, a 1989 paperback anthology. In their introduction to the Ballard piece, *Semiotext(e)*'s editors kindly provided their address for Ms. Fonda's lawyers. Re/Search had originally intended to include this story along with the earlier surgical fictions in their expanded edition of *The Atrocity Exhibition*, but it never appeared. Re/Search's expanded version of the book was adopted in the UK by Flamingo, who brought out their own large-format paperback edition in 1993. This included the sidebar annotations, but no illustrations; of the additional stories included by Re/Search, only "Princess Margaret's Facelift" and "Mae West's Reduction Mammoplasty" were incorporated. Later Flamingo editions have been normal size paperbacks in which the annotations have been relegated to separate sections at the end of each chapter.

The prototype for the surgical fictions: "Coitus 80: A Description of the Sexual Act in 1980" from *New Worlds* (1970).

By the time *Crash* was published in 1973, the flow of stories emanating from Ballard's attempt to make sense of the 1960s appeared to have run its course. Later works might cover similar subject matter, but not with the personal intensity that marked *The Atrocity Exhibition*: "I'm conscious of the fact that in the mid-sixties something happened to me... I think I was trying to make sense of my wife's death by taking as a subject matter the world of the '60s, particularly that around Kennedy's death, and trying to make sense of it, trying to find in a paradoxical way something good. Now I know that's a sort of nightmare logic, but that's what *Atrocity Exhibition* is, a book of nightmare formulas... Desperate, desperate measures—I suppose the whole of *Atrocity Exhibition* and *Crash* is summed up under that heading. A kit of desperate measures, desperate devices." (JG Ballard, interview with Alan Burns, circa 1974)

The Atrocity Exhibition: A Selected Bibliography

The Atrocity Exhibition
As *Grusomhedsudstillingen* (Rhodos, Denmark, 1969) Danish Translation, Paperback, World First Edition
   - Ditto - as *The Atrocity Exhibition* (Doubleday, US, 1970) Suppressed and Destroyed
   - Ditto - as *The Atrocity Exhibition* (Cape, UK, 1970)
   - Ditto - as *Love And Napalm: Export U.S.A.* (Grove Press, US, 1972)
   - Ditto - as *The Atrocity Exhibition* (Panther, UK, 1972) First UK Paperback Edition
   - Ditto - as *The Atrocity Exhibition* (Re/Search, US, 1990) Large-Format Paperback, with annotations, illustrations, and four additional stories
   - Ditto - as *The Atrocity Exhibition* (Re/Search, US, 1990) Signed Hardback, with annotations, illustrations, and four additional stories, 400 copies
   - Ditto - as *The Atrocity Exhibition* (Flamingo, UK, 1993) Large-Format Paperback, with annotations and two additional stories

The Individual Sections
"You and Me and the Continuum" in *Impulse* #1, March 1966
"The Assassination Weapon" in *New Worlds* #161, April 1966
"You: Coma: Marilyn Monroe" in *Ambit* #27, [Spring] 1966
   - Ditto - in *New Worlds* #163, June 1966
"The Atrocity Exhibition" in *New Worlds* #166, September 1966
   - Ditto - in *Encounter*, March 1967
"The Assassination of John Fitzgerald Kennedy Considered as a Downhill Motor Race" in *Ambit* #29, [Autumn] 1966
   - Ditto - in *New Worlds* #171, March 1967
"Plan for the Assassination of Jacqueline Kennedy" in *Ambit* #31, [Winter-Spring] 1966/1967
"Notes Towards a Mental Breakdown" (as "The Death Module"), in *New Worlds* #173, July 1967
"Why I Want To Fuck Ronald Reagan" (Unicorn Bookshop, Brighton, [January] 1968) Pamphlet, Signed and Numbered, 50 Copies
   - Ditto - (Unicorn Bookshop, Brighton, [January] 1968) Pamphlet, Unsigned and Un-Numbered, 200 Copies
   - Ditto - in *International Times* #26, 16-29 February 1968
   - Ditto - in *Ronald Reagan: The Magazine of Poetry*, [Summer/Autumn?] 1968
"Love and Napalm: Export U.S.A." in *Circuit* #6, June 1968
   - Ditto - in *The Running Man* #2, July/August 1968
"The University of Death" in *Transatlantic Review* #29, Summer 1968 (UK/US)
"The Great American Nude" in *Ambit* #36, [Summer] 1968
"The Generations of America" in *New Worlds* #183, October 1968
"The Summer Cannibals" in *New Worlds* #186, January 1969
"Crash!" in *ICA Eventsheet* (Institute Of Contemporary Arts, London), February [1969]
   - Ditto - in *Aspen* #7: British Box (Roaring Fork Press), Spring-Summer 1970 (US), Multi-Media Magazine in Box
   "Tolerances of the Human Face" in *Encounter*, September 1969

Additional Stories included in the 1990 Re/Search Edition
"Princess Margaret's Face Lift: An Intersection of Fiction and Reality" in *New Worlds* #199, March 1970
"Mae West's Reduction Mammoplasty" in *Ambit* #44, [Summer] 1970
"Queen Elizabeth's Rhinoplasty" in *Triquarterly* #35, Winter 1976 (US)
"The Secret History of World War 3" in *Ambit* #114, [Autumn] 1988

Related Material
"The Terminal Beach" in *New Worlds* #140, March 1964
The Burning World (Berkley, US, 1964) Paperback
   - Ditto - as *The Drought* (Cape, UK, 1965)
"Confetti Royale" in *Rogue* Volume 11 No.1, February/March 1966 (US)
   - Ditto – as "The Beach Murders: An Entertainment for George MacBeth" in *New Worlds* #189, April 1969
"Notes From Nowhere: Comments on Work in Progress" in *New Worlds* #167, October 1966; Article discussing his recent fiction
"Coitus 80: A Description of the Sexual Act in 1980" in *New Worlds* #197, January 1970
"Journey Across a Crater" in *New Worlds* #198, February 1970
"The New Science Fiction" in *The New SF*, Ed. Langdon Jones (Hutchinson, UK, 1969); Transcript of a 1967 radio interview
Crash (Cape, UK, 1973)
   - Ditto - (Farrar, Straus & Giroux, US, 1973)
[Project For A New Novel] in *New Worlds* #213, Summer 1978; Textual collages produced circa 1958
"Jane Fonda's Augmentation Mammoplasty" in *Semiotext(e) SF* (Autonomedia, US, 1989)

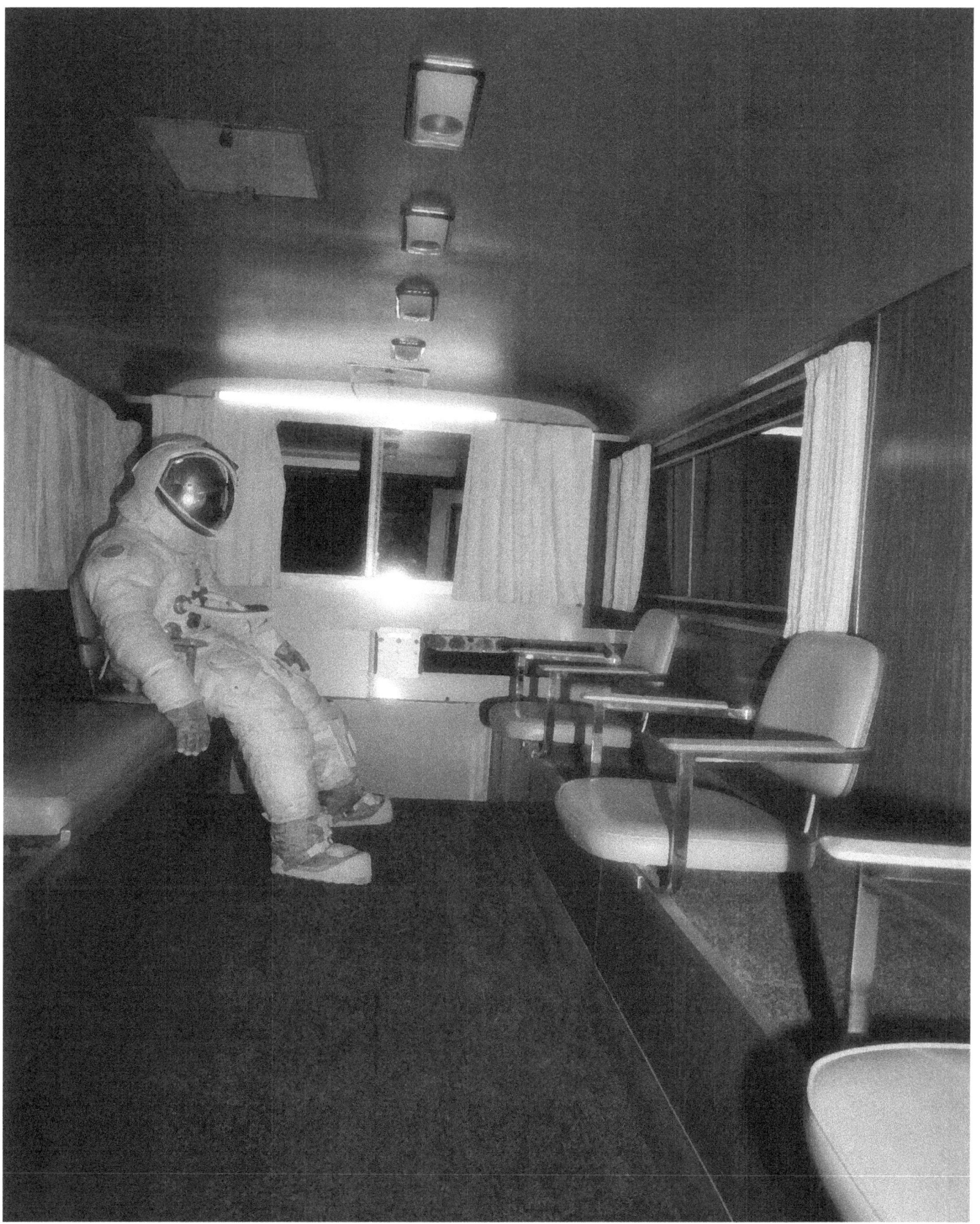

ANA BARRADO
Astronaut on bus to launch site, KSC Museum, 1995

Visualizing the Ballardian Image

by Rick Poynor

JG Ballard is unusual among writers of fiction for being perceived primarily in terms of his imagery. The term "Ballardian," now in wide critical use, has become shorthand for a particular kind of location, object, conjunction of objects, or atmosphere. As many interviews with Ballard have made clear, his principal influences came from visual artists and he sometimes spoke of himself as a frustrated painter. Images and ideas drawn from Surrealism and Pop informed his writing to a degree that sets him apart from other contemporary writers operating at a similar level of imaginative intensity.

All of this might seem to offer highly promising source material for anyone whose task is to represent Ballard, his oeuvre or specific works in the form of a visual image. This essay explores the ways in which Ballard's worlds and worldview have been represented as visual imagery in the media. My focus is not on the texts, but on their visual interpretation. Book covers are central to this discussion, though I also consider other kinds of illustration, photography and typography, concentrating in particular on *The Atrocity Exhibition* (1970). These images, which are not usually given any critical attention at all, can be understood as a form of evidence for the meanings the books hold for their audiences. They can also be seen as a kind of highly condensed commentary on the texts, especially in their cumulative effect over time. Many of Ballard's covers circulate on websites run by enthusiasts and collectors and they are often used in articles about his work on the Internet.

 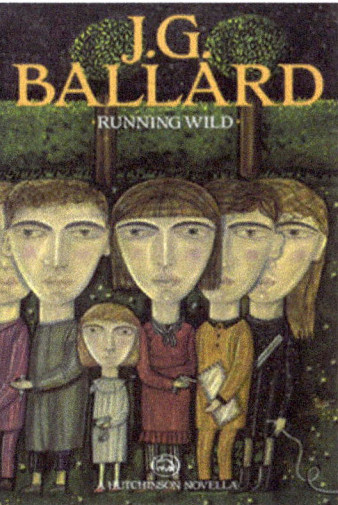

Left: Design by Bill Botten, Jonathan Cape, hardback, 1982.
Right: Design by Craig Dodd. Illustration by Janet Woolley, Hutchinson, hardback, 1988.

When it comes to his book covers, Ballard has not been served well by most of his publishers. Simon Sellars, introducing an interview with Ballard collector Rick McGrath on his Ballardian website, describes them as "the trashiest covers this side of Philip K Dick." A commenter on the thread agrees: "If there were an award for Writer Most Abused by His Publisher's Designers, Ballard would have to receive the lifetime achievement award [...] It's a real testament to his prose that you stomach some of those cover illustrations to read it." I share these views. I bought hardback editions of Ballard's books as they were published between 1979 and 1991 with an unvarying sense of dismay at the covers' failure to match my perceptions of the writer they represented—or rather misrepresented. Rather than assemble a rogue's gallery of the many Ballard cover disasters (the two opposite are typical), I would rather concentrate here on cases that seem more purely Ballardian.

One might ask, of course, whether it matters much anyway. Is a book cover anything more than superficial packaging, a kind of advertisement that has no purpose other than prompting a purchase? While that might once have been a literary person's view of covers, it is no longer adequate, particularly where a visually knowledgeable writer such as Ballard is concerned. (To explore this issue properly would require a lengthy detour into the history and development not just of book design but of late 20th century graphic culture.)

Ballard certainly understood the importance of the visual for contemporary audiences. In an interview published in 1981 he explained:

> I've always been conscious since I started writing that the tide was running the wrong way for the writer, whereas the visual artist, the painter or sculptor, was in a seller's market; the direction of the twentieth century was ever more visual. I sensed way back in the late fifties when I started that the tide was running away from the written word towards the visual mode of expression and therefore one couldn't any more rely on the reader, you couldn't expect him to meet you any more than halfway.

Ballard signalled his allegiance to Surrealism in his novels, and in his essay "The Coming of the Unconscious," published in *New Worlds* in 1966, he goes so far as to specify six key Surrealist paintings with a "direct bearing on the speculative fiction of the immediate future" by De Chirico, Dalí, Magritte, Domínguez and Ernst, listed twice for *The Elephant of Celebes* (1921) and *The Eye of Silence* (1943-44). One Surrealist painting not included in the *New Worlds* list, *The Palace of Windowed Rocks* (1942) by Yves Tanguy, had already surfaced on a Penguin paperback of Ballard's *The Drowned World* (1965)

Left: Detail from *The Eye of Silence*, Panther, paperback, 1968.
Right: Detail from *The Palace of Windowed Rocks*, Penguin, paperback, 1965.

where a detail is used (for some reason the picture has been flipped). This was most likely chosen by Penguin's art director, Germano Facetti, who had a brilliant eye for selecting paintings that encapsulated the mood of a text.

In 2004, in a letter, Ballard told me that he had forced his British publisher, Jonathan Cape, to use *The Eye of Silence* on the hardback cover of *The Crystal World* (1966)—one of only two Cape covers that satisfied him ("the design dept. hadn't the faintest idea what I was about"). The image was used again on the paperback. Two decades later, another Ernst from Ballard's pantheon, *Europe after the Rain* (1940-42), appeared on the American cover of *Memories of the Space Age*, though it is a half-hearted design, with poorly matched

Detail from *City of Drawers*, Jonathan Cape, hardback, 1970.

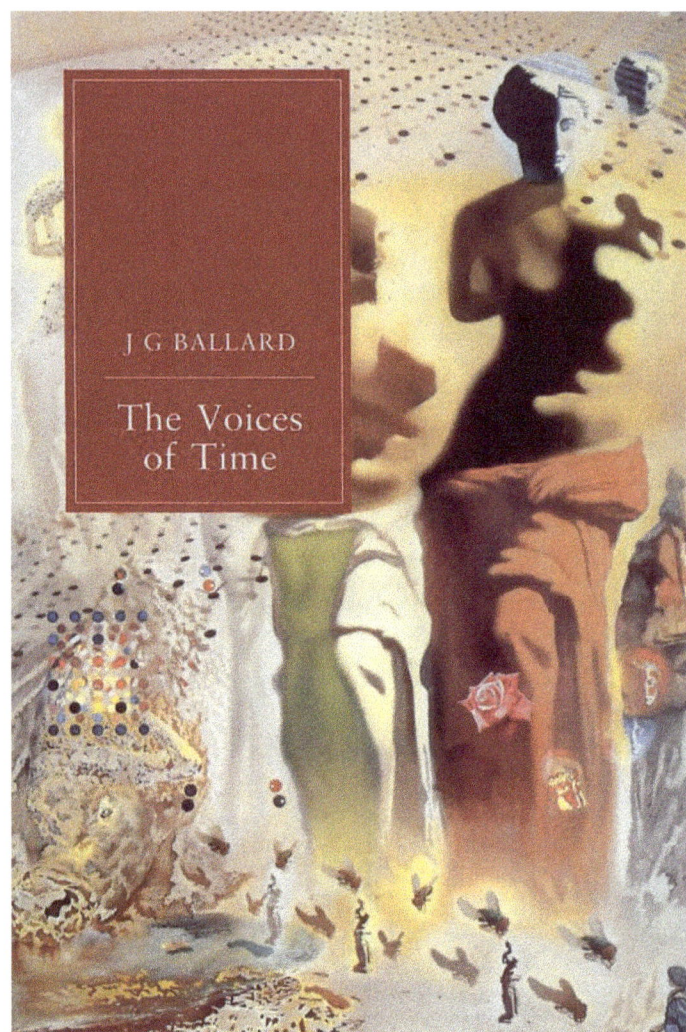

Detail from *Hallucinogenic Toreador*, Orion, paperback, 1992.

typography. Ballard was also able to persuade Cape to use a detail from Dalí's pen and ink drawing *City of Drawers* (1936) on the UK hardback of *The Atrocity Exhibition*. Seen in the round, the jacket has undeniable power and it was unusual, especially for its time, in reserving its principal content—the woman's bizarre cabinet-of-drawers torso—for the concealed back cover. Yet the image has only a tangential relationship to the book, as does the psychedelic Dalí, *Hallucinogenic Toreador* (1968-70), used on a reissue of *The Voices of Time* in 1992.

Designs based on canonical Surrealist images can be seen as a kind of amplified citation, or a confirmation of Ballard's allegiance to Surrealism, rather than as an interpretation of the book itself. They are Ballardian by association rather than Ballardian in essence.

Four covers published by Penguin in 1974 are among the most purely Ballardian images to be found on any of his books. David Pelham, art

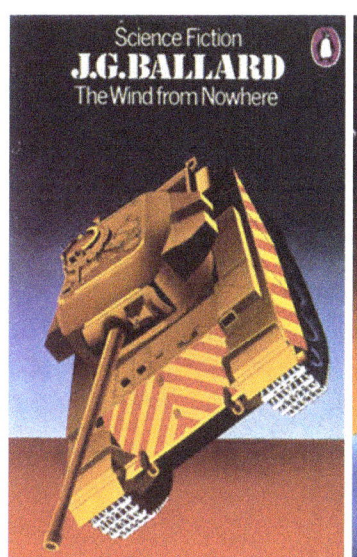 

Left and right: Design and illustration by David Pelham, Penguin, paperback, 1974.

Design and illustration by David Pelham, Penguin, paperback, 1974.

Replica of the Fat Man atomic bomb dropped on Nagasaki in 1945.

director of Penguin in the 1970s, designed them and created the airbrush illustrations. *The Terminal Beach*, the strongest of the quartet in my view, unites two Ballardian motifs, the sand fused by weapons tests in the title story and the Fat Man bomb dropped on Nagasaki, standing here for all atomic weapons. Graphic design is a form of rhetoric and one reason this image works so well is that it has been realized so perfectly. Pelham's illustration is grounded, like Ballard's prose, in meticulously precise observation, but he has given this scene of becalmed destructive power an intensified, hyper-real quality, most obviously in the use of color. The image is simplified and stylized yet luminously sharp and exact. The tonal gradations and shadows endow the bomb with a presence both menacing and fetishistic: it is not just a bomb in the literal sense, but an avatar of psychic unease. The centered type is flawlessly placed and weighted in relation to the image below, and the stencil typeface carries a military association that fits the subject matter of the title story. The lack of resonance in later editions of *The Terminal Beach* underlines the conceptual and aesthetic accuracy of Pelham's cover. The 1974 edition attracts attention, as a book cover should, while reflecting with considerable insight the nature of the texts inside. It satisfies the needs of both the potential buyer, at the moment of purchase, and the committed reader, who will live with the book.

Pelham worked elegant variations on this basic structure and even Ballard's first novel, *The Wind from Nowhere*, later suppressed by the writer, achieved temporary respectability. The Ballard series was, in addition, a sub-series that developed from Penguin's superbly visualized science fiction series

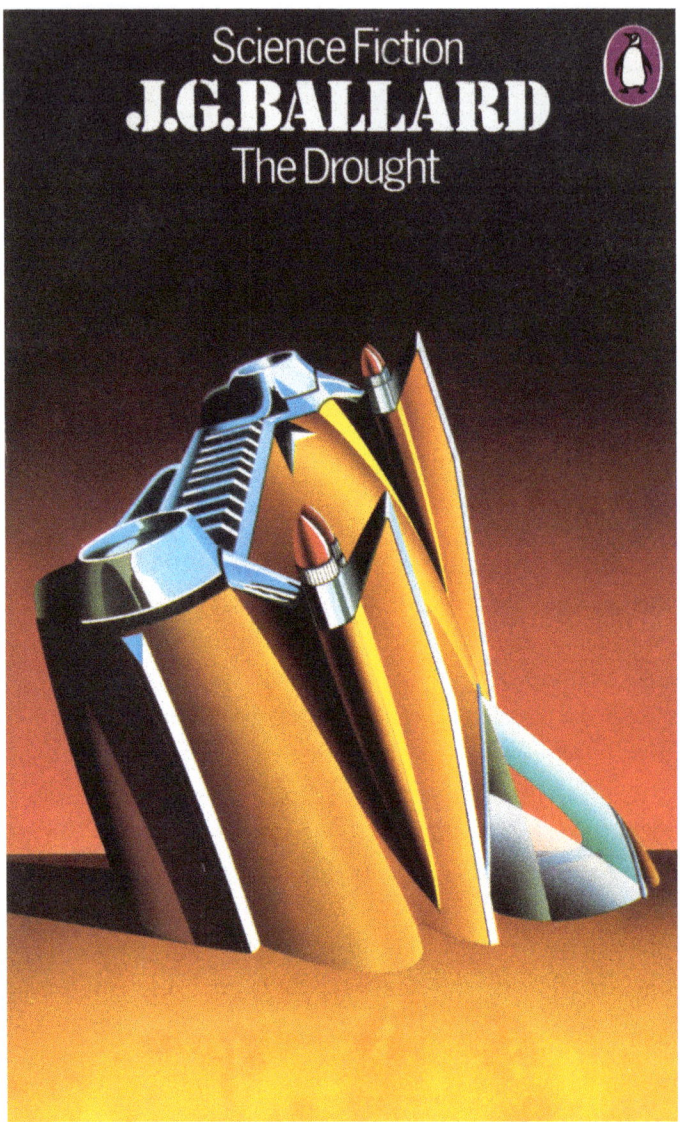

Design and illustration by David Pelham, Penguin, paperback, 1974.

introduced Pelham to Ballard and Pelham showed him a postcard-sized trial image for *The Drought*. Ballard gave his approval and they discussed the other titles.

Although I don't propose here to examine the cover treatments of *Crash* (1973), which I have done elsewhere, it must be clear that *The Drought*'s iconic, entropic car body could have functioned just as suggestively to represent *Crash*. Once again, the hardware's obsessional and fetishistic qualities, the eroticized gleam of the car's accentuated chromium trim, the eerie light and sickly plasticity reminiscent of Dalí's pictures, without simply quoting one of them, seem utterly Ballardian.

The writer's love of 1960s American car styling is, in any case, a matter of record. Airbrush, also used at the time on the cover of a paperback translation of Barthes' *Mythologies*, proved to be exactly the right tool to evoke an overlit, affectless realm of celebrity, mass media and seductively styled consumer design—a lurid, stripped-down, Pop Art update of Dalí's old-masterish oil paint illusionism. It's also interesting to note the use of montage to represent themes in Barthes' essays.

A similar technique was applied to the first British paperback edition of *The Atrocity Exhibition*, published by Panther in 1972. The typeface, with its exceptionally deep x-height and abbreviated ascenders, has a ferocious bite, suggesting seriousness and rigor, while the unusual stepped arrangement of the title and author's name gives the cover an air of instability.

of the early 1970s, also designed by Pelham—the consistent panel at the bottom becomes the ground and horizon on the Ballard books.

Pelham was both an excellent designer and an enthusiastic reader of Ballard's writing. Unlike so many of Ballard's designers, he understood these books. In *Penguin by Designers* (Penguin Collectors Society, 2007), Pelham explains how the covers came about: "I was very familiar with Ballard's work, having been a great admirer from way back. I admired the bleak style of his catastrophe novels [...] and their heartless depiction of human and technological breakdown and decay. Grim perhaps, but wonderfully written. Drawn to the romance of his apocalyptic imagery, I wanted to illustrate his covers myself."

Ballard's friend, the artist Eduardo Paolozzi,

 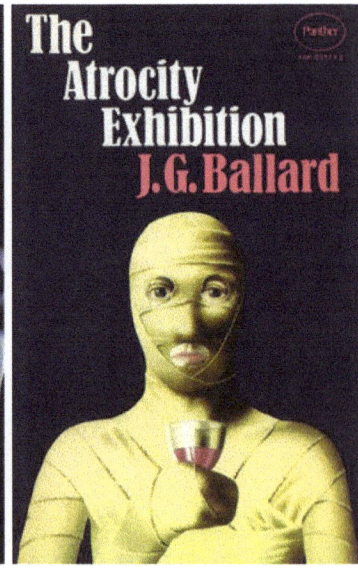

Left: Illustration by Phillip Castle, Paladin, paperback, 1973.
Right: Illustrator uncredited, Panther, paperback, 1972.

As so often, the image bears only a tangential relationship to the central incidents, themes and tropes of the book. Whatever the illustrator had in mind, it is clear that Ballard is still being characterized in relation to Surrealism, although the slightly jocular image entirely lacks the power and conviction of the real thing. Later paperback cover treatments of *The Atrocity Exhibition*, published in 1979 and 1985, continued to visualize the book in terms of waxily smooth imagery created with an airbrush.

The repeated failure of editors, designers and illustrators to engage intellectually with *The Atrocity Exhibition* is all the more remarkable because the book offers a litany of Ballardian images: bunkers, concrete causeways, jutting balconies, crashed bombers, a drained sculpture fountain, a deserted beach resort, rubber mannequins and plastic dummies, as well as more ambiguous images such as a "conceptual auto disaster" or a "spinal landscape"—quite apart from its erotic content. The many artists Ballard invokes by name or by artwork title also suggest visual possibilities, particularly the contemporary artists: Kienholz, Segal, Wesselmann, Warhol, Paolozzi. Above all, there are the book's numbered lists, conceptual image-kits assembled, according to Ballard, by free association. These read like an artist's notes on components for a painting or print and any one of them could provide an image-maker with the elements for a provocative montage. Montage was a modernist invention, in use since the 1920s, and Ballard was well acquainted with *Just what is it that makes today's homes so different, so appealing?*, Richard Hamilton's seminal, proto-Pop collage of 1956.

Paolozzi's screenprints are also intricate montages—Ballard owned at least three, including a copy of *B.A.S.H.* (1971) seen on his wall behind him in a frequently used publicity shot from the 1980s—and the artist produced occasional book covers. They were both contributing editors at *Ambit* magazine. Moreover, covers for fiction based on montage, with multiple focal points, were not unknown in British publishing by the mid-1980s.

One of the more significant moments in the evolution of Ballard studies came with the publication of Re/Search's special issue about Ballard in 1984. It remains an essential document, most obviously for its interviews. Ballard had for several years been a key figure for post-punk musicians

Left: Cover concept and photograph by Bobby Adams. Design by Rebecca Wilson, Re/Search, 1983. Right: Design by Rebecca Wilson. Photograph by Ana Barrado, Re/Search, 1984.

and the book was the most complete expression to date of a particular view of Ballard that zeroed in on everything that was most acutely Ballardian for hardcore fans—with *The Atrocity Exhibition* and *Crash* at the center—and harnessed this to a branch of subcultural inquiry obsessed with extremes of all kinds. Based in San Francisco, the founders began by publishing *Search & Destroy*, a punk newspaper, and previous issues of *Re/Search* had been devoted to William Burroughs and to industrial culture and the music of experimental bands such as *Throbbing Gristle*, Cabaret Voltaire and SPK.

Apart from its content, much of the impact of the Ballard issue comes from the typography and layout, which is radically different from the tastefully well-mannered professional design of its day. The designer, Andrea Juno, buttresses, brackets and constrains the text with heavy bars and panels and kick-starts paragraphs with emphatic black squares. Photographs by Ana Barrado and Bobby Adams of rockets, concrete block houses and

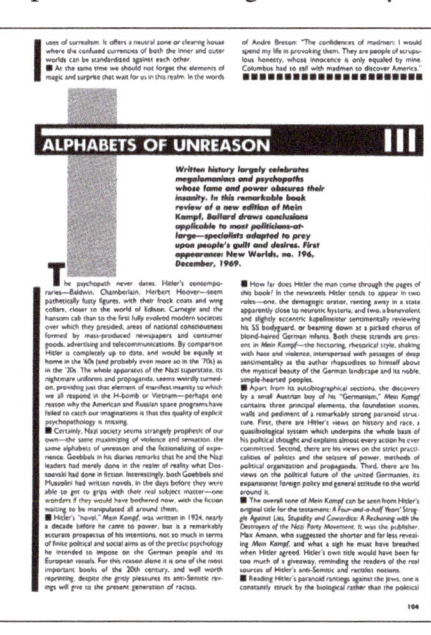

Page design by Andrea Juno, Re/Search, 1984.

121

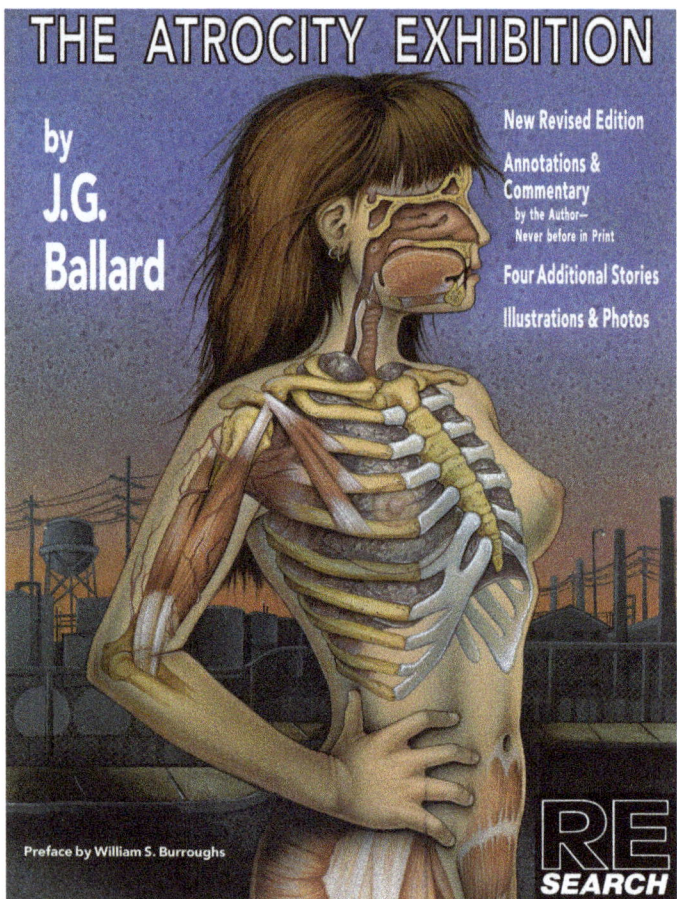

Design by Andrea Juno. Illustration by Phoebe Gloeckner, Re/Search, 1990.

palm trees compose a monochrome travelogue of Ballardian America, electrically charged yet at the same time ethereally removed. The combined effect is so forceful and unsettling as to stamp Ballard with a new framework of visual references such that even the strangely over-articulated typography comes to seem in some curious way Ballardian.

Juno applied essentially the same repertoire of brutally industrial graphic devices to the expanded edition of *The Atrocity Exhibition* that Re/Search published in 1990, with annotations by Ballard. While the startlingly aggressive and disturbing cover image by Phoebe Gloeckner, a medical illustrator and comic book artist, is let down by some clumsy typography, her series of 10 illustrations inside is the most intensive and forensic visual investigation in printed form of any text by Ballard, showing a willingness to emulate its cold, pornographic stratagems that reminds us just how wide of the mark most publishers' interpretations have been. In their introduction, Re/Search's publisher/editors V Vale and Andrea Juno suggest that the realism of the images "dismantles 'pornography' like Ballard's text: as a series of fragmentary, alienated, passionless responses to a set of stimuli."

The uncompromising Re/Search edition of *Atrocity* presaged a small shift in publisher awareness and an American edition of *Crash* produced in 1994 features one of the most apposite Ballard covers to date (see my essay about cover treatments of *Crash*). Most crucially, the design at last recognizes the representational possibilities of fragmentation and montage—albeit tightly gridded—a direction that remains to be deployed more fully across Ballard's oeuvre. When a large-format annotated edition of *Atrocity* was published in Britain in 1993, with a mini-montage on a billboard on the cover, it did not include Gloeckner's illustrations. British publishers seem determined to make this demanding, complex, recalcitrant work look as innocuous as possible. The latest cover design (2006), part of a series, is a bland, spray-paint graffiti illustration of Marilyn Monroe—Ballard Banksy-fied—that couldn't do less to direct attention to the book's disquieting kit of images and fragmented narratives.

For a more convincingly Ballardian use of imagery in recent years, we need to leave commercial bookselling and return to the cultural margins. The packaging of the *Atrocity Exhibition* DVD, released in The Netherlands by Reel23 in 2006, in a non-standard slipcase made of card, is a rare occasion when an entirely contemporary design approach has been applied to a Ballard-related commodity. The design accepts that the most likely buyer of the DVD will know Ballard's work and will identify with the same elements of difficulty and extremity that engage Re/Search's audience, and that mainstream publishers seem unable to handle with any boldness or coherence. Reel23 has also released David Cronenberg's early films *Stereo* and *Crimes of the Future*, and *The Atrocity Exhibition* slipcase relates to the graphic styling and identity used for the company's website, as well as its other DVD titles.

The apocalyptic imagery, drawn from director Jonathan Weiss's film—via Ballard—is relatively understated, compared to the norms of DVD packaging, and most of the impact comes from the largely monochromatic graphic framework and the fractured, dysfunctionally letter-spaced typography. The sheets of computer print-out, recalling the waste material Ballard received in the 1960s from his friend Dr Christopher Evans' wastepaper basket

DVD Slipcase. Design by Bas Mantel, Reel23, 2006.

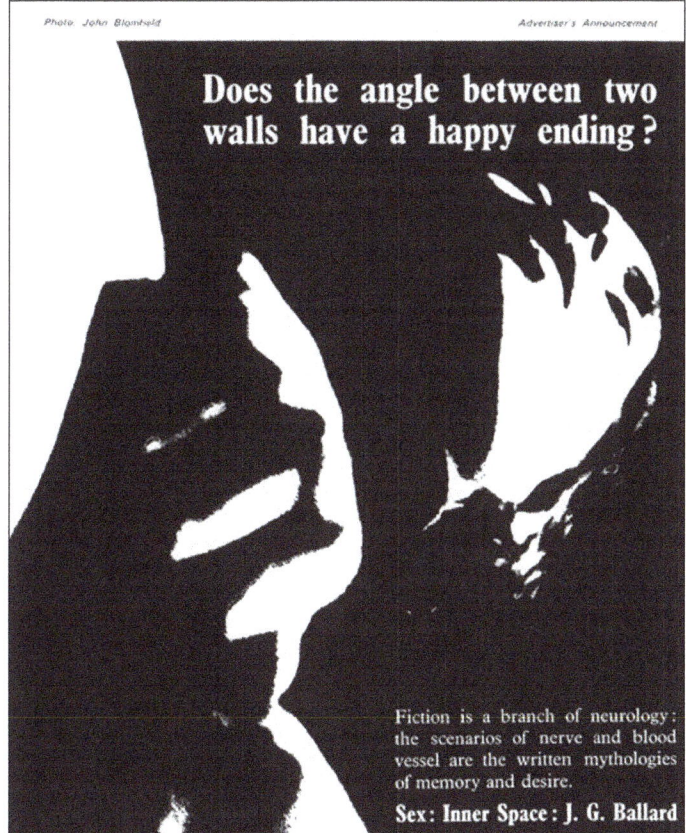

"Advertisement" written and designed by JG Ballard, *Ambit* No. 33, 1967.

at the National Physics Lab, are a textural representation of the scientific language that pervades novel and film.

Again, we might note how unusual it is—Re/Search aside—for typographic material to be used as any kind of signifier in relation to Ballard, even in the 1990s when the new digital design tools provoked an international trend for typographic experimentation, widely seen in the United States and Europe in CD packaging, advertising and magazines such as *Ray Gun*. Bear in mind, too, that Ballard had experimented in the late 1950s with typographic collages for a new kind of fiction and had later published a series of "advertisements" in *Ambit*. His original plan was to apply these techniques in *The Atrocity Exhibition*, but Jonathan Cape took fright at the idea.

What these examples make clear is that, when it comes to visualizations of Ballard, his admirers and fans, as close readers of the texts, have a much better idea of what an adequately Ballardian image requires than Ballard's official mediators in publishing. Perhaps the most striking demonstration of the perspicacity of Ballard's fans can be seen in the community-based, image-sharing website, Flickr. The site allows members of the public, mostly amateur photographers, to upload their own pictures. These images can then be tagged with a range of keywords so that the photos will show up in different Flickr collections. Thousands of pictures have been classified with the tags "Ballardian" and "JG Ballard" and there is a Ballard group, founded in 2005, consisting (on 3 February 2011) of 585 members. They provide a brief mission statement: "This group shall collect images that evoke the narrative of JG Ballard. Drained swimming pools in suburban landscapes, gated communities with their security video surveillance, highway embankments, deserted airport concourses, the post industrial nightmare of the end of the western empire."

Some members upload dozens and even hundreds of pictures on these themes. While many are mundane, limited by the photographer's eye and skill, the best attain a high level of intensity and resonance. Inevitably, there are smashed cars but covers of *Crash* have often displayed the same literalism. Other images of cars attain a heightened realism—a Surrealism—that might recall the dream car buried in the sand on the cover of *The Drought*.

Photo by Stephen Teso, JG Ballard group on Flickr, 2010.

Some pictures display a Ballardian relish for the deserted, empty, drained, ruined and abandoned. Many photographers venture under the concrete roadways to document the immense stanchions and soaring thoroughfares.

The flyover has become a defining Ballardian image in publishing and commentary, so there is a sense, here, of the image-makers affirming their perception of Ballard and the personal meanings that his texts hold for them by adding their own versions of these images to a potentially limitless library of scenarios and epiphanies, which any Ballard reader with visual inclinations might share.

As with Ballard's writing, the visual repetitions become hypnotic, compelling the reader (or viewer) to keep returning for reasons that, as literary critic Roger Luckhurst suggests in *"The Angle Between Two Walls": The Fiction of JG Ballard*, cannot ultimately be explained. The most interesting pictures embody this sense of uncanny Ballardian immanence in more oblique types of subject matter and image. A photographer with the name "Hoodlum Scientist"—a reference to Ballardian characters such as Vaughan in *Crash*—titles one picture "The Angle Between Two Walls," a verbal image taken from one of the "advertisements" Ballard published in *Ambit*. The Ballard group photo pool contains pictures that are far more effective as personally felt evocations of the writer's vision than many of the images used over the years on his covers.

My motivation for exploring the visual representation of Ballard's writing stems, as I have said, from a feeling of dissatisfaction with the way so many of his books were presented. Why didn't he do more to ensure that his book covers expressed his aims better? His enthusiasm for art would seem not only to have qualified him for the task, but to have made it a personal necessity.

In his early days as a writer, Ballard did make efforts in this direction, though he was usually thwarted. In correspondence with me, he was particularly dismissive of Cape, saying that he was "very poorly published" by the company. He also noted that, "Jacket design is a vast and contentious subject, and authors can be a nightmare for jacket designers." Yet his subsequent UK hardback fiction publishers, Gollancz and HarperCollins, and his paperback publishers, didn't serve him much better. It is common today for writers, especially successful writers, to have a say in their covers. Could it be that Ballard overlooked design and in particular graphic design as an area of ever-increasing significance, despite his immense sensitivity to so many aspects of visual culture?

It might seem improbable, yet there are very few references to any kind of design in Ballard's interviews. His neglected domestic environment at his home in Shepperton, so often commented upon by journalists, suggests someone for whom art as an idea remained separate from the many opportunities for visual meaning and satisfaction possible in one's everyday surroundings.

I approached Ballard twice in connection with

Photo by Chris Beckett, JG Ballard group on Flickr, 2011.

the visual dimension of his work. He offered some help, but both times declined an interview, leaving me with the impression that this was not an area of particular importance to him, despite his early recognition that culture was becoming increasingly visual. Ever since *Empire of the Sun* (1984) brought Ballard a wider audience and a new level of acceptance among reviewers, his British book covers have tended to be middlebrow and lacking in direction—the opposite of what he stood for—and they rarely live up to the books' provocations.

Compare the paperback cover of *Millennium People* with William Gibson's *Pattern Recognition*, also published in 2004. Gibson's publisher, Penguin, was carefully positioning him for a hip, plugged-in, visually aware, trend-monitoring, modern audience. And Ballard? What could an uncommitted browser deduce about the novel's darkly sardonic view of Britain's middle classes in revolt from this tepid conglomeration of stylistic signals?

Thus far in this essay I have explored the idea of the Ballardian image and the ways that some designers and image-makers have interpreted it. Now, I want to consider a German-born artist based in France whose paintings are the most Ballardian I have ever seen. So far as I am aware Peter Klasen has never been discussed previously in relation to Ballard or his writing. There are good reasons for supposing that Ballard was unaware of Klasen's work and I have found no evidence to suggest that the artist was aware of Ballard, though it remains a possibility. The remarkable overlap in their thinking and practice at a critical moment in the 1960s is a matter of synchronicity, not influence.

Ballard's impact on the art world has been a subject of growing interest, which was given an additional spur by his death in 2009. His readily acknowledged debt to Surrealism is already well covered and critical attention has recently moved to his friendship with the artist Eduardo Paolozzi.

In February 2011, a conference at Manchester Metropolitan University, organized by David Brittain (author of *The Jet Age Compendium: Paolozzi at Ambit*), focused in part on this relationship, and some notable Ballard-watchers were in attendance. In 2010, the Gagosian Gallery in London mounted the exhibition "Crash: Homage to JG Ballard." This included artists Ballard is known to have admired—Dalí, De Chirico, Paul Delvaux, Edward Hopper, Ed Ruscha, Francis Bacon, Eduardo Paolozzi, Tacita Dean—as well as artists felt by the curators to share concerns with the writer, including Richard Prince, Jeff Koons, Cindy Sherman, Jake and Dinos Chapman, Douglas Gordon and Damien Hirst. Peter Klasen wasn't among their number in the Gagosian's big show, although his work has far more in common with Ballard's than did many of the pieces in "Crash."

This oversight didn't surprise me at the time because I, too, was completely unaware of Klasen's work. A few months later, in a bookshop in Arles in France, I noticed a thick new monograph titled *Peter Klasen: Oeuvres 1959-2009*, published in 2009 by the imprint Actes Sud (in French only). Turning the pages and seeing these extraordinary images for the first time, I felt something like the excitement an anthropologist might experience having just unearthed a crucial missing thigh bone. As luck would have it, an exhibition of recent works by Klasen was showing at a gallery around the corner.

In the 1960s, Klasen was loosely classified as a Pop artist. More accurately, he belongs to a tendency the French call "narrative figuration"; in 2008, there was a major retrospective of the movement at the Grand Palais in Paris. Klasen has had a distinguished career in France and Europe, with many exhibitions and earlier monographs, including one by the theorist Paul Virilio, but he seems not to have exhibited in the UK and Anglo-American critics have never taken much interest, though later he had shows in the US. Lucy R Lippard gives Klasen two lines without a picture in her study *Pop Art*, first published in 1966, noting only that his work is reminiscent of Richard Hamilton's. In *Pop Art: A Continuing History* (1990), Marco Livingstone has slightly more to say, though again no image, observing that Klasen, "incorporated rather mechanistic renderings of real objects in his pictures, and sometimes even the objects themselves, but generally he did so in order to heighten the sexual connotations of the images of women featured as his primary subjects; although his works of the late 1960s closely resemble certain aspects of American Pop, his art remained at odds with the impassive stance of its prototypes because of its fetishistic tenor."

This sounds a bit like a scholarly put-down. Everything Livingstone says is true so far as it

Peter Klasen, *Les Bruits de la ville* (*The Noises of the City*), acrylic on canvas, 92 x 73 cm, 1966.

but just as often he paints the entire "montage" as a seamless unit. The component images are shattered into fragments and here Klasen differs from an American Pop artist such as James Rosenquist whose image quotations tend to be more complete, continuous and celebratory. The resemblance to Richard Hamilton, whose painterly probes of popular culture also fused image-sections into new aesthetic configurations, comes in the way Klasen deploys these fragments across the picture plane, allowing zones of unoccupied space to open up between them. Although traditional commercial Pop iconography sometimes appears (a hotdog, a bowl of food, a lipstick), Klasen's overriding concern is the equivalence between female body parts drawn from advertising and glamour pictures—lips, eyes, breasts, elbow—and the manufactured or mechanical elements, which include taps, valves, plugs, handles, switches, syringes, steering wheels and car windows. He presents both types of image on equal terms within the painting's symbiotically organized structure. Several of the same image fragments recur from picture to picture and Klasen's color-drained image-world becomes a semiotic pressure chamber in which new forms of control (and desire?) subordinate the erotic presence of the female subjects.

In an interview in 2008, Klasen recalled the influence during these years of Jean-Luc Godard's approach to film-collage, his essayistic abstractions, disruptive inter-titles and anti-cinematic moments of rupture. A graphic montage using sources also favored by Klasen can be seen in a poster from 1966

goes, but the traits he identifies are not a limitation—they're the point. In a famous axiom, Ballard declared, "sex times technology equals the future." In the period from 1966 to 1973, which saw the appearance of the texts later collected in *The Atrocity Exhibition* (1970), and the publication of *Crash*, Ballard focused obsessively on this theme. Much the same could be said of Klasen, who locked onto target a year or two earlier, except that he kept on going—similar themes are still present, though differently expressed, in the septuagenarian artist's recent work. "I believe…in the elegance of automobile graveyards," wrote Ballard in a lyrical litany of private obsessions. The final picture in Klasen's monograph is a photo of the white-haired artist standing in a breaker's yard, a predatory Nikon slung around his neck, in front of a twisted hillock of rusting machine parts.

The three paintings shown here are typical of Klasen's work in the mid-1960s. All of these images utilize a combinatorial system derived from modernist montage of the 1920s. Occasionally Klasen glues images and small objects to the canvas,

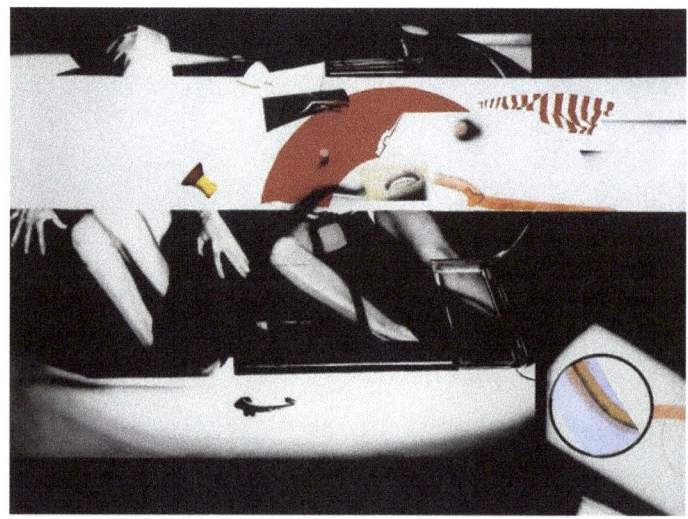

Peter Klasen, *Une rencontre a bien eu lieu* (*A Meeting Took Place*), acrylic on canvas, 130 x 162 cm, 1965.

Peter Klasen, *Anatomie du plaisir* (*Anatomy of Pleasure*), acrylic and oil on canvas, 81 x 65 cm, 1964-65.

for Godard's *Two or Three Things I Know About Her* about the life of a prostitute in Paris. If Klasen's pictures are still "sexy" to us, despite their coldness and extreme, disassociating fragmentation, then it's a violently ultra-modern kind of sexiness.

Now consider this passage from a chapter titled "Notes Towards a Mental Breakdown" in *The Atrocity Exhibition* (first published with the title "The Death Module" in *New Worlds* No. 173, July 1967):

> **Operating Formulae.** Gesturing Catherine Austin into the chair beside his desk, Dr Nathan studied the elegant and mysterious advertisements which had appeared that afternoon in copies of *Vogue* and *Paris-Match*. In sequence they advertised: (1) The left orbit and zygomatic arch of Marina Oswald. (2) The angle between two walls. (3) A "neural interval"—a balcony unit on the twenty-seventh floor of the Hilton Hotel, London. (4) A pause in an unreported conversation outside an exhibition of photographs of automobile accidents. (5) The time, 11:47 a.m., June 23rd, 1975. (6) A gesture—a supine forearm extended across a candlewick bedspread. (7) A moment of recognition—a young woman's buccal pout and dilated eyes.

This is one of Ballard's celebrated image lists found throughout *The Atrocity Exhibition*. The items that comprise the "operating formulae" can be seen as a miniature exhibition list, as an extreme form of conceptual montage, and as a forced marriage of apparently unrelated images (a classic Surrealist stratagem), which replicates the scrambled structure of the narratives within each chapter, and the way these non-linear chapters ultimately cohere as a work. At the same time, it would be possible to use Ballard's image kit as a set of instructions to assemble a montage on paper that might then resemble a painting by Klasen (zygomatic arch, angle between walls, balcony unit, accident photos, forearm, dilated eyes, etc.). What both Ballard and Klasen share at this point in the mid-1960s is a cold, appraising, analytical eye. It's impossible to tell how they feel about what they show, or to know what they want us to feel, if anything at all. Their findings are disturbing and perhaps even repellent from a humanist perspective, yet the new aesthetic forms they use to embody them are, even today, exciting, provocative and tantalizingly difficult to resolve.

Ballard's experiments with condensed collage-novels in the late 1950s have received increasing attention and they were shown at the Gagosian Gallery; the "Advertiser's Announcements" he presented in *Ambit* from the summer of 1967 appear in the catalogue. A few months earlier, in *New Worlds* No. 167 (October 1966), Ballard published a series of comments on his new experimental texts, under the title "Notes from Nowhere." He considers the intersection of three kinds of planes: the world of public events, the immediate personal environment, and the inner world of the psyche. "Where these planes intersect," he writes, "images are born." In Ballard's attempt to locate himself, by calling on "the geometry of my own postures, the time-values contained in this room, the motion-space of highways, staircases, the angles between these walls," the intersection of planes again suggests Klasen's surgically precise combinatorial technique. Ballard goes on to propose that it might one day be possible "to represent a novel or short story, with all its images and relationships, simply as a three-dimensional geometric model." Then, just a few lines later, in a curious unedited moment that seems to express his ambivalence, he says that he is worried that a work of fiction could become "nothing more than a three-dimensional geometric model."

By the early 1970s, Klasen had severely reduced the number of image fragments and the agitated visual complexity seen in his earlier montages. In a development that actualizes Ballard's conception of a new kind of three-dimensional fiction, Klasen's constructions, while still wall-mounted, become fully three-dimensional with projecting pipes and bathroom fittings. The unrelenting hygienic cruelty of this work, its absolute concentration on a few fetishistic motifs to the exclusion of everything else —breasts and basin, waist and switches, lips and bidet—bears comparison with the strange mental journey Ballard would undertake as he worked on *Crash*, the ultimate statement of his ideas about the sexualization of our relationship with technology. "Nothing is spontaneous, everything is stylized, including human behaviour," he said in 1970, in an interview with Lynn Barber in *Penthouse*. "And once you move into this area where everything is stylized, including sexuality, you're leaving behind any kind of moral or functional relevance."

Also in 1970, in a brief manifesto, reprinted in his latest monograph, Klasen set out his aims (my translation from the French):

- Play on the dialectic of a photographic reproduction and its pictorial transposition.
- Play on the magical and poetic power of an object out of place.
- Respond to the aggression of society with another aggression.
- Show that beauty is everywhere, in a bathroom, for example.
- Demonstrate that a bidet, a washbasin, a switch can exercise the same fascination on the spectator as the mouth, the body of a woman or a racing car.
- Return these images and objects to the spectator-consumer, allowing him to react to these object-tableaux and to project his own fantasies onto them.
- Stimulate his awareness by providing him with aesthetic and ideological information about himself and the world that surrounds him.

"Respond to the aggression of society with another aggression": this is exactly what Ballard had done in *The Atrocity Exhibition*, responding to what he called the "death of affect"—of ordinary emotional responses to events—by playing it out within the glinting, recursive, multi-planar architecture of his book, returning society's images to the "spectator-consumer," with their inherent characteristics pulled to the surface and intensified, as a morally ambiguous invitation to know oneself better. Ballard, too, had found a perverse kind of beauty in this material, which is one reason why his writing of this period continues to exert its extraordinary hold on readers.

There is no indication that Ballard knew of this kindred spirit across the sea. Klasen was at the start of his career, like Ballard, and had no reputation in Britain, and unfortunately still doesn't. Ballard made journeys to France, from the 1960s, but if he had ever come across Klasen's work, which would have been more likely later, he would surely have mentioned it somewhere—he wrote regularly about art. If the critical aim now, as the Gagosian Gallery show suggests, is to map more fully Ballard's visual thinking and wider connections to the art world, then Klasen's body of work deserves close attention. A couple of his previously unseen paintings, had they been shown at the Gagosian, could have made a great impact; the reason for their inclusion would have been much more readily apparent than it was for some of the over-familiar art the curators selected.

The overlapping concerns of Ballard and Klasen in the mid to late 1960s represent one of the great might-have-beens of contemporary art and literature, but a belated union is still possible. It's hard to imagine better images than Klasen's, ready-made or otherwise, for the covers of future editions of *The Atrocity Exhibition* and *Crash*. It's strange that the French, great admirers of both these books, haven't cracked this one already.

ANA BARRADO
Neon Flamingos, Flamingo Las Vegas, 1992

JG Ballard: Time Out of Mind

by Peter Brigg

"... instead of treating time like a sort of glorified scenic railway, I'd like to see it used for what it is, one of the perspectives of the personality, and the elaboration of concepts such as the time zone, deep time and archaeopsychic time." JG Ballard, "Which Way to Inner Space?"

The full implications of the nineteenth and twentieth centuries' discovery of human subjectivity are only now beginning to unfurl. While it is a commonplace to assert that each man sees the world in his own way, there remains an unwritten and unstated assumption that the world remains an objective entity and that one is reasonable or sane if one "sees it the way it is." But in the cloudy chaos of our times, in the shadows of missiles and technological future shocks, the real implication—that there are as many realities as there are individuals—begins to come home.

To James Graham Ballard an important part of the task of the writer is to demonstrate the implications of the absolute individuality of the world that each man sees and to extend those implications to the production of responses. He consistently asserts in his fiction that we see things for ourselves and then act according to our lights. His fiction asserts (contrary to some critical observations) that the strange behaviors of his characters are right, that they act according to the internal absolutes of their own reasonably processed observations. Through the lenses of these consciousnesses, the odd geographies of Ballard's fiction—deserted landscapes, pathological implications of automotive and space technologies, the seemingly distorted jungles of the modern urban life-style—may herald the moment when, for a particular character, the external world corresponds perfectly to internal meaning, when one can both see and act. To paraphrase the prophet, "to every man there is a season," and Ballard's protagonists identify their moments, are at ease within them, and act according to their necessities.

It cannot be stated firmly enough that this is not some sort of fabricated justification for aberrant behavior. It is a statement that there really is no such thing, an ultimate acceptance of the absolute privilege of the individual-particularly situated against the plastic and chrome kaleidoscope of our times to define reality and act accordingly. Nor is it an amoral position, privileging people to assassinate, do violence, or remain impassive in the face of extremities of suffering. For individuals respond within the framework of biological imperatives (colored, on occasion, by whimsical intellectual affectations), but the world they respond to is the world *as they understand it to be.*

The key to the characters' perceptions of their needs, situations, and consequent actions is time in both the senses of clock time and occasion. Just as Dali has pictured the soft time of his distorted watches, so Ballard shows characters responding to time as they understand it, often appearing to float through external reality with little consideration of such necessities as sleep, food, and the other regular features of life. This is frequently acutely pointed by the characters being placed in worlds where the regular forms of existence are collapsing, the science fiction realities where the "normal" world has suddenly ceased to function. But unlike so many of the science fiction stories from the mainstream, in which the rational, often militarily oriented scientist figure triumphs in making sense of strange situations and taking them over, Ballard's central characters interact with strangeness, becoming different in their goals and, in many cases, realizing that they are now in a world that frees them to fulfill their inner natures. In the time that they have found, there is a curious mixture of vagueness and neglect for the movement of clock time combined with an underlying sense of identity between the man and the time, a sense of having arrived in one's own time when the world is comprehensible and the course of action obvious and simple.

"The Voices of Time" (1960) is perhaps the most powerful of Ballard's early treatments of time, containing as it does not only a time-centered plot but the special atmosphere characteristic to these stories. It is set against a pattern of images of galactic, evolutionary, and geological time. In its overwhelming, monstrous shadow the human protagonists, Powers, an experimental brain surgeon, and Kaldren, an experimental artist, are dwarfed by the insignificance of the individual human life and even of the life forms that populate the Earth, motes in the galactic infinity.

Set in the American desert, the events of the story form not so much a plot as a pattern. People are beginning to succumb to narcoma, sleeping longer and longer each day, until they become terminals, sleeping without dreams until their deaths. Powers himself is succumbing, but he is also continuing the experiments of Dr. Whitby, who, before his suicide, was exciting the silent genes of various species via X-rays and in so doing was trying to push these species through some sort of evolutionary barrier to a higher level. Congruent to all of this are the discoveries of changes taking place in different species naturally, or perhaps as an outcome of the atomic age, which suggest adaptation to radical changes in the Earth's environment that may come about. Thus Powers finds a common frog enclosed like an armadillo in a shell made very heavy by a high lead content, as though preparing for a radioactive environment. Whitby's experimental creatures, such as a sea anemone which has developed a primitive nervous system, seem to be preparing to see in the ranges of infrared or X-ray.

Kaldren is paying particular attention to the radio astronomy and the cosmic outer frame of events. From different sections of the galaxy vast countdowns, diminishing numerical progressions, are being recorded by radio observatories. One of these sequences, coming from Canes Vanatici near the galactic core, is expected to reach zero at the moment of the death of the universe. The countdowns are the "voices" of the title: "These are the voices of time, and they're all saying good-bye to you. Think of yourself in a wider context. Every particle in your body, every grain of sand, every galaxy carries the same signature."

An additional datum from space is the brief history of the Apollo Seven, whose astronauts did not return from the moon after claiming to have spoken to beings from Orion who told them something about "telemeters."

Everywhere in the landscape, time expresses its presence in the story. Powers "sees" the time in the rock strata of the valley he drives through, millions of years of hard time layered around him. A gigantic sunflower, one of Whitby's mutations, grows with varying speeds according to whether it is surrounded by ancient limestone or modern polyvinyl chloride because its strange new organs seem to "see" time. Various perspectives on the meaning of this pattern of events are offered in the story through observations by the characters or through the third person narration. Powers replays a tape by Whitby in which Whitby suggests that the human race has simply worn out the pathways of evolution, that the genetic templates are failing and the race is succumbing to narcoma as its way of dying out. The "dying out" is offered as an eerie and haunting phenomenon, a sort of vast parody of the human expectation of death. While science is struggling with it there is no suggestion in the story that anything can really be done beyond providing vast, dimly lit wards for the terminals to lie in. Humanity, like the dinosaurs, cannot change its genetic makeup in an individual lifetime, nor even in the short term, and is therefore presumed to be doomed by the inexorability of change. This is in tune with the larger context of the dying universe and with Whitby's attempts to break through with his experimental mutants, all of which are failures in that they might cope only with a strange surrealist world of hard radiation and different light frequencies. In fact, they cannot be seen as evolutionary progress in any conventional way because they are offering adaptations before the conditions warrant them. One of the haunting connections mentioned in the story is that all of the early terminals have the silent genes, as though the human race was unconsciously surrendering its last genetic opportunity.

The central characters of the story, Powers and Kaldren, are faced with this unsettling mixture of factors and information and make of it what they can. Ballard renders this in a highly individualized form: what is true for one person is not true for another. Kaldren has had an experimental brain surgery performed by Powers that renders him unable to sleep. (It is not made clear in the story whether this was to offset the onset of the narcoma in Kaldren.) He is discovering that this is a damnation in its own ways, forcing him to fill time and presumably cutting him off from the psychic comforts of the dream life. Powers has developed the narcoma, and if the story has a linear plot at all it is the sequence of his ever-shortening days until he chooses a quixotic death. Submerged in Powers and Kaldren's situations are powerful paradigms for the alternate ways of facing human life. Kaldren is the conscious and intellectual figure, sleeplessly facing the world and, through his art, organizing it. Powers, although he is a scientist, is driven by the world of sleep and forces of subconscious response over which he has no rational control. Powers's responses range from the straightforward, acute human fear of death to complex, darkly driven actions that seem so out of place when viewed against "reality." His continuation of Whitby's experiments and his preservation of Whitby's curious vivarium of mutants seems to have no possible outcome, particularly in light of Whitby's estimates that the research only proves how the human race is coming to an inevitable end.

Powers makes a 16-mm film of himself sleeping for three hours, a strange auto-memento mori that mirrors the common dream and fantasy of seeing oneself dead. But the heart of his response to his crisis (which, importantly, is the crisis he shares with the universe-entropy) is his response to the messages of the countdown from the stars.

Powers gets the countdown from the stars through Kaldren, who initially delivers the seemingly meaningless large numbers as postcards or chalked on Powers's house gate and later shows Powers the ticker machines printing out the results of radio telescope monitoring. Powers's response is to act, unaware of what he is doing, to build a vast concrete mandala at an abandoned weapons range on the valley floor. He does not do this while in the narcoma sleep, but he does not remember it either, a fact shown by his mystification over concrete dust in his beard and demands to pay for bags of concrete that he cannot remember buying. When it is constructed he goes to Whitby's laboratory, gives himself a massive dose of X-rays, and drives back to stand on the mandala and listen to the heavens until he collapses and dies. But this mechanical description of his actions does not begin to describe what Ballard implies happens to him during these events. First, as he drives through the dawn from Whitby's lab to the mandala, he sees the time encapsulated in the landscape:

> Closing his eyes, Powers lay back and steered the car along the interval between the two time fronts, feeling the images deepen and strengthen within his mind. The vast age of the landscape, the inaudible chorus of voices resonating from the lake and from the white hills, seemed to carry him back through time, down endless corridors to the first thresholds of the world.

When he gets to the mandala there is a "resolution" of the forces of the universe and the inner self.

> Like an endless river, so broad that its banks were below the horizons, it flowed steadily toward him, a vast course of time that spread outward to fill the sky and the universe, enveloping everything within them... Watching it constantly, he felt his body gradually dissolving, its physical dimensions melting into the vast continuum of the current, which bore him out into the

> center of the great channel, sweeping
> him onward, beyond hope now but
> at last at rest, down the broadening
> reaches of the river of eternity.

It is clear that this extraordinary moment, positioned as it is in the absolute terms of omniscient description that brook no arguments about Powers's subjectivity, is intended to bring together the strands of the story and suggest the satisfactory nature of Powers's demise. Affected by the X-radiation, he can see time in the valley and hear the very voices of time beamed at him from the stars. The vague inner clues of his psychic time that have driven him through the story are suddenly seen as positioning him where his fear of death is resolved ("beyond hope now but at last at rest") as he stands at the center of a cosmic clock, seeing and feeling time in a strange harmony with the cosmos itself as its sweeps toward its ultimate extinction. This meeting of a single individual with a moment that he can grasp and be at one with, strange as that moment may be to others or to the reader, is the essence of Ballard's sense of deep time. It is in some sense biological time, as seen here in the way a dying man communes with a universal entropic tendency. It is also psychological time, of course, and Ballard keeps to the external narrative to permit readers to understand what is passing through the characters' minds. The prose in this passage is highly metaphoric and highly colored. It works because the story has led us to it, using Ballard's characteristic mixture of hard science, artifacts, and information spun together seamlessly so that a dying man has this experience standing on the mandala he has patiently built while in a state of unawareness. The reader is left with the powerful image of the center of the mandala, a point of meeting focus between universal and private time.

Kaldren does not achieve the empathy with time that Powers does. This implies the importance of the subconscious in self-knowledge, because Kaldren, unable to sleep, is symbolic, if not the actual model of, the human ego—the rational self. He tries to get at the meaning of things through a variation of the artist's function as the organizer of reality. In creating his "Terminal Documents," a private artistic exhibition, Kaldren juxtaposes visual signposts of the contemporary human position such as an EEG tape of Einstein's alpha waves, the tapes of the countdowns from the stars, and the transcripts of the Apollo Seven's last transmissions from the moon. This attempt is supposed to lead to some sort of sense. As Kaldren asserts, "They're endprints, Powers, final statements, the products of total fragmentation. When I've got enough together I'll build a new world for myself out of them." But the tag end of the story, which describes Kaldren puzzling over the documents and the events of the narrative for months afterwards, is sufficiently inconclusive to suggest that he can never achieve the synthesis Powers does. Whereas for Powers all of the elements of the voices of time, internal and external, coalesce and take on their full meaning as he stands on the mandala, Kaldren is forever excluded from this ironic wholeness in the moment of dissolution.

"The Voices of Time" is a vivid expression of the way in which the whole inner being of a particular individual, in this case Powers, can come into a perfect correspondence with the external reality of the whole universe. It is the story's achievement to generate, through its range of approaches varying from the mutants to the terminal documents to the mandala (symbol of cosmic and personal wholeness) to the voices of the galactic center, a vast scope in which Powers has a place. Within the context he does what he must-the right thing. And while Ballard stands back, maintaining a slight ironic distance so that readers will not be proselytized, it is clear that this is a triumph for Powers, a representation of the furthest and deepest satisfaction and understanding that is possible for a human being.

Ballard's first four novels form a "disaster quartet" portraying catastrophe by wind, *The Wind from Nowhere* (1962); by flood, *The Drowned World* (1962); by drought, *The Drought* (1964); and by time, *The Crystal World* (1966). The true disaster of time comes to all things, of course, in the inevitable entropic change and the cessation of organic life. *The Crystal World* posits the spread of a sudden transformation, a rapid, initially localized but clearly soon-to-be-universal change in forms.

> ...We now know that it is time... which is responsible for the transformation. The recent discovery of anti-matter in the universe inevitably involves the conception of anti-time as the fourth side of this negatively charged continuum. Where anti-particle and particle collide they not only destroy their own physical identities, but their opposing time-values eliminate each other, subtracting from the universe another quantum from its total store of time... As more and more time "leaks" away, the process of supersaturation continues, the original atoms and molecules producing spatial replicas of themselves, substance without mass, in an attempt to increase their foot-hold upon existence.

The immediate outcome of these events is the crystallizing of an area of jungle in French West Africa and the Echo communications satellite (and reports of similar events in Florida and the Pripet Marshes). Trees, animals, buildings, and even people who stay still become encased in glittering carapaces of crystals and are held in a strange state of suspension outside of or without time. While the "explanation" quoted above has obvious flaws, not the least of which is that the phenomenon appears to have been triggered throughout the universe by the human postulation of antimatter, it is far more elegant and simplified than the conglomeration of circumstances in "The Voices of Time." It offers, moreover, an immensely strong mythic aspect, a scientific transmutation of the shining jeweled garden of Yeats's "Byzantium" in which the vitality of living beings is exchanged for eternal preservation. Scientific reality replaces the artist-craftsman of the Pygmalion sculptor, the Byzantine craftsman, and Renaissance sonneteer as the agent who can offer the powerful transmutation of life into a sort of "art," the stable, glittering, many-faceted, but at best only passively alive, frozen version of the living universe.

To the characters caught up in this strange deformation of reality as time deliquesces out of the universe, it is not so much a question of what to do in this situation as a question of what to feel, of internal and emotional positioning. Although there were really no possibilities for reversing the processes outlined in "The Voices of Time," there was a semblance of attempts to impose human authority and actions: Whitby's experiments, the research on the terminals, Kaldren's attempts to "make" reality through art. In *The Crystal World* there is really only the desultory response of the military and civil officials of a French equatorial colony and the explanation of the situation offered above. All of the stress, all of the real "action" of the novel lies in the varied responses of the different individuals as they establish their private contacts with the myth of crystal eternity.

The novel chronicles a voyage into the jungle by Dr. Edward Sanders, who is going in search of his former mistress, Suzanne Clair. She and her husband, Max Clair, are, like Sanders, doctors engaged in the care of lepers. Also going into the jungle are a priest returning to his mission, Father Balthus; Ventress, a half-mad architect who has come to recover his young bride, Serena, from Thorenson, a mine-owner; and the lesser figures of Louise Perez, a French journalist, and Captains Radek and Dragon, members of the military party dealing with the crisis.

It emerges that Suzanne Clair has fled to the jungle because she herself is developing leprosy and is driven by the desire to leave her lover before he sees the changes in her as well as by the attraction of the forest. For Suzanne and the group of lepers she finally leads in a strange dance through the jungle there are a series of half-articulated correspondences between the crystallizing world and leprosy. Captain Radek points one aspect of this out to Sanders:

"It seems to me that the business here and your own speciality are very similar. In a way, one is the dark side of the other. I'm thinking of the silver scales of leprosy that give the disease its name'. And Ventress suggests its connection to time: 'Surely leprosy, like cancer, is above all a disease of time, a result of over-extending oneself through that particular medium?' Suzanne herself draws on Shelley's *Adonais* to explain its importance to her: "...what's happening in the forest—I mean in the widest sense—to all our ideas of time and mortality. How can I put it? 'Life, like a dome of many-coloured glass, stains the white radiance of eternity.'"

The passage from Adonais is of great interest, for the rest of it, which is not offered by Suzanne, reads,

> Until Death tramples it to fragments. — Die,
> If thou wouldst be with that which thou dost seek!

She is clearly implying the fascination of the crystallization for herself and the other lepers. It would make them the "domes of many-coloured glass" that would stain eternity, their brilliant jeweled scales replacing the pale ones of their disease. And it would evade death, for she does not quote the lines in which Death crushes even the domes of glass, as the deliquescing universe must eventually destroy even those held in the static glittering forms in the forests of light. For the lepers the hope of arresting the inexorable, disfiguring change shines more brightly than the possible price of being frozen in place in the jeweled jungle.

The other lady of this shimmering heart of darkness is Serena, who lies dying of the other great wasting disease, tuberculosis, in the care of Thorenson, who had earlier stolen her from her husband, Ventress. Much of the actual action in the novel involves these two obsessed men hunting each other in the jungle with Dr. Sanders vaguely attached to one or the other. Serena, meanwhile, lies propped in a gilded four-poster, dying slowly amidst her mane of prematurely white hair. Thorenson brings her jewels in the scene in which

Sanders first meets her, and they bring her warmth when she is suffering from the cold. In refusing to take her outside to a sanatorium, Thorenson assures Sanders that he is doing the best thing possible for her, which the reader realizes is the eventual course of preserving her at least partly alive in the crystalline state. When Sanders last sees her she is lying beside Thorenson, who has shot himself, but she lives on in the suspended crystal sleep. Thorenson's objective has been the prolongation of life, the cheating of decay in the cold sleep of the crystal sheath. In Serena and in Suzanne, Ballard is picturing the response to human entropy, to the diseases that are emblems of the eventual wasting away to death which comes to all those who live out their spans. Rather than age and change and fade it is their deepest inner desire to freeze themselves, to become immobile for a seeming eternity.

The indication of what it is like to be in this state comes from the character who passes in and out of it, Captain Radek. Radek becomes lost in the jungle and is found crystallized by Sanders, who tears him free and leaves him partly submerged in a fast-running stream in hopes that the crystals will fall away. He does this despite Ventress's warning that he is taking something from Radek, and when Sanders meets Radek again he is horrified by what he has wrought. In the first place Radek is severely damaged where the crystals surrounding him were fractured when Sanders tore him free, so that part of his face and shoulder are missing. It is clear that the crystals do not merely form atop the victim but are the victim. Moreover Radek violently orders Sanders to take him back, suggesting that there is something desirable about the crystalline suspension. In this he echoes the longings of Suzanne Clair, who has expressed surprise and dismay at Sanders's comments about being trapped in crystal.

But of all the characters it is Sanders himself who has the most complex relationship to the process. He arrives unaware of it and initially sees it as a danger and a scientific problem. But as he sees the beauty of the forest he becomes half in love with the idea. The omniscient narrator hints at this early in the novel: "Ventress had referred to the Matarre forests as a landscape without time, and perhaps part of its appeal for Sanders was that here at last he might be free from the questions of motive and identity that were bound up with his sense of time and the past." Sanders has come to see Suzanne as a vague gesture toward recovering their affair, but the insincerity of this is suggested by the ease with which he falls into a brief affair with Louise before he has even found Suzanne. While he is not yet fully ready for the crystal world, he expresses its fascination for him in a letter he writes to the director of the leper hospital where he had previously worked.

> It's obvious to everyone now that in the forest life and death have a different meaning from that in our ordinary lack-lustre world. Here we have always associated movement with life and the passage of time, but from my experience within the forest near Mont Royal I know that all motion leads inevitably to death, and that time is its servant.

For Sanders the crystal world reveals the paradox of time, in that the very motion that is its hallmark is the agent of dissolution, the annunciation of entropy. As he rushes through the forest, staying in motion to keep from becoming a glittering statue, he has around him the examples of Suzanne, Radek, Serena, and Father Balthus, who choose to cease their motion and accept the inevitable. For Sanders, the forest explains the relationship between time and death, with the added confusion that there are clearly advantages in being forever still and, in some strange sense, forever alive. The surrender he speaks of as he closes his letter is the one he chooses, to give up his conventional physical and temporal identity by returning to the forest to accept a strange immortality.

In *The Crystal World* Ballard offers a vision of the freezing of time. This vision haunts the reader because of the balance it strikes between motion and stasis and the appeal it makes to the image of the frozen garden of perfection, the archaic memory Sanders refers to in his letter. The novel accelerates and pauses with the rhythm of a dream, and the dreamlike feeling is accentuated by the acute sensuality of the images of light and color mixed with physical sensations of cold and heat. Its stylistic ancestors are a mixture of the romantic intensity of Coleridge and Keats and the clinical dreams of the surrealists. Not only is the meaning of time under examination in the narrative situation and the observation of the characters' responses, but the novel itself is a transport to the realms it portrays, glittering and many-faceted both in motion and at rest.

At first glance *Hello America* (1981) appears to veer from the preoccupation with time which characterized "The Voices of Time" and *The Crystal World*. Yet while it lacks the eerie surreal shocks and much of the psychological manipulation of the reader of the previous works, it offers an archaeology of the future that bounces time, history, and the inner clocks of the characters and the readers off one another. Set in 2114, the novel describes the adventures of a party of explorers crossing an America that has been abandoned after a vast failure of national will caused by the failure of the dreams of prosperity and technology brought about in turn by an energy crisis. After it has been abandoned, the construction of the Bering Straits Dam has revised the climate of America so that east of the Rockies is desert and west of the Rockies is rainforest. Thus the eastern portion of the continent is preserved intact, but has been empty except for a handful of nomads (riding camels that escaped from zoos). The perspective of the book, which is often tongue-in-cheek, is a looking back over the gap of 150 years on the greatness and the flaws of America of the third quarter of the twentieth century.

Ballard brings this to life through a series of time

tricks, using the overall structure of the book with its movement to the west (which ends in the tattered and shattered dreams of surrealized jungle Las Vegas) as a frame for vignettes based on the objects and people the travelers meet, combined with an exploration of their "inner geographies," the desires they all privately harbor as descendants of those who emigrated from America to the gray reality of a socialized and controlled Europe.

Atop this structure sits the plot secret of the book, the existence of a madman, calling himself President Charles Manson, who has established himself after the pattern of Howard Hughes in the sterile suite at the Desert Inn Hotel and has begun to revitalize the west of America in the image of the old United States, with emphasis on armaments and a pathological xenophobia. As Manson plays with mile-high holograph projections of John Wayne, Mickey Mouse, and the Starship *Enterprise*, Ballard is able to bring the icons of our time into the future, casting them in relief against the desert and the jungle. In addition, the very language of the novel, speaking of "porcupine pie" and "uneasy riders," is laden with cross-references between our times and the twenty-second century.

When Wayne speaks of his "once and future father" the phrase carries a key to this whole novel. As with American author T.H. White's retelling of the Arthurian legend, Ballard is concerned in *Hello America* with the recurring dream of America's greatness, a dream that exists in history, in future possibilities, and in the inner makeup of the "Americans" as a people. There are continual references to the pilgrims and pioneers in the novel, from the fact that the Apollo expedition (the name given the ship that brings them to America) touches first at Plymouth to the pattern of westward travel that dominates the book and is brought into focus when the explorers are in Washington deciding on their course of action. "'No, Gregor, we're not going south—not for all the swimming-pools in Miami. We're not going south because that isn't an American direction. When Americans started to move south everything went wrong.'…'West,' Wayne said." The second wave of American greatness, the revival of Camelot, is represented in the novel by the memories of our own age, of the Kennedy presidency, the Apollo moon shots, the detritus of the great age of Detroit and military-industrial ascendancy and the cultural hegemony of Monroe, Mickey Mouse, and the Starship *Enterprise*.

A third and tentative level is the actual experience of the crossing of America by the ever-optimistic pioneers who are the characters in the tale. The final level is the renaissance of America offered, perhaps ironically, in the closing pages of the novel. As the mad Manson launches the last of the Titan missiles at himself and Las Vegas, destroying the garish leavings of the old America of greed and crime, the Chicano children who have been his forces and the surviving explorers take off in the miraculous Sunlight Fliers, created by the aging scientist who may be Wayne's father, and "set sail at a brisk seventy knots for the safety of California and the morning gardens of the west."

There is a high level of ambiguity in the novel's observation of this recurrent pattern. As with all pattern theories of history, there are powerful implications of predestination, in this case of the inevitable failures implicit in the history of America. Nor does the romantic escape from the destruction of the dream tarnished by Manson and the greed of Las Vegas necessarily imply an escape from this circle of time and history, for it is dependent upon more technology, the sun powered aircraft, and on the faint hopes that the curious and varied party who fly in them will show more sense than all of the previous waves of pioneers and more sense than they have shown locked in their private dreams throughout the novel.

It is these private dreams that tie *Hello America* to the "The Voices of Time" and *The Crystal World.* The novel makes clear that the central characters are driven and controlled by their dreams, that their inner sense of themselves as Americans waits to be played out on the continent, regardless of the changes in climate and times. These inner agendas are suggested from the beginning of the book— "Nor was McNair alone in this—the Apollo carried an invisible cargo of dreams and private motives"—and work themselves out as Ricci becomes an Italian-American gangster, Anne Summers puts on the heavy makeup and clothes of a movie star, McNair becomes the all-conquering amazingly ambitious American industrial engineer, and Steiner becomes the John Wayne lone gunman, tight-lipped and slightly mysterious. Wayne himself plays out the myth of the poor boy, in this case a stowaway, who seeks to become president of the United States. Ballard tells us of the whole of the adventure: "Under the guise of crossing America, as Wayne soon discovered, they were about to begin that far longer safari across the diameters of their own skulls."

This makes, in the end, for a fascinating interplay between the transcontinental trek and the voyage into the personal visions of the characters as reborn Americans. They become progressively more lurid as they go west, smeared with old lipsticks to keep off the desert sun and scrambling from motel to motel to scavenge water from ancient boilers. Yet they preserve their own sense of the pilgrimage to the source of their dreams and seem at home until the last moments as participants in Manson's mad dream of rebuilding and preventing the "viruses" of foreign invasion from penetrating America. Wayne comes to his senses only as the Titan is about to threaten Las Vegas: "He realised that time had begun to leak from Las Vegas like the last music from an antique record player." At this point all of the old dreams and inner hopes that have driven the characters-who have found in these landscapes and situations the same overwhelming connections with their inner selves as Powers and Sanders and those who surround them-collapse, and reality seems to pour in. But the close of the novel once again taps the inner dreams, and the romantic children of the "renewed" America of the Sunlight Fliers fly off into the western sunset.

This renewal of the dream, the assertion that the inner sense of time and the meaning of history is dominant, is, in the end, treated quite differently in *Hello America* than in the previous stories considered. In them the gap between the characters' inner senses and the reader's external observations was absolute. While the characters coped with death or eternal stasis the reader could see how they were responding to their sense of the identity between inner "time" and external "historical" reality, but the nature of that identity was bizarre in the extreme.

In *Hello America* the inner reality is more playful, itself a dream partly realized in history in which the characters seem to select and live out roles. This leads to the ambiguity of the ending, when Ballard allows hope for that other aspect of time, the future, while he has, in fact, to a considerable extent already denied the dreams of the future that the reader of our day might hold. While still concerned with time, *Hello America* is far more interested in the paradoxes of history, the game to be played with the once and future dreams of America, than with the apocalyptic dreams that come to life in the earlier fictions.

"The Voices of Time" is not a pessimistic story, for it asserts the essential Ballard premise that the service of the inner sense of time and purpose is more important than more conventional human expectations. But there is a sense in which the reader is disappointed by the way entropy overcomes Powers, for it is very hard to accept the final triumph of time over the protagonist, the Earth, and the universe. One of Ballard's most recent stories, "News From the Sun" (1981), seems at first to be a variation on the earlier story, but closer examination suggests that he is now speculating that the end of time may be a uniquely human possibility and that it may lead not to dissolution but to a strange and possibly satisfying eternity.

"News From the Sun" is set in the reductio of the Nevada desert, where Franklin, a psychologist, has been attempting to solve the mystery of a narcoma that has begun its spread with the astronauts (space exploration has ceased as a result) and gone on to those who prepared them and to those who watched. The condition exhibits itself in fugues that begin by lasting for only a few minutes and extend until they are continuous. When in fugue a person freezes, often dangerously, as evinced by people standing immobile in the middle of roads or in the blazing sun.

One of Franklin's patients is Trippett, the last of the astronauts to have even fragments of wakefulness. Ursula, Trippett's daughter, visits him and eventually takes him to Soleri II, an experimental solar-powered town with a vast array of mirrors that capture sunlight. Slade, whom Franklin had rejected as an astronaut on mental grounds, buzzes Franklin in a microlight aircraft and enlists Marion, Franklin's wife, in his campaign against Franklin.

"News from the Sun" is unlike "The Voices of Time" or *The Crystal World* in that Ballard has found a new focus on man's power to initiate and, to some extent at least, control his destiny. The story asserts that man has, albeit accidentally, brought about the narcoma: "[Franklin] had helped to put the last astronauts into space, made possible the year-long flights that had set off the whole time-plague, cracked the cosmic hour-glass..."

There is sort of sin involved here, not one against God but against either nature or fate: "The brute-force ejection of themselves from their planet had been an act of evolutionary piracy, for which they were now being expelled from the world of time." But if there is a "sin" involved, there is also a possibility of going forward in this situation, a need for assertive action that goes beyond the good fortune that earlier Ballard characters find when they happen to be synchronized to the "timeframe" of their modified worlds. Franklin, Slade, and Ursula conquer the change to varying degrees and in varying ways. Slade uses his psychosis to drive himself through the barrier of his narcoma, and Ursula is taught to break through by Franklin toward the end of the story. The reader gets to see Franklin working out the possibilities as he continues the struggles against the narcoma he had begun as a physician and carries on in the private darkness of his own personality. Franklin is experimenting with a perimeter camera that creates images of the outlines of the body in very slow motion, moving the element of time into the perception of the self.

He even sees the same effect as he imagines the contours of his wife's body migrating to the tiled walls of the bathroom. Franklin gradually ceases to use clock time, but when the fugues are coming so often that it is virtually impossible to drive, he goes in brief bursts and then waits for the temperature gauge on his car to indicate cooling so that he will know that sufficient time has elapsed to allow him to proceed. He seems to be actively seeking alternatives to time in the realm of the other senses and spatial dimensions.

Indeed, when Franklin begins to have an existence within the fugues it is in terms of the perception of things: "A weird world, spatial change perceived independently of time."

He gradually becomes "awake" in the fugues, in a new sense of the word. He is able to cook and feed Ursula, Trippett and himself and, when threatened by Slade, he is able to retain his consciousness to resist. The story ends not with Franklin's death but with him awaiting a new and strange future and what amounts to a whole new range of the perceptions of space and time. Through Franklin Ballard presents a series of suggestions as to what this different state might portend. Central to this description is the idea that time as we know it is not an absolute but man-made, and the events of the story may mark a release rather than an imprisonment.

> 'Clock time' is a neurophysiological construct, a measuring rod confined to homo sapiens… If time is a primitive mental structure we have inherited, then we ought to welcome its atrophy, embrace the fugues…

There are indications that the events of the story support this radical proposition. First Trippett and later Ursula and Franklin see the Nevada desert blooming around them as though they were able to see it in a time frame embracing either the future or the past. Franklin muses about the adjustments his psyche is making to a new grasp of the eternity of which all things and all events are a part:

> The whole process of life is the discovery of the immanent past contained in the present. At the same time, I feel a growing nostalgia for the future, a memory of the future I have already experienced but somehow forgotten. In our lives we try to repeat those significant events which have already taken place in the future. As we grow older we feet an increasing nostalgia for our own deaths, through which we have already passed. Equally, we have a growing premonition of our births, which are about to take place. At any moment we may be born for the first time.

This remarkable speculation—the making concrete of the idea of all reality simultaneously existing while we are locked in the present until the possibility of being released by the narcoma—represents an amazing step forward in Ballard's musings on the nature of time.

Of course the new situation is unclear in that it hovers on the borderline between "physical" and "mental or subjective" reality. That has always been Ballard's terrain in fiction and particularly in the treatment of time. But whereas the mental time of the characters has always engaged his respect and, if anything, has been given a higher place in his scale of values or importance, in "News From the Sun" there is a confident assertion that there is a place to go outside of time, an evolution of understanding into which man might be forced by circumstance and where subjectivity would actually triumph. At the close of the story Franklin has survived a long journey on foot through the desert while dwelling in the fugue state and has proved himself capable of sustaining himself rather than succumbing to the narcoma. For him it is an escape *to* rather than an escape *from* reality.

In his fictional examinations of time, Ballard has always sought the fullness of the apocalypse, the end that is transmogrified into a new and wonderful beginning. In "The Voices of Time" and *The Crystal World*, light began to be a central concept, just as for the contemporary physicist it lies in the clutches of time at the intersecting point between matter and energy. The reality that could be frozen, albeit as lifelessly as Keats's urn, gives way in the blinding glare of the American desert and the glittering Las Vegas to the energy of the Sunlight Fliers moving off into the future of *Hello America*.

In "News From the Sun" the desert sunlight comes to greet Franklin as he emerges from time into a living eternity. There is an opening out, a blossoming, in Ballard's treatment of the theme of time. Not only are the characters now aware of their inner realities and acting within them, but Ballard is aggressively asserting that the realities of his characters may be substantially more real than the worlds we take for granted.

Ballard has long followed Dali and the surrealists on the journey to inner space, but in his fictions about time he has moved to the assertion that the internal is coming to dominate the physical universe, to shape the future of the cosmos. While there cannot but be an aspect of the metaphorical in the making of that assertion today, its power is the power of the imagination to overcome reality, and it certainly is reality in at least some senses of the word.

Ballard gives to eternity a local habitation and a name in the sleep that begins in the glittering jungle or the burning sun of the American desert.

JG Ballard's Shanghai

by Rick McGrath

The smiling doorman touched his cap and turned, deftly flicking a finger at a dragon line of orange and yellow cabs patiently waiting to ingest their next fare. I stepped from the crisp confines of the hotel lobby, gasped at the sudden hot kiss of humidity and smog, and quickly cocooned into the back seat. The driver pulled away as I smoothly called out my destination. Sure, I did. In actuality, I handed over my written address: 508 Pan Yu Road. We were off to the newly opened *SH508* restaurant, and today's lunch menu featured an irresistible special—an expedition to discover what, if anything, was left of JG Ballard's childhood home, that gilded cage of Victorian family formality which constituted his first experience of living behind gated walls.

Looking down Amherst Avenue (Xin Hua Lu). *Andy Best Photo*

Off we crept, swerving slowly through the chaotic traffic as I peered out the hazy windows and tried to imagine Ballard's mythic home town without all the cypher-like skyscrapers, mad is bad drivers and swooping freeways. It was September 13, 2007, and we were heading west through the International Settlement along Nanking Road, but I wanted to travel back in time as well, back to the 1930s when Pan Yu Road was called Columbia Road, and it was just another cross street on Amherst Avenue, the then-main suburban thoroughfare for an enclave of rich Europeans who lived the cozy crazy expatriate life on the outskirts of a death-filled, dangerous city once crammed with capitalists, crooks, and hot & cold running coolies.

As traffic and pedestrians jostled in the white light outside my improbable time capsule, I thought of the young Jim Ballard in his family's Packard as Yang drove the streets and street urchins tapped the car's windows, calling out, *No mama, no papa, no whiskey soda…*

I also remembered the many steps I had taken to find myself this far along the road to the Ballard family home, a journey begun in January, 2006. That was when I met Canadian Englit Professor Peter Brigg. We hit it off—one Ballardian to another—and at that first meeting he kindly gave me five pictures he had taken of the Shanghai Ballard home, and photocopies of three letters from Ballard about his Shanghai roots. Intrigued, I asked Peter how he came to have taken these photos. As deep assignments would have it, in the early 1980s Peter had decided to write a critical analysis of Ballard's work for use in American university courses.

By 1984 Peter had the book nearly finished, and he was living in Shanghai, teaching at the Shanghai Institute of International Economic Management. In 1984 *Empire Of The Sun* was published, and Peter, somewhat astonished to find the novel is set in Shanghai, sent Ballard a congratulatory postcard.

On December 29, 1984, Ballard replied to Brigg expressing obvious surprise that Brigg would be in Shanghai, and coyly sending out feelers about tourism and a suggestion to visit Lungua Pagoda. "Many thanks for your postcard," he wrote, "and the kind comments on *Empire of the Sun*—it's an odd coincidence that you should be reading it in Shanghai… it occurred to me that I ought to write to you while you were still in Shanghai to get some kind of first-hand information about how easy or difficult it might be for me to visit the sites of the novel, and my own childhood, if I ever travelled to China—or whether, in fact, these sites still exist at all."

Peter wrote back that he would indeed venture

36 Old Charlton Road
Shepperton
Middlesex
England
29 Dec 84

Dear Peter Brigg:

Many thanks for your postcard and the kind comments on Empire of the Sun -- it's an odd coincidence that you should be reading it in Shanghai. I've been interested to see your letters in David Pringle's JGB News, and it occurred to me that I ought to write to you while you were still in Shanghai to get some sort of first-hand information about how easy or difficult it might be for me to visit the sites of the novel, and my own childhood, if I ever travelled to China -- or whether, in fact, those sites still exist at all.

The only map I have of present-day Shanghai is that in the Encyclopaedia Britannia, where the street and place names are in Chinese. The road scheme doesn't altogether follow that of the 1940's layout -- Keswick Road, which then marked the western perimeter of Shanghai, ran a few yards from the Shanghai Hangchow Ningpo railway line, but on the eastern side of the line, whereas in the Britannica what seems to be a huge ring-road, Chung Shan Pei Street, lies on the western side of the track. Amherst Avenue ran into Keswick Road, and was roughly half a mile or so from Siccawei Cathedral. If one set off east along Amherst Avenue one eventually joined the Avenue Joffre, which now seems to be called Huai Hai Chung St.

I don't know if you ever visit the former western suburbs of Shanghai. Keswick Road and Siccawei marked the urban limits of Shanghai to the west and south-west, but presumably the open fields have long since been covered by the sprawl of Metropolitan Shanghai. Does Lunghua Airfield still exist? The camp lay a mile or so to the south of the airfield, and was a former teacher training college. Many of the buildings were substantial cement structures and may still be standing. I think Hungjao aerodrome is now the site of Shanghai International Airport.

What are the chances of a private visitor, without any kind of official assistance, actually being able to travel to these sites? Presumably most western visitors get little further than Nanking Road, the People's Park (ex-Shanghai Racecourse), and the Old City, plus an assortment of approved tourist locations. Would I be able to travel more freely? I speak no Chinese, and it would be almost impossible to explain to a taxi-driver where I wanted to go. What are the chances of entering the former Country Club (in the Bubbling Well Road) or the French Club? And what about Pootung and Hongkew?

I look forward very much to your book —

I'd be extremely interested to hear your views on all this. People have told me that the Shanghai of the 1940s has enormously expanded, but the central core may well be intact -- the Bund, judging by newsreels, seems hardly to have changed at all.

Lunghua Pagoda is well worth a visit, if it still stands, as I imagine it does. As I describe in the book, it was a flak tower during the war. A picnic there would be rather fun....

All the best,

J.G. Ballard

out, and on February 3rd, 1985, Ballard wrote back to Peter: "Very many thanks for your letter and all the fascinating information, and for the map—it was kind of you to go to the trouble of marking it up. The last thing I want to do is put you to any trouble, by the way—the notion of going back to Shanghai is a bit of a pipe-dream, an ambition for the long term which I mean to fulfil one day, but not yet."

To help Brigg with his explorations, Ballard drew a map to locate the Ballard House: "We had taken the bus out—around four or five miles from The Bund—and happily found Amherst Avenue right away after taking a fork from the main road (I believe it was Bubbling Well Road) and going two short blocks to Amherst. The lane from Amherst was more like a paved path wide enough for an automobile and heavily tree-lined.

"We walked down the lane to 31A and we could see a big house behind a high wall, but the door in the wall was locked and we couldn't get onto the property. What to do? Was there a back door? We went back to the main road, turned right, and then found a parallel street, and this took us to the side of the house, where there was a door and reception office. We were met by several Chinese, none who spoke any English, but my partner spoke some mandarin, and she was able to explain why we were there. They let us go around the outside of the house and I took pictures of the house from the back garden, but our glances inside revealed the ground floor was in use as offices and storage for boxes.

"The house was being used as a warehouse... a book depository. And the kinds of books? Technical manuals for industrial machinery! They showed us one but it was all Chinese to me. I thought that was an appropriate legacy for JGB."

The photos Brigg took offer us the first look at the house and property since the Ballards had been forced to abandon it in 1942. Brigg sent the photos off to Shepperton, and Ballard soon replied: "Very many thanks for the remarkable photographs, which I've been gazing at with all sorts of strange feelings, as you can imagine—it's generous of you to have the prints made and, of course, to have set off on the original expedition in the first place, or expeditions plural—the last thing I wanted was to burden you and your wife with the task of trundling miles across the city, whether to Lunghua or Amherst Avenue."

Most noteworthy in this letter is Ballard's announcement of plans to film *Empire of the Sun*, and his realization that if they shoot in the UK at Shepperon studios, "my neighbours will be recruited to play the internees, the wheel will have come full circle..."

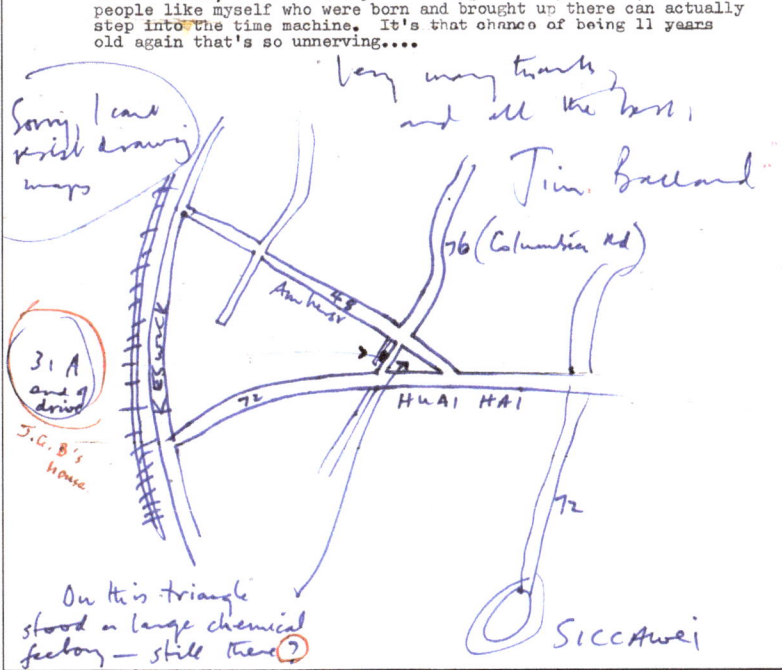

Ballard responds to Brigg's photos: "That is the lane in from Amherst Avenue, though as you surmise there were no trees in 1945, and I remember the front door vividly—as I do the house from the garden, though again there were no trees that close to the house. The upstairs awnings look as if they might be the 1930s originals, and presumably the bamboo structure replaces the perished awnings below. I'm not sure where the new entrance to the house can be —in 1945, as one stood facing the front door, there was a brick 2-car garage attached to the house on the left, with the tradesman's doorway to the left of that." *Peter Brigg Photos*

J. G. BALLARD
36, OLD CHARLTON ROAD
SHEPPERTON
MIDDLESEX
TW17 8AT

TEL: WALTON-ON-THAMES
225692

4 Oct 85

Dear Peter Brigg:

Very many thanks for the remarkable photographs, which I've been gazing at with all sorts of strange feelings, as you can imagine — it's generous of you to have the prints made and, of course, to have set off on the original expedition in the first place, or expeditions plural — the last thing I wanted was to burden you and your wife with the task of trundling miles across the city, whether to Lunghua or Amherst Avenue.

However, I'm glad you did — that is certainly the house, though it looks almost ramshackle (the Chinese, as I remember, were never very good at property maintenance, a trait I must have picked up from them). That is the lane in from Amherst Avenue, though as you surmise there were no trees in 1945, and I remember the front door vividly — as I do the house from the garden (all thanks to your wife, by the way), though again there were no trees that close to the house. The upstairs awnings look as if they might be the 1930s originals, and presumably the bamboo structure replaces the perished awnings below. I'm not sure where the new entrance to the house can be — in 1945, as one stood facing the front door, there was a brick 2-car garage attached to the house on the left, with the tradesman's doorway to the left of that. The latter led to the servant's quarters and the kitchen. Perhaps the garages have been removed and there is an entrance into the side wall of the house.

Still, all this is of no interest to anyone but myself, and I'm grateful to you for the fascinating details about the present occupants. I will keep your letter carefully, and take it with me if and when I visit Shanghai. Complex emotions surge around, the whole thing could be a complete let-down, leaving me with an unfillable void in place of my present nostalgia...

Fascinating too to see Lunghua pagoda. This I walked to from the camp in August 1945, and remember it as a large and massive stone structure — the Japanese mounted anti-aircraft guns on its decks and it was virtually a flak tower covering the airfield two miles to the south. Apart from a very small village at its foot of shabby earth hovels, the pagoda was surrounded on all sides by open country. Lunghua airfield had no fixed perimeter — we stepped through the wire of the camp and walked through long grass until we reached the runways. Sadly, neither of the Lunghua photos was is of the former camp buildings but they weren't too dissimilar.

Curiously, I had a phone call a couple of afternoons ago directly from Shanghai, from the American producer at Warner Bros who hopes to film Empire of the Sun, and was there for a week with the director, Harold Becker, and the British playwright Tom Stoppard, who is writing the script. They were very excited by it all, and said that it was like travelling fifty years back in time, this 30s city more or less perfectly preserved. They had identified most of the down-town locations — the Bund, Nanking Road etc — and had been to Lunghua pagoda, but said they had been refused permission to enter the airfield or the remains of the camp — I assume the concrete buildings are still standing and are now part of some military installation. A pity. They had not yet tracked down the Amherst Avenue house, though I may have misled them by saying that 31A was the second house on the left down the lane — as it was in 1945; there was then a plot of about ½ acre between the first house, on the corner of Amherst and Columbia, and 31A, and presumably this has now been built on. (An ironic touch: I asked Shapiro, the producer, if they were planning to film there, and he said, "Oh, no — the camp scenes we will film in England." I thought, oh my God, Shepperton studios, my neighbors will be recruited to play the internees, the wheel will have come full circle..)

Anyway, many thanks again for all the trouble — I appreciate it. I look forward to reading your book, and wish you all the best. Of course I'll let you know my thoughts on the book, and will let you know if I visit Shanghai during the period you'll be there.

All the best to you and your wife,

Jim Ballard

Part Two:
The Ballard House is Visible from Space

A year has gone by since my meeting with Peter Brigg, and the only result of any research has been the discovery of a video, *Shanghai Jim*, done by the BBC in 1991 of Ballard's only return to the scenes of his youth.

In a white suit and hat he happily visits his old Shanghai haunts, recounting in vivid terms what his life was like and how much Shanghai, and especially Lunghua, affected him.

It is still a fascinating revelation, suddenly explaining so much about Ballard's strangely compelling art. Suddenly, the thought just popped into my head: why not see these places for myself? Nobody else seems interested.

A trip is organized and scheduled for September 2007, and in anticipation satellites are called into play as I try to find the Ballard Shanghai home from space. After zeroing in on the city, I was able to cruise over the appropriate parts of the area west of the International Settlement and quite easily found the area Ballard indicates on his map to Peter Brigg from 1985.

The satellite map was quickly printed and mailed off to Ballard. He wrote back: "Yes, I think you've found it—it's absolutely amazing what computers/satellites can do. Next time, feed in Atlantis, El Dorado and the Promised Land and see what Google comes up with."

J. G. BALLARD
36, OLD CHARLTON ROAD
SHEPPERTON
MIDDLESEX
TW17 8AT

TEL: WALTON-ON-THAMES
225692

19/3/07

Dear Mr McGrath:

Yes, I think you've found it -- it's absolutely amazing what computers/satellites can do. Next time, feed in Atlantis, El Dorado and the Promised Land and see what Google comes up with.

When I was last in Shanghai in 1991 the building boom had just begun, but already I feared that my old family home would soon be replaced by a high-rise block of flats. It's good to see that it's still there. I've marked Amherst Avenue and Columbia Road, and the narrow lane that ran from Amherst Avenue to our house, 31A Amherst Avenue. The original front door opened onto the lane, but in 1991 was disused. A new entrance to the property had been constructed off the former Columbia Road, at what is now 508 Pan Yu Road. Assuming you take a taxi, that is the address you should give the driver. A recent visitor to the house tells me that the entire property has been refurbished. In 1991 it was in a very shabby state.

Since my own visit in 1991 the chemical factory in the triangle of roads to the right has been demolished and replaced by a park. One thing you will notice is the huge number of trees, planted as a conservation measure during the 1970s, I believe. Lunghua Camp, as it were, is filled with them, though there can't have been more than half a dozen in all during the war.

Tracking down the former Lunghua Camp could well be difficult and expensive. You will almost certainly need to take a taxi. It is now The Shanghai Highschool (all the other highschools in Shanghai are numbered) and the original buildings have been refurbished and added to. I suggest you try your Google spy camera, and search the area some three miles due south of Lunghua Pagoda. There is a large water tower in the north-east corner of the site.

I'm afraid I don't recall Betty Barr or Tess Johnston. Do remember that many of the former internees were very young children during the war, and their memories of the camp are based on recollections handed down to them by their parents. Many of the former internees who protested against my picture of Lunghua in Empire of the Sun turned out to have been 4 or 5 at the time, and I suspect that quite a few of the 'diaries' were concocted from hazy memories, perhaps in response to the novel's success, decades after the event.

Yes, Jeannette Baxter has told me of the huge response to the Norwich conference. I'm very grateful to her for the immense amount of work she has put into the conference, and to everyone else, like yourself, who is making the huge journey to attend. Sadly, I won't be able to attend -- I've been seriously ill for the past year and more, and spend a great deal of time visiting hospital, having tests and various programmes of medication. I appreciate your interest in my writing, and I'm sure you understand that I'm not strong enough to meet anyone.

[signature: J G Ballard]

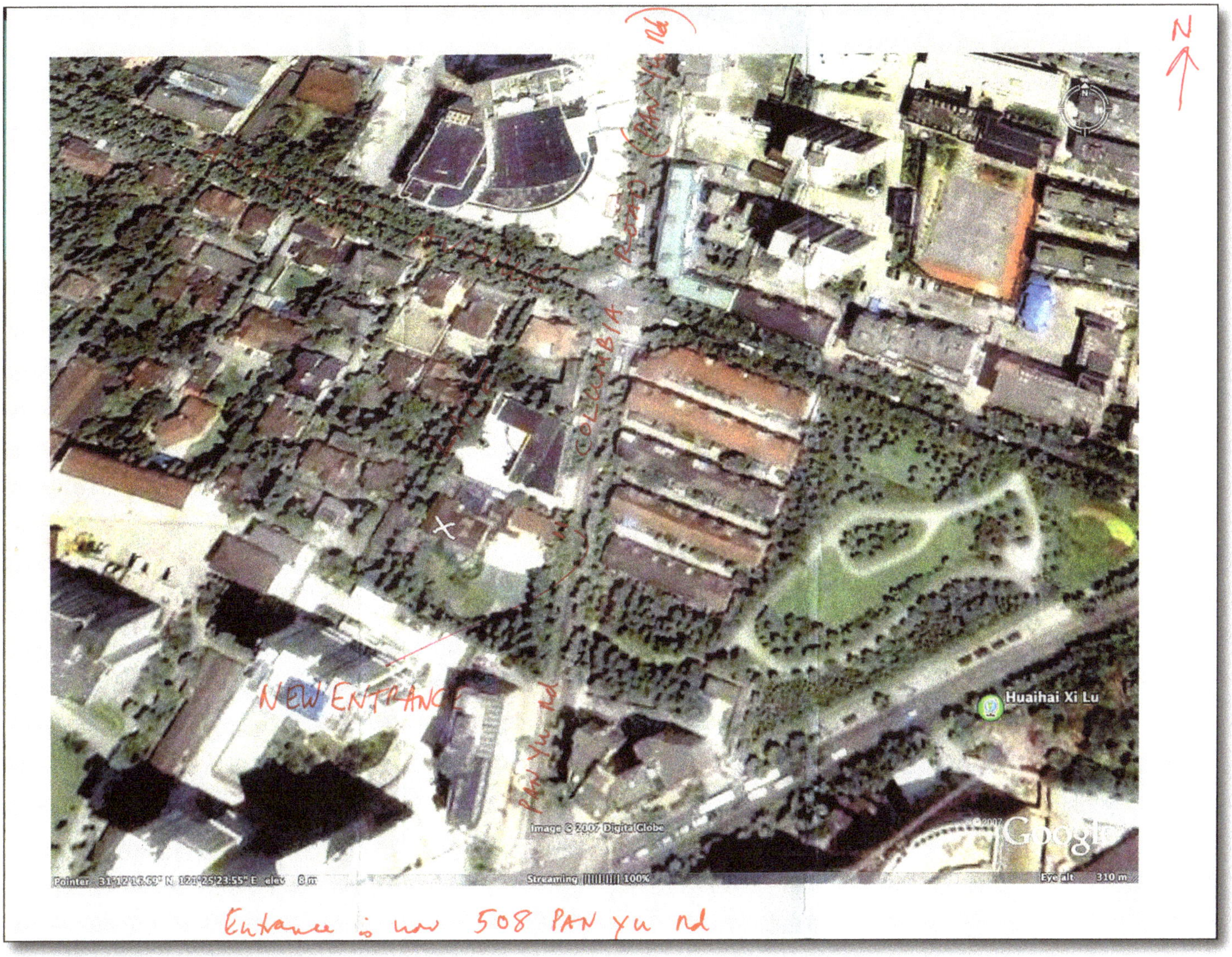

Ballard also filled in the details of the map I sent him: "I've marked Amherst Avenue and Columbia Road, and the narrow lane that ran from Amherst Avenue to our house, 31A Amherst Avenue. A new entrance to the property had been constructed off the former Columbia Road, at what is now 508 Pan Yu Road. Since my own visit in 1991 the chemical factory in the triangle of roads to the right has been demolished and replaced by a park. One thing you will notice is the huge number of trees, planted as a conservation measure during the 1970s, I believe."

Part Three: A Shanghai Contact Appears

Andy Best

And then... like a parachuted canister full of food, an email arrives from out of the synchronous blue: "I have been living in Shanghai for six years now. I saw your site showing maps and a satellite image of Ballard's house in Shanghai and got a shock. It's round the corner from my house here and I have passed it every day for three years without knowing. It has been turned into a restaurant called SH508. Probably you're aware of all of this? If not, would you like me to send photos or something? Andy Best."

Very cool. A fellow Ballardian intimately familiar with the area. We converse immediately and he agrees to take some pix. This was the first he sent:

By this time I had finalized the trip and Andy had agreed to be my guide, meeting me at the restaurant/former home and then checking out the neighbourhood. I wondered: which one of us was on deep assignment?

I was curious as to the layout of the house—how much had they changed it? how would I know?—so I wrote to Ballard, informing him of my impending trip to Shanghai, and that his house was now a restaurant. I also asked him if he could draw me a floor plan map to compare with the house when I visited it. Ballard replied, incredulously: "What next? I wonder if your Shanghai contact has the right house—when I was there in 1991 the house was in a state of some dilapidation, but I suppose someone may have felt it was worth restoring. If it is a restaurant, let's hope it's a McDonald's or KFC." And he did draw me a fantastic map of the main floor:

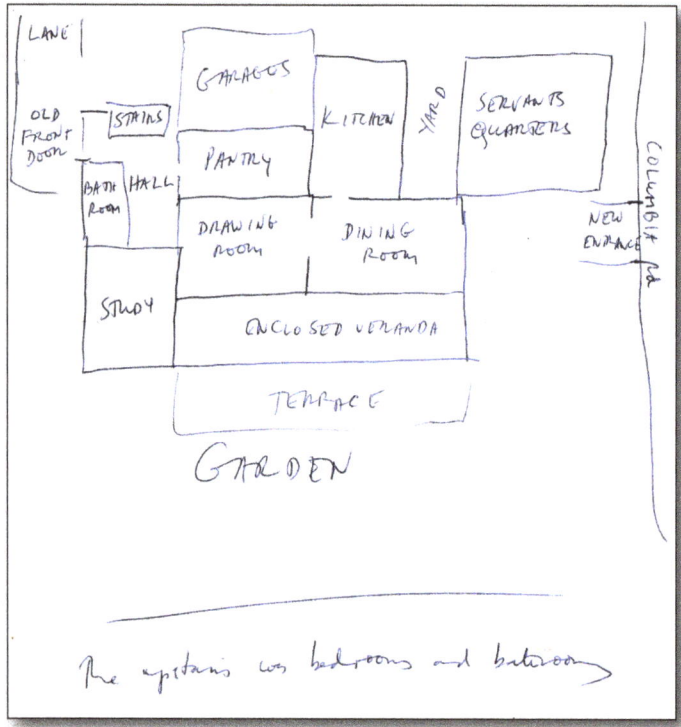

Part Four:
The Ballard Home, 31A Amherst Avenue

A lack of honking horns snapped me out of my reverie and I looked outside. The traffic had finally picked up speed and we were now on the western edge of the old International Settlement. Street signs are no help, as all the old western names are gone. Amherst Avenue is now called Xin Hua Road, and the cabbie made a vicious turn off it onto Pan Yu Road and came to a screeching halt in front of an impressive iron gate, just opening for the day's trade.

This was it. After years of planning, I was here. The house at 31A Amherst Avenue. JG Ballard's childhood home—now, a big, T-shaped, three-storey blend of period house and commerce, with a new main extrance door welcoming the hungry under a neon sign reading SH508, with its own parking lot and expensive garden behind the same high wall that protected and isolated young Jimmy Ballard 70 years earlier. There was no swimming pool. It certainly was not, as Ballard had hoped for, either a McDonalds or KFC. Quite the opposite.

My host and guide for the day, Andy Best, was already there. I paid the cabbie and excitedly disembarked into the heat and light. After brief introductions we stood and gazed at the sight before us. Yes, by this time I had seen many pictures of the place. From Peter Brigg's 1985 shots to Andy's more recent pictures, but it was still an amazing feeling to be standing in such an evocative area.

I was itching to enter, but Andy suggested we take in the surrounding neighbourhood before going in for lunch. OK, I agreed, and we set out north to Amherst, turned east, walked for a minute and then came across the long, narrow laneway that once led to the Ballard house front door. Barren in the 1930s, pleasantly lined with tall trees in the 1980s, the alley from Amherst down to the Ballard front door had changed again with the infill of progress: large, branchy trees lined the lane, long sheds covered lineups of Shanghai's ubiquitous motorbikes, new power-driven iron gates were closed, barbed wire atop high brick walls kept out the curious, and an army of white-faced air conditioners hung on walls like heat-seeking jellyfish lost on the reef of some new electric sea.

The Ballard house is at the very end of the lane,

and as we approached the terminus the city's air raid sirens suddenly began to sound. The humidity shook with a series of long, anxious blasts. I searched the skies, unsure whether to look for Japanese or American bombers. "Do you believe in synchronicity?" Andy asked. "That's the 10 o'clock signal for today's national anniversary. Sirens are blowing all over the country right now." He leaned in, looked up and down the alley, conspiratorially. "It was precisely 70 years ago today the Chinese withdrew from Shanghai and the Japanese took over: September 13, 1937." I looked up and down

the alley, too. That makes today, 70 years ago, the beginning of the end for everyone living around here. And Jim's already barely-normal childhood.

I was dumbfounded. No, gobsmacked. What were the odds of this happening on the one day I was here? It was like some temporal shift was taking place, and I was being swept along in a sort of dual timeline. The walls were coming together to form an angle. Yes, it was that corny a moment. Being there helped.

The three-storey original façade of the Ballard manse towered above us. The old front door, now bricked-in and mortared-over, I had seen in pictures, but I was still surprised to note the new undoor was capped by a tile and wood peaked roof. Oddly, the house seemed a lot closer to the wall and door than I had imagined—perhaps a twist of visual perception—and for the first time I noticed just how nondescript this side of the building was, given

its prior role as the front of the house. Looking out were just three windows—one on the third floor and two on the second—and I couldn't help but flash on how this secretive face has the same introspective look as its once-youthful occupant. On the other hand, fewer street side windows are a good defense against midnight ramblers.

With the ebbing echo of the nostalgic sirens fading into the past, Andy and I retraced our steps and began exploring the alleys up and down Amherst. Noting that most of the grand old houses had long since been converted into an anthill of small flats, I realized that by renovating the Ballard house into a restaurant, it had avoided the fate of these other mansions, and had retained its rooms and garden as a complete whole. And the insight occurred it was now most fitting that Ballard's home was dispensing food. Nourishment was the most precious substance (save the imagination) in the obsessive hunger of *Empire of the Sun*—for the body and the mind.

By now it's just noon, and only Andy, myself, mad dogs and Englishmen are subjecting themselves to the empire of this merciless sun, which has now cooked the air to the consistency of hot jello.

Andy pointed out many of the homes now had plaques designating them as Heritage Architecture. Apparently the local officials decided to identify these old houses as symbols of the city's quickly disappearing decadent colonial past, and began erecting these signs in 1999. We stopped beside a large gate and Andy pointed to the wall: "Check it out. This plaque says: 'English garden residence on Amherst Road. Built in 1925.' Note they got the 'road' wrong. And this one? 'English country style garden residence on Amherst Road. Completed in

1930. Brick-and-concrete composite structure.'" He looked up appreciatively at the faint remains of the mock-Tudor structure. "These places are now worth a lot of money." I wondered if this was the house belonging to the Belgian dentist, and if the rows of teeth still ornamented the glass cases in its study.

We hailed another cab, and Andy spoke to him in Mandarin. "Are we going to the camp?" I asked. "You'll see." After driving for about 15 minutes along a confusing network of twisting roads, past Shanghai's new 80,000-seat stadium (you can see it from space!), suddenly a tall pagoda appeared over the rooftops to the cab's left. Was this the pagoda at the end of Lunghua Aerodrome that once bristled with anti-aircraft guns?

"Yes. But don't believe your eyes. The tourist guides say it's 10th century Buddhist, but Shanghai was the centre of the Cultural Revolution and everything was ripped down and destroyed in the 1960s. All the temples you see in Shanghai have been rebuilt. They call it renovation. This is the Lunghua pagoda, all right, but they rebuilt it quite far from its original site." I laughed. Crazy commies. But at least I knew we were going to the airport. A short distance away from the ersatz pagoda we came across a railway line. Hah. What else but the Shanghai-Hangchow Railway, the same line that hosted the death march to Nantao when the Japanese cleared out Lunghua at war's end.

It still looks evil. An ancient guardhouse stands on the road beside the tracks, and it was easy to imagine a Japanese Corporal lounging on the tiny verandah while a Chinese coolie sang himself to death lashed to a telephone pole.

Another five minutes and the airfield arrives. No longer the grass aerodrome that young Jamie almost donated his bones to, but a concrete strip that stretches north/south beside the Huangpu River.

There's not much to see here, so we're back into a cab and off to Lunghua Camp. Andy thought he could pull some strings to get us past the gates of what is now Shanghai High School, but classes were running and this is a repressive society, capitalism or no. Casually we walked up to the big padlocked gate and Andy began pleading in Mandarin. Surprisingly, Andy's description of the "crazy Canadian" had some effect and the gates miraculously opened. One shot of G Block, where the young Jim and his family lived, and that was it…

Left: current new Lunghua Pagoda; right: the original Ballard saw as a youth, covered with anti-aircraft guns.

G Block, where the Ballard family were interned at Lunghua Camp. This building was destroyed in 2010 to make a swimming pool.

no exploring of the premises. As the gates clanged behind us I remembered what JG had told me in his last letter: "an immense amount of time has gone by and the Lunghua you visit will not be Lunghua Camp." Prescient as always, JG was right: the real Camp only exists in the minds of a diminishing few, its no doubt fascinating real history repressed in rather mundane books such as *A Curious Cage* and

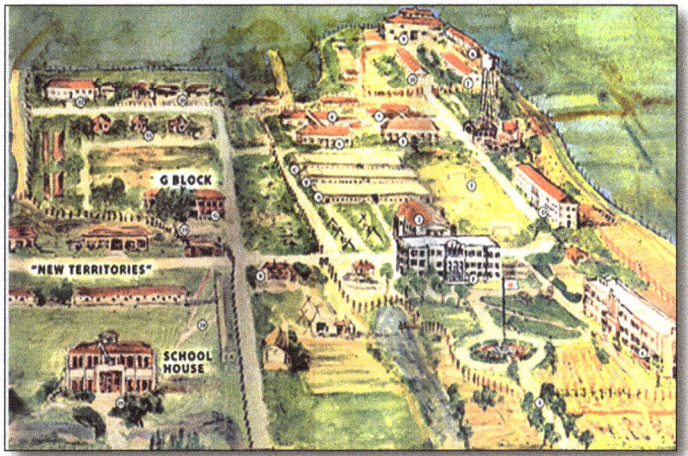

An internee's drawing of Lunghua Camp during the war years.

Life in a Japanese Internment Camp, both of which propose a Lunghua as ficticious as the one described in *Empire*. I suspect Ballard felt that twinge of disappointment when he finally visited the Lunghua in 1991. You can't go back.

By now it's just noon, so we hail another cab and point northeast, back to the house/restaurant.

It was, I'll admit, even more of a thrill to finally enter the house after this extended dance around its perimeter. I had Ballard's hand-drawn floor plan, a hardcover copy of *Empire Of The Sun*, and a desire to explore as much as I could, not just the main floor. This was the first time since Ballard visited in 1991 that someone who knew the building's history was on the loose. The rooms, apparently, are just like the original—the dining room, drawing room, enclosed verandah, terrace and study are all the same, and the old kitchen and pantry are still there.

I couldn't check out the garage to see if it still contained an old Packard, with Yang polishing the chrome, but the drawing room and dining room run beside a long east/west hallway, which I assume is original, although it's not shown on Ballard's drawing. An easy oversight after so many years.

This hallway runs the length of the house, and has steps to the second floor at each end. So, the main floor is seemingly untouched—no doubt because all the walls are supporting.

Upstairs the second floor is dominated by one huge, long room, with three smaller rooms opening off it, each facing the back garden by looking out over the roof of the verandah. At the other end of the long room is a doorway that leads to a wide hallway with another room over the first floor study that overlooks the garden. Off the hall are steps going down to the main, and up to the third floor, where I find a T-shaped room that leads off to a large room and a smaller room which both overlook the garden. It would seem most likely the young Ballard would have been in the largest room.

The ceilings were all original, done Tudor-style, with open edgewise planks over white plaster, and the crossbeams look old enough to have had model airplanes dangling from them.

Down the stairs and I'm out through the old study's French doors (after pausing to admire a rather fancy fireplace), and onto the terrace, which leads down to the garden.

There's no swimming pool any more, drained or otherwise, and all has obviously been feng shui redesigned to allow for the luckiest playing of scenic events like weddings and other contract signing celebrations.

The original property wall is still there, and walking around the perimeter I got the feeling of just how big this estate was… half an acre? Big.

I wandered the yard, thinking back on all the times Ballard had mentioned his imaginative games acted out on this selfsame turf. I could almost hear the rat-a-tat of youthful heroics, until I realized a waiter was clearing off one of the terrace tables.

Spell broken, I wandered back in the house to find Andy ready to explore. I tell him I've already taken the tour, and ask about the bill. Turns out he's already paid it. Hey, does it get any better? Well, yes it does, as this time I get to show Andy around the place a second time.

Just before we leave I have the presence of mind to ask if any promotional literature has been prepared for the restaurant, and am pleasantly surprised when I'm handed a slick glossy brochure. "May I have two?"

When I returned from China I put together a package of stuff and mailed it to Ballard. He wrote back, clearly indicating the house had been altered much more than he had originally thought.

His letter follows:

J. G. BALLARD
36, OLD CHARLTON ROAD
SHEPPERTON
MIDDLESEX
TW17 8AT

TEL: WALTON-ON-THAMES
225692

16/10/07

Dear Mr McGrath, Many thanks for taking the trouble to send me the remarkable photos of your Shanghai trip — I much appreciate it — I've already spent hours studying every detail, a kind of long-range reconnaissance, though I'm not sure what I'm really looking for — some trace, probably, of a previous existence — as you say in your very interesting report, everything has changed, & there's now scarcely a trace of the old Ballard home — the SH508 management should adopt as their slogan — "Forget about Shanghai Jim — just enjoy the dim sum!"

The curious thing is that all these changes have taken place in the very recent past — in 1991 the house was a near ruin, but was still recognisably its 1945 self — the new owners have extended it in various ways — the original upstairs floor plan more or less duplicated the ground floor arrangement — there were three bedrooms, each with a bathroom, off a corridor that ran east-west — the long room you mention didn't exist — the open veranda on the garden side, directly above the enclosed veranda below, has also been enclosed — the former bedrooms and bathrooms have been torn out and turned into your long room — the small bedrooms you mention occupy the former open veranda. There was originally only one staircase, which you photograph, rather touchingly — it's virtually unchanged — and no corridor on the ground floor — they probably used part of the large pantry (larger than the kitchen) —

All this is of no interest to anyone, I fear, & I don't know why I've gone on at length, like some demented estate agent — houses are constantly being altered — many of the world-famous houses, by architects of the Richard Neutra/Schindler 1920's generation, in Los Angeles, have been enlarged and reshaped, like many of Corbusier's houses in France, some even fitted into pitched roofs!

I'm glad you made it to Lunghua — In 1991 the children were on holiday, and the BBC had arranged our visit to the site with the Shanghai TV management — we were able to move all over the camp site, though again there had been enormous changes — not just to the former camp, but to the surrounding terrain — it's hard to believe that in 1945 there was nothing but open fields between our house & Lunghua Camp five miles to the south.

It was interesting to hear from Andy Best (please thank him for me) about Lunghua Pagoda — the war-time pagoda was a large structure that carried anti-aircraft guns, and when we filmed around the pagoda in 1991 it seemed to me to be a much smaller and slimmer structure —

In an odd way it's quite reassuring that everything has changed so much — the Shanghai I knew, along with

31 Amherst Avenue and Lunghua Camp, only survives inside my head —

Thank you again, + for the photos of the neighbourhood houses (none of which I recognised) — your letter from Da Li — what next? — arrived on the same day as the photos —

All the best

JG Ballard

Part Five: The Changes Continue

Within two years of my visit to Shanghai word arrived from Andy Best that the building, which at least retained the bones of the Ballard home, was again under renovation: "The SH508 people have sold the house and moved to a new location around the corner. The house is currently under renovation of some kind. Will keep my eye on it, but, in Shanghai, despite the government 'protection' of old houses, every time one of the villas changes hands there's a 50 percent chance it goes, at least in it's original form."

Nick Darsley Photo

A month later photos of the renovation arrived from Dan Butterfield, then making a trip through China: "I just returned from a trip through China. Made it to Beijing, Shanghai and Hong Kong. I stopped by JG Ballard's boyhood home in Shanghai. It's currently undergoing a major renovation. The construction workers were aware of the historical significance of the home. Hopefully it will be finished with respect to its origins."

In 2010 another traveler, Nick Darsley, sent an update. "Haven't got much of a story to tell—to visit the Ballard home, I came out of Hongqiao Road metro station, and headed northeast along Huahai Road for about ten minutes, before turning left into Pan Yu (Columbia Rd before the war). The house is clearly visible behind a wall and electric fence. At first glance, it looks pretty much like the original house, but almost nothing original remains of the old place.

"The renovations seemed to be pretty much complete, but I was not able to tell what the building is intended to be now. It might be another restaurant, or it could equally be a private dwelling. I didn't have time to try and ask around to find out, so I headed around the corner into what used to be Amherst Avenue (now Xinhua Rd). As I saw the old driveway to JG Ballard's home, I thought of the old beggar lying dead in the snow on the corner, and the wheels of the car going over his foot as it turned out into Amherst.

"There is a little cabin with a security guard at the entrance of the drive, but I just walked by and waved at him—he nodded back and didn't seem to mind me being there. At the end of the drive I looked at the original site of the Ballard front door. It is completely sealed off by a new brick wall, and

Ben Lin Photos

unless you knew, you wouldn't imagine this was once the front of the house. The window above the old door remains."

In 2011 another traveller, Ben Lin, visited the house. "Looking at JG's drawing, it looks like the dining room, drawing room, and enclosed veranda have been combined into the main dining room of the restaurant. The kitchen appears to be the original kitchen, and expanded into the servant's quarters. I asked the waitress if she knew anything about history or ownership of the building, and she told us that a lot of English and Germans come in and talk about an author who is famous in the West that used to live there, but that was all she knew, which was actually more than I expected.

"The lane in the back must have been wider in the 1930s-1940s, because I can't imagine it being wide enough for a car of the period to get in and out of the garage gate. Today, it's barely wide enough for a modern car, which has a much smaller footprint than cars of the 1930s. It appears that the house has been built all the way up to the outer wall, and the only way into or out of the premises into the lane is through the garage gate. What was the front door is totally sealed up to the outer wall."

So, what can a literary traveller looking for traces of JG Ballard find in Shanghai today? The original family home is now an ersatz copy, and even Lunghua camp, Ballard's most influential "home" as a child, has now lost most of its associations with the war and the 2,000 people who lived there for three years. There may not be much of the original, but for many the mythic will suffice.

In July, 2012, daughter Fay Ballard and family made the trip to Shanghai. Fay reports: "The JGB tour has been superb. Last night, strong cocktails at the Peace Hotel. Today—the house, fully explored, birthplace hospital, townhouse, Cathedral school and camp, F Block and Assembly Hall. *The city is JGB*. Wish he could have returned after WW2."

Ballard himself was circumspect about all these changes. In 2007, two years before his tragic death, Ballard wrote to me and simply summed up his feelings: "In an odd way it's quite reassuring that everything has changed so much—the Shanghai I knew, along with 31 Amherst Avenue and Lunghua camp, only survive inside my head."

And in literature, Mr Ballard, and in literature.

JG Ballard's Shanghai in Maps

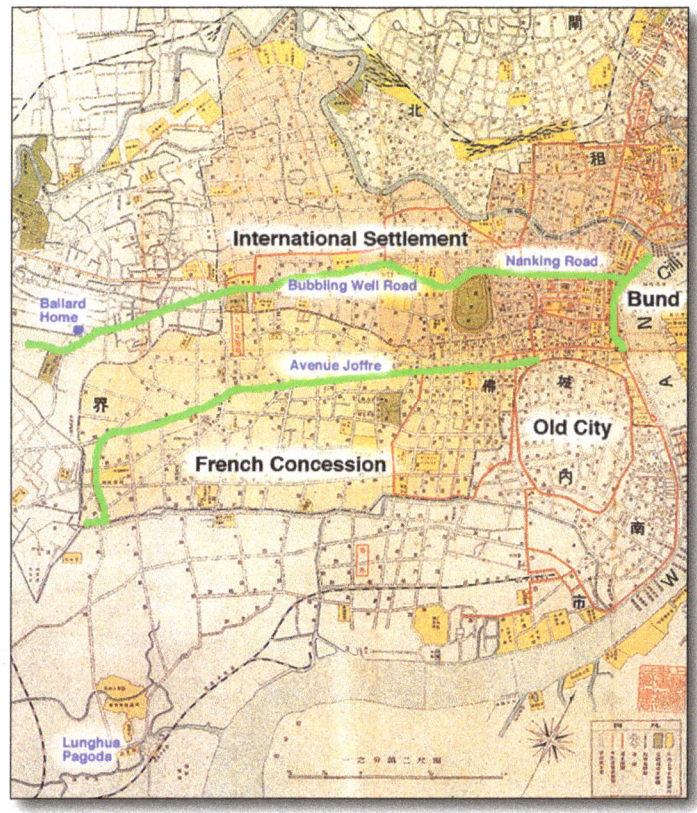

Where everything is in relation to each other.

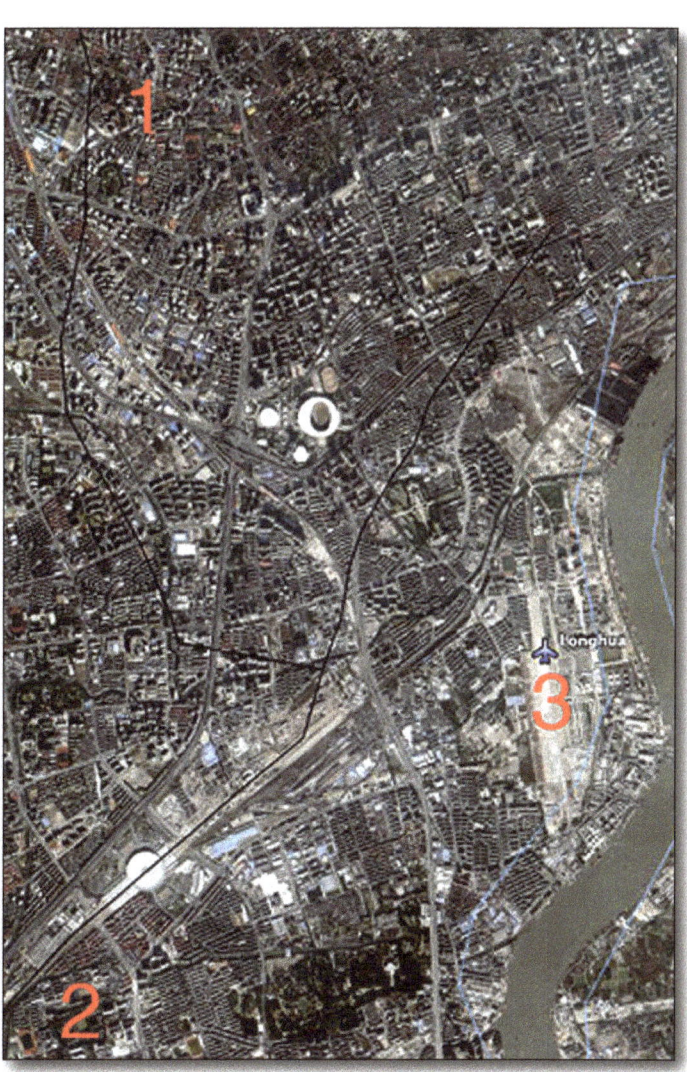

(1) Amherst Avenue (2) Lunghua Camp (3) Lunghua Airport (the big O is the new Shanghai stadium).

Lunghua Airport (top right) and Lunghua Camp.

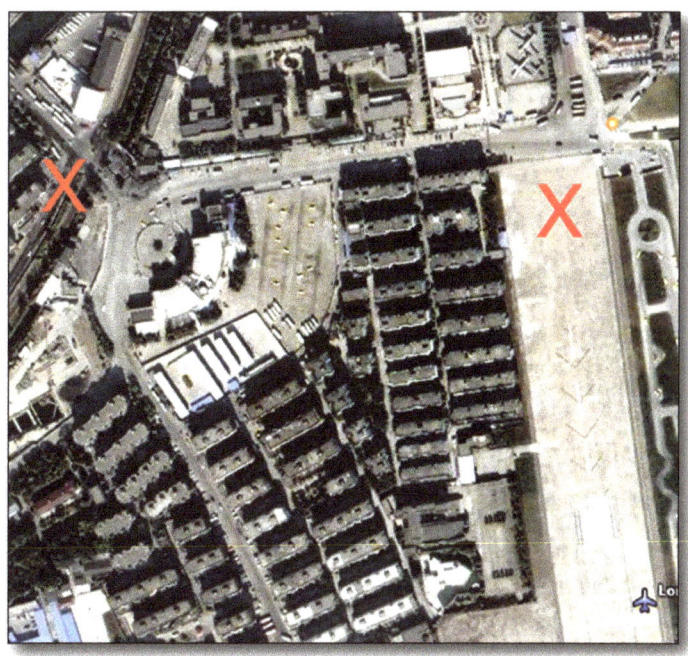

(Left) Guardhouse on the Shanghai-Hangchow Railway (right) Lunghua Airport.

Ballardoscope:
Some Attempts at Approaching the Writer as a Visionary

by Jordi Costa

1. "How do I look?," asks David Carradine, in the guise of the fierce killer Bill, aka the Snake Charmer, in the final minutes of *Kill Bill, Volume 2* (2004), a film that JG Ballard didn't like at all. "You look ready," Uma Thurman replies, possessed by the abstract character of The Bride, after tapping her lover/executioner in the middle of his chest using the five-point-palm exploding heart technique. When you reach the end of *Miracles of Life*—which is the last book Ballard leaves us with us—the Ballardian reader feels they are in a similar situation: over a 50-year, unflagging literary career, the writer has applied to our subconscious the five-minute technique which will project us into the future.

And there is no going back, There is no doubt that the Ballardian reader is prepared to decipher the profound structure of the world they inhabit and to foresee, with a scant margin of error, the internal logic of the immediate future.

Ballard is a writer who came from the limits of human experience—his years in Shanghai—touched by the secret power of reading the visionary present, to tell us what the next five minutes (or next 50 years) are going to be like. This means that being a Ballardian reader is a blessing and a curse at one and the same time: the blessing of understanding exactly what is happening—or what is being hatched—and the curse, which has its counterpart in Ray Milland's character in Roger Corman's *The Man with the X-Ray Eyes* (1963), who is unable to look at life other than with a Ballardian gaze. Just like David Carradine in Tarantino's film, the Ballardian reader is, in fact, preparing for what is ahead: he also knows that, in the next five minutes, there is only space (or time) to take a few last steps before the inevitable happens.

2. This Ballardian reader recalls his keen childhood admiration for an author who he only read through expurgated texts or adaptations to the language of the comic strip or cinema: Jules Verne. At that time, Verne was, without a shadow of a doubt, that prophet of the last century who had seen a future of submarines, journeys to the moon, and skies dotted with aerial devices which now formed part of the present. In his adult life, the Ballardian reader has no alternative but to attribute the same prophetic precision to Ballard, a writer who is able to dazzle, define and catalogue another form of future. Not the technological future, but something more intangible and complex. The spiritual future, our coming states of mind. Ballard hasn't stopped revealing layers of our future until the stopwatch has reached zero: when the writer put the final full stop on the last page of *Miracles of Life*, the world had become something essentially Ballardian, something foretold from the very first sentence of *The Drowned World*: "Soon it would be too hot." Bruce Sterling summed it up much better in the pages of *Time* magazine in 1999: "Ballard never predicted events or devices; instead, he described future sensibilities—how it might feel, what it might mean. A bizarre contemporary event like the paparazzi car-crash death of Princess Diana is perfectly Ballardian. No flow chart, no equation, no profit projection could ever have predicted that, but if you've read Ballard, you swiftly recognize the smell of it. I dare say that's the best the SF genre will ever do—and no more should ever be asked of it."

There are many ways of reading Ballard, but only one of them adopts the form of a journey of semi-initiation, punctuated with strategic twists and discoveries leading up to the all important final revelation: the path must run through his entire body of work, in an exhaustive, ordered and chronological way. Not for nothing—however dreamlike, inverted or perverted—is logic one of the guiding concepts of Ballardian sensitivity, and the writer's discourse has always advanced (against the tide, upstream) without making any concessions to arbitrariness. Today, many books later, the Ballardian reader can affirm that everything, absolutely everything, has been necessary: even the repetitions, the bombshells disguised as apparent changes of genre, the succession of veils and masks leading up to the concise final autobiography... When Ballardian readers reach the terminus station of this imaginary universe, they understand that, in principle, Ballard is a science fiction writer—he has no other destiny other than to become what he had always been, deep down: a realist writer. It could be argued that he is even a hyper-realist writer, because his raw material has always been hyperrealism, or realism intensified or heightened by this ability to see and understand that is reserved for a few. In a certain sense, at the end of his journey, the Ballardian reader is a little like Charlton Heston at the end of *The Planet of the*

> *Herein lies the key to understanding why Ballard is a poet who writes like a forensic scientist. Someone who remembers, narrates and weaves together a fiction like someone performing an autopsy on themselves.*

Apes (1968): the traveller who finds himself on the start square of a board game, who assumes he never moved from there. A Ballardian character (and, by extension, a reader) would never succumb to the final angry outburst by the heroic Heston, because the journey would have helped him understand that there was no other possible solution to the equation: the interesting part doesn't lie in showing resistance, but in exploring the new horizon of possibilities from this terminal beach.

3. We can summarise Ballard's life's career as the bare essentials, until we come to the moment when the pages of his autobiography *Miracles of Life* formulate something akin to poetry: Ballard was born in Shanghai on 15th November 1930, to an affluent, influential family living in the British colony on the west side of the city. The splendour of Shanghai—a synthetic city *avant la lettre*, a hedonistic limbo that looked like the blueprint for the soon-to-be-built Las Vegas, a mediatised landscape before Ballard himself thought up the concept—bewitched his childish gaze, although the poverty, illness and death that marked its streets worked as a counterpoint and early source of transmitting guilt. Shortly afterwards, the underlying hell was unleashed with the outbreak of the Sino-Japanese War, opening up a linked sequence of horrors which continued with the Second World War and the internment of the British settlers—including the Ballard family—in prison camps. From March 1943 to August 1945, the Ballards were confined to the Lunghua Camp, where the future writer found a sort of private and perverted Arcadia, a gated mirage of tranquillity in the midst of the desolation and chaos of war. Towards the end of this anomalous initiation phase, the white light of the atomic bomb—which was to become part of the agreed mythologies of the 20th century as a synonym of the horror—was interpreted by the young Ballard as a sign of liberation.

Four years after the bomb was dropped, Ballard was studying medicine at Cambridge University. He was yet to become a writer but, when he looked back over his career in *Miracles of Life*, he realised that he had found his poetics at this stage: "Now, in 1949, only a few years later, I was dissecting dead human beings, paring back the layers of skin and fat to reach the muscles below, then separating these to reveal the nerves and blood vessels. In a way I was conducting my own autopsy on all those dead Chinese I had seen lying by the roadside as I set off for school. I was carrying out a kind of emotional and even moral investigation into my own past while discovering the vast and mysterious world of the human body." Herein lies the key to understanding why Ballard is a poet who writes like a forensic scientist. Someone who remembers, narrates and weaves together a fiction like someone performing an autopsy on themselves. Or the autopsy of what is still to come: he has been able to see our future as a dead body and it has taken him a lifetime (and an entire body of work) to dissect it, to diagnose its diseases and to catalogue even the—seemingly—most unimportant organs.

4. The paradigm of the cult writer, loved by minority groups of readers who were quick to set up something similar to a circle of initiates in a secret society—all of them tourists in perpetuity at the health spas of *Vermilion Sands*. white as a fossil skeleton—Ballard has also experienced one of the clearest forms of glorification that mainstream culture can provide: to see his work adapted as a superproduction directed by the so-called King Midas of Hollywood, Steven Spielberg. We can thank the director of *Empire of the Sun*, the film (1987), for the fact that the name of the author of *Empire of the Sun*, the novel (1984), triggered a spark of recognition among those who had never been—and may never be—Ballardian readers. Nevertheless, the most hardcore faction of Ballardian readers opined that Spielberg's saccharine gaze had softened and devalued the extreme harshness of the original novel. In part—for instance, in the scene when Lunghua becomes almost like a theme park where Jim runs around to the emphatic sounds of John Williams' soundtrack—they were right, but perhaps they should have spotted a fundamental detail: light, one of the aesthetic identifying signs of Spielberg's films, which has traditionally been associated with some kind of mystical or religious epiphany, expanded (or modulated) its meaning in the extraordinary sequence in which young Jim, in Nantao Stadium, which the production design team were able to transform into a purely Ballardian space, thinks he is seeing the flash of the atom bomb. Basically, Spielberg's light, this light that makes us think of God taking a photograph, still meant the same thing—the moment of epiphany — but the Ballard factor revealed its own footnote—its cargo of death and destruction—which redefined it as the foundation of this ambiguous and troubling future which Ballard's works will never cease to explore. Spielberg is perhaps living proof of an irrefutable truth: it is impossible to approach Ballard without being transformed in essence.

Empire of the Sun, the film, is, basically, the perfect opposite of the films Spielberg branded onto the collective imagination between the late 1970s and early 1980s: faced with the conquest of an Arcadia of immaturity through the precise handling of a sense of wonder, *Empire of the Sun* talks of the premature, traumatic death of the inner child, of the early entry into adulthood by the Jim who was to become Ballard. Until then, the children in Spielberg's films had represented the spectacular form of our own inner child, but Christian Bale in *Empire of the Sun* brought about the extreme transgression of the archetype: he is the one who buries his inner child with his own hands, while still a child. The metaphor becomes explicit in the scene which, in Ballard's own words in *Miracles of Life*, condenses the essence of his novel: the attempt at resurrecting the dead kamikaze pilot who, for a few seconds, becomes the corpse of the child Jim once was. It is one of the two scenes in *Empire of the Sun* which make it clear that Spielberg's film is basically about the birth of a writer.

The other is perhaps the best known and most often quoted scene in the entire film, the one in which Spielberg saw the film he was going to (and wanted to) make: young Jim being dazzled by the Mustangs bombing Lunghua Camp. At the end of the scene, Dr Rawlins—who is called Dr Ransome in the original novel—rescues Jim from the roof. Jim starts talking to him in a highly emotional and excited state about the landing strip being paved with the bones of the prisoners. The same landing strip which could also have been paved with Jim and Dr Rawlin's bones, had things worked out differently. The doctor grabs his arm and shouts at him "Try not to think so much! Don't think so much!" There are two possible definitions of a writer. Or at least of the writer Ballard: a) someone who has been condemned to think too much, not to look at reality without interpreting it, without getting right to the bottom of it; b) someone who strives to bring something dead, something that has been lost, back to life. Even though what has died or been lost is, in fact, oneself. Or one of the forms of oneself.

5. Ballard's writing, which some—with a certain degree of short-sightedness—have defined as functional, has its own canonical form—something like the buzzing, the background noise which the characters in Ingmar Bergman's *The Serpent's Egg* (1977) listen to but are not aware of; a canonical form which, at times, has released eruptions of baroque, bejewelled and sensory lava—*The Crystal World* (1966) was the paradigm of this—and, in other cases, has become fractured through the effect of inner earthquakes of a considerable scale. The most severe of these earthquakes is the one that resulted in Ballard's most radical and insular work: *The Atrocity Exhibition* (1969), a collection of short stories or an atomised novel, which was paginated and printed at the exact moment when it burst onto the scene—a constantly exploding book—or a set of atonal variations on an obsessive theme. The narrative model that is repeated over and over again in the book could be linked to one of the (many) possible readings of a film that fascinated the writer: Alain Resnais' *Last Year at Marienbad* (1961). Some people interpret the elusive narrative of the film, directed by Resnais and written by Robbe-Grillet, under the light of the psychoanalytical mechanics geared to create the emergence of a traumatic event the memory has suppressed: in other words, what happened "last year at Marienbad" between X and A—two characters who, like Ballardian figures, function as numbers on an abstract landscape—may

> *The first true science fiction story, and one I intend to write myself if no one else will, is about a man with amnesia lying on a beach and looking at a rusty bicycle wheel, trying to work out the absolute essence of the relationship between them.*

have been, for instance, a rape which A has tried to forget and which X wants to replay in the form of a therapeutic ritual. This model recurs obsessively in the different chapters of *The Atrocity Exhibition*: a character with a fractured identity—who will keep changing his name in his different manifestations—moves towards the cathartic, ritualistic and spectacular representation of his trauma, between the demiurgic gaze of a mysterious doctor and the magnetisation of what might well be the Ballardian version of the femme fatale in the film noir genre. Just like a film by David Lynch deciphered by Žižek, Ballard's characters always sound like film noir archetypes recycled as functions of the subconscious: passion, which in the classic film noir model usually drives the plot, here becomes a fossil that has seen its meaning eroded in a desert of affection.

In *The Kindness of Women* (1991), the second of Ballard's pseudo-autobiographical—or, if you prefer, falsely autobiographical—books, the author seems to read the adaptation of *Empire of the Sun* in a similar key. This traumatic event, which the writer took 20 years to forget and a few more to remember, was exorcised in the most spectacular way possible: as a Hollywood super-production with the interiors shot near his home in Shepperton, where many of his neighbours at the time were hired as extras. Ballard's life, between his years in Shanghai and the premiere of *Empire of the Sun*, could be the expansion of one of the fragments from *The Atrocity Exhibition*: his entire body of work until then could be read as a sequence of rehearsals leading up to the Grand Final Performance. What remains afterwards is the Real which, at that moment, has already become something tremendously Ballardian: the cycle that opens with *Running Wild* (1988) and closes with *Kingdom Come* (2006), a guided tour of the landscapes of contemporaneity that bring about that death in life that is an invitation—a provocation—to a traumatic awakening.

6. Ballard states that the protagonist of *Empire of the Sun* is perhaps his most sophisticated literary invention. Jim is and isn't Ballard, in the same way that Ballard is and isn't the homonym of the Ballard who is the main character in his novel *Crash* (1973), just as Ballard is and isn't Travis, Talbot, Traven, Talbert, etcetera... in *The Atrocity Exhibition* Ballard's work is a succession of masks culminating in the sober, moving and anti-climatic nakedness of *Miracles of Life*: its pages make us aware, once and for all, that there was invention in *Empire of the Sun* and *The Kindness of Women*, but we confirm that the psychological and literary truth of both works is completely safe. *Miracles of Life* doesn't contain scandalous revelations, or excessive digressions with regard to what we already knew: the important thing, as always, is in the details, in the subtle variations and in the way the gaps are finally filled and all the pieces fit together. The Ballardian reader who is writing this text was, at any rate, surprised at the keenness of the burgeoning young writer Ballard to provide a new voice, to forge his own style, to avoid the tautology of what has already been said. From the very outset, nothing has been done by chance. Ballard's singularity isn't the result of chance, but of a painstaking search, of his connection to the responsibility of the writer to the spirit of his age.

Martin Amis associated the cautiousness with which some Ballardian readers received the (supposed) change in register of *Empire of the Sun* with the disappointment the public would feel if a magician revealed the machinery behind his tricks. The novel revealed that some recurrent images in Ballard's imagination—empty swimming pools, abandoned hotels, desolate landscapes, planes—had their origins in experience: nevertheless, the magician who reveals his tricks would be unable to explain fully the meaning (or meanings) inherent to these images as they emerge from the darkness of the subconscious. The interesting thing about Ballard's work is the way in which everything always looks the same, to reveal itself in the end as different: the meanings are modulated, twisted, mutating... in short, only their appearance and rhythms are enriched in their perpetual, languid and indolent movement.

In "Myths of the Near Future" (1982), the story that opens the anthology of the same name, Ballard seems to propose a summa of Ballardian motifs: there is, for instance, the recurrent post-noir triangle formed by the Ballardian anti-hero, the wicked doctor and the enigmatic woman, as well as by the empty swimming pools, an abandoned Cape Canaveral, the strange geometries of desire abandoned by passion, the flying devices, the dead astronauts, the lysergic visions, the unruly vegetation, the exotic birds, the phosphorescent night club... On the one hand, Ballard's literature is the writer's long negotiation with his own founding trauma: with his own premature death. On the other, Ballard's literature is also the gradual recycling of images, motifs, themes and symbols which he has been able to draw from his own well of trauma in order to put together, as the title of the story underlines, a universal mythology for the imminent future: that moment when we will close all the doors to the outside world in order to devote ourselves, with a psychopathic zeal, to the inner tourism on the landscape of our obsessions. In other words, the (future) moment when our (present) death will become clear.

When Ballard closes his case (so to speak) by attending the premiere of *Empire of the Sun*, he sees —to put it in Monterrosian terms—that the dinosaur is still there. Or that reality has caught up with his imagination. Deep down, everything had been there from the very beginning: the gated communities in *Running Wild*, *Cocaine Nights* (1996), *Super-Cannes* (2000), *Millennium People* (2003) and *Kingdom Come* (2006) are the echo of that British colony in Shanghai encapsulated in its social rituals, cocktail parties and games of golf, completely removed from the background noise of Shanghai, from its dazzling lights at night, and the horrors of the poverty in its streets. A mirage of order, peace and civilisation that will be reproduced, by other means, in the Lunghua Camp, with its paths named after streets in London, and its signs mimicking the logotype of the Underground network.

The Lunghua Camp survivors took exception to the book *Empire of the Sun*: according to them, the routine they managed to establish inside the camp—which included an educational plan, theatre performances, sporting activities and other echoes of life in peacetime—bore witness to the strength of this community which was able to rebuild itself in adverse conditions. To their mind, Ballard's way of looking at these years applied a veneer of alarmism

> *The imagination according to Ballard is the source of redemption and transcendence— what makes us fly— but it also contains the dangers of obsession and self-destruction— what absorbs our identity and reduces it to nothing.*

which bore no resemblance to the reality. Perhaps something else happened: inside this limbo (this gated community of codes, rituals and ordered behaviour), young Jim encountered another possible world, his private universe, his "Enormous Space," peopled with pilots in flames, wanderings through the undergrowth and panoramic vistas of the underlying landscape of the fight to stay alive, and human misery. Once again, Ballard saw the profound structure of the thing. In a by no means literal, but probably revelatory, sense, the young JG Ballard was to the Lunghua Camp what the tennis player Bobby Crawford is to the Marbella resort town of Estrella de Mar in *Cocaine Nights*: the one who reveals what lies beneath, the one who activates what nobody wants to see.

7. When the calendar marked the turn of the new millennium, the orthodox readers of science fiction had the childish reaction of feeling they had been conned: of all the things they had been promised, the only one that had become a reality was the ersatz tricorder first seen in *Star Trek* (1966-1969) which we know as the mobile phone. A device which, in the long run, turned out to be much more sophisticated and versatile than the original model. The Ballardian reader, however, knew that this future that had already been conjugated in the present was exactly as the Prophet had told us it would be, right down to the last detail. A future that was more like a film by Antonioni than a space opera, with characters immobilised in a temporary limbo, as if in a pan shot from *Last Year at Marienbad*, while they consider the different geometric possibilities of the dissolution of their identity. Basically, the infinite views of a surrealist landscape, where the fossils of the everyday project the shadow of new calligraphies that are ready to be deciphered. Everything seems quiet in this image of the future: the important thing is in the interior, with these psyches polished by the incessant erosion of a barrage of images in which the assassination of

Kennedy merges with Marilyn Monroe's pubis, and the napalm showers over the Vietnamese jungle, and the enlarged effigy of Mickey Mouse, and the regular orbit of a dead astronaut, and the erotic angles of a crashed car, and the after-effects of a terrorist attack on the sex life of an affluent middle-class family, and the images of boring sitcoms that will conquer outer space while, at the same time, down here, a chosen few can at last feel they are the masters of their no less enigmatic and ungraspable inner space. Ballard once said that the future would be fundamentally boring: a suburb of the soul inhabited by ghosts who have become disconnected from their instincts. The writer has also repeatedly denied that he is a pessimist: utopia is beating in the background of his works, although it might not be pleasant or comfortable. Once again, the interesting thing is inside: in the landscapes of disconnection there continues to exist the overwhelming potential of the imagination, obsessions and psychopathology. In short, the parallel universe of unlimited possibility which, of course, also has its venomous side.

8. "What our children have to fear is not the cars on the highways of tomorrow but our own pleasure in calculating the most elegant parameters of their deaths," observes Ballard in his introduction to *Crash*. In this text, the author articulates another possible poetic form, developing some of his postulates which are already present in his important founding essay "Which Way to Inner Space?" published in the magazine *New Worlds* in 1962. In it, Ballard confronts the members of his tribe—science-fiction writers—advocating a generic model open to experimentation, and focusing on the immense speculative possibilities of subjectivity: "The first true science fiction story, and one I intend to write myself if no one else will, is about a man with amnesia lying on a beach and looking at a rusty bicycle wheel, trying to work out the absolute essence of the relationship between them." This story suggested by Ballard could have become "The Terminal Beach" (1964), an important point of inflection in his career and the first (successful) essay of his career based on this aesthetic of fragmentation which is sublimated in *The Atrocity Exhibition*, *Crash* and many short stories written afterwards.

In the introduction to *Crash*, Ballard is no longer affirming himself in the face of the philotechnological trends of current science fiction, but he wishes to restore science fiction as the central discourse in a literary context that must free itself from the inheritance of 19th-century literature in order to face up to the demands of the 20th century, with all the consequences this entails. Ballard tries to deal with one of a writer's most onerous responsibilities: to find the voice of his era. And his era is, precisely, the most problematic of territories: a place where fiction has poisoned everything and the novel (or fiction) has no other way out other than to become the only space of reality.

The dizzying leap that realising this entails and, to a great extent, resolving it, bears out Ballard's true importance in the context of 20th-century culture and, by extension, the turn of the millennium. With *The Atrocity Exhibition* and *Crash*, Ballard shapes the voice of his era and, inevitably, a sort of literature of the boundary which reveals the impossibility of going any further. Ballard's career could be read as the trajectory in a straight line towards the radical disintegration expressed in *The Atrocity Exhibition* and *Crash*, followed by a fascinating corollary of variations and revelations designed so that the Ballardian reader will gain a deep understanding of all the meanings and implications of the journey.

The tandem formed by *The Atrocity Exhibition* and *Crash* also attests to the fact that some of the inherited concepts used to assess his work are no longer valid. It is surprising that, at the end of the introduction to *Crash*, Ballard underlines the fact that "the ultimate role of *Crash* is cautionary", because, as the sentence which opens this section allows us to understand, morals are no longer useful in order to decipher the spiritual state which these novels take us to. In the world described by these works, logic has supplanted morals and, at the same time, it becomes clear that this logic is new, it isn't the one we once knew, maybe because, until that time, the logic had always been subordinate to morals.

Ballard's literature reveals that there exists a logic which moves in the opposite way to the one that has articulated our knowledge until now: this is why, everything that appears in his fiction takes on a Ballardian meaning that cancels its previous significance passed on by tradition. It is an irresoluble question to decide if Ballard is a moralist or just perverse: the only certainty is the ambiguity, and a good example of this are the subtle variations—applied, for instance, to something as important as the ideological context—which the same template of conflict in Ballard's most recent novels is subject to. However, neither morals nor ideology are the right instruments for approaching Ballard. Anyone who reads his early novels about disasters and tends to believe that the writer predicted, in a poetic key, climate change, has not yet found the right key in order to enter the Ballardian sphere: ecology is a concept that cannot be applied to inner space.

The author uses the extreme metaphor as the instrument whereby his literature can take us to that (a)moral territory where we would never go, following the dictates of our reason, although, without us knowing it, we are already submerged in this territory. Ballard definitively conquers this spiritual sphere announced by the Compte de Lautréamont when he suggested introducing prostitution into the family home. De Lautréamont's fantastical vision needs to find in Ballard its geometry in order to show itself to be truly effective. Logic is the only strategy that can bring each extreme metaphor to a satisfactory conclusion.

This is the secret of Ballard: the primitivisation of the sophisticated building in *High-Rise* (1975) is true to life, because, at no time has he strayed from his own logical guidelines, such as the passage from *Concrete Island* (1974), a traffic island cut off from the rest of the world by the road network, to the limitless landscape which the protagonist will travel on the back of an animalised giant… If the only possible reality which demands to be turned into literature, here and now, is inside us—the world of our imagination, dreams, obsessions and psychopathologies—only the particular logic of each subjective landscape can provide the right road map in order to travel it.

There is a stunning novel by Ballard which translates all these codes into the universal language of the adventure story: *Hello, America* (1981), a western, pure and simple, which, in reality, is a western in reverse. The adventure no longer lies in the discovery and conquest of virgin territory, but in the rediscovery of a culture in ruins, formulated as an inner landscape. The geography has mutated in order to adjust to the new parameters: the desert begins in New York and the road ends in the leafy jungles of Las Vegas, which are so similar to the destination in *Heart of Darkness* (1899).

9. When Ballard had written his first novel—which, in fact, it wasn't: he wrote *The Wind from Nowhere* (1961) before but has made every effort to forget about it—his publisher Victor Gollancz took him out for lunch and rewarded him with one of those double-edged compliments that would lower the self-esteem of any budding author: "It's an interesting novel, *The Drowned World*. But of course, you've stolen it all from Conrad." Ballard hadn't read Conrad at the time, but he soon filled the gap and saw in this long journey from Marlow to Kurtz the pattern that could govern the movement of every Ballardian (anti)hero: always heading upstream, on course for destruction or horror, or self-knowledge. After *Empire of the Sun*, the novel that revealed the secret driving force behind his fictions, which widened his readership and opened the doors of literary recognition to him, Ballard wrote *The Day of Creation* (1987), one of his strangest, most unfathomable books, almost like a mirror image of *Heart of Darkness* in the key of metaliterary self-exploration. The central character in *The Day of Creation*, Dr Mallory, believes he is responsible for the birth of a river—a third Nile—which could reshape the surrounding landscape. Mallory embarks on a delirious odyssey in search of the source of the river, and becomes caught up in the confrontations between two rival factions in a local war: in the end, the last drops of this figment of his imagination dry up in his hands, heralding the final triumph of the desert. The Ballardian reader soon realises that *The Day of Creation* is a book about the act of writing, about the potential for madness and self-destruction inherent in the act of creating, about the tragedy of tracing and taming the fruits of our imagination. Its denouement may talk about the inevitable exhaustion of every creative source: Ballard makes out the death certificate of his own imagination and prepares the Ballardian reader for the culmination of the discourse in the territories of the real. In the end, the wonderful creator of metaphors used to explain our era, creates the twilight metaphor of himself.

Ballard as a metaphor is also the core subject of a previous novel, whose title echoes self-definition in a corporate key: *The Unlimited Dream Company*

(1979), another mysterious interlude on the road, between the steel and cement phase and before the off-course excursion *Hello, America*. In *The Unlimited Dream Company*, the main character, Blake, crashes a stolen plane into the waters of the Thames, by the riverbank near Shepperton, and emerges from the water like a lubricious, pan-sexual Messiah, who can fertilise the vegetation with his own sperm and teach all the inhabitants in the neighbourhood to fly. *The Unlimited Dream Company* is a sort of perverse gospel, which describes the passion, death and resurrection—not necessarily in that order—of an apostle of the febrile imagination who seeks to be deciphered as an extreme metaphor of Ballard himself. *The Unlimited Dream Company* is the shining face of *The Day of Creation*: both novels in which the author invents himself, providing substantial keys in order to understand the beneficial (and terrible) properties of his literature and, by extension, of literature. The imagination according to Ballard is the source of redemption and transcendence—what makes us fly—but it also contains the dangers of obsession and self-destruction—what absorbs our identity and reduces it to nothing.

10. A car explodes inside the Guggenheim Museum in New York and multiplies into successive forms of itself, which rise up through the central atrium of the rotunda to the top floor. That was the spectacular welcome the exhibition *I Want to Believe*, by the Chinese artist Cai Guo-Qiang, gives to the visitor: one of the many Ballardian traits that anyone could detect in lands which are not necessarily aware that our era has been lucky enough to have had someone like Ballard, who embodies a sensitivity and a gaze that are in a permanent viral expansion. The Ballardian reader who is writing this text doesn't know if Cai Guo-Qiang has ever read Ballard, but he has no doubt that opening an exhibition which freezes the explosion of a car in space and time is something unequivocally Ballardian.

Likewise, Cai Guo-Qiang's theory, which interprets the archetype of a suicide bomber as a ready-made artist, or his paintings which bear the traces of burnt-out gunpowder, or the huge, unfeasible projects which dream of drawing a Wall of China in flames on the surface of the Moon on a night when there is an eclipse, or digging an inverted pyramid out of the lunar surface which, while it is orbiting the Earth, will align itself perfectly with the angles of the Pyramid of Giza.

When Ballard wrote in *The Atrocity Exhibition* that "in the post-Warhol era a single gesture such as uncrossing one's legs will have more significance than all the pages in *War and Peace*" he was also intuiting the sensitivity which, many years later, would crystallise in this Louis Vuitton boutique placed in the middle of the exhibition the Brooklyn Museum devoted to the Japanese artist Takeshi Murakami. While some sectors of the press were being scandalised at Murakami's witty exhibit—which was nothing more than the inevitable corollary of Warholian logic—the London Barbican was bringing together a selection of contemporary artworks following the also highly Ballardian criteria of applying the linking thread of the anthropological gaze of a hypothetical extraterrestrial civilisation.

In a scene from *High-Rise*, Ballard describes a female character with varying levels of dishevelment in her physical appearance, "as if she were preparing parts of her body for some gala to which the rest of herself had not been invited."

To a certain degree, all of us, Ballardian readers or those who have never been (or ever will be), are as unsuitably attired as this character is to attend the night-time gala that is the future (or, already, the present) according to Ballard. This is why we tend to think, with a clear margin of error, that our world is becoming increasingly Ballardian, that reality is taking on the forms of a fiction imagined by Ballard. And we don't want to realise that the answer has always been there: it isn't life that imitates Ballard, but Ballard who has had the gift of seeing life as it was going to be. As it already is. As it was already written on the body of that dead child he left buried in Shanghai.

In other words: the only person who is dressed appropriately for the occasion is this quiet gentleman, who lives in Shepperton, who, for a long time now, has been waiting for us in the doorway to the future, slowly savouring a glass of whisky with ice, telling us with his dry humour what was going on inside at the party, with the calm and assuredness of someone who knows that, sooner or later, we will all get there, because, as Criswell would say, the future is where you and I are going to spend the rest of our lives.

ANA BARRADO
Gas pump after Hurricane Andrew, Tamiami Airport, 1992

JG Ballard: A Few Brief Queries (Interview)

by Samuel Francis

In the spring of 2005 I was midway through writing a PhD thesis at the University of Leeds under the lofty title *A Critical Reading of "Inner Space" in Selected Works of JG Ballard*. I was trying to examine how far Ballard's novels published between 1962 and 1979 fulfilled the exploration of "inner space, not outer" trumpeted in his well-known *New Worlds* manifesto of 1962. At my supervisor's prompting, I wrote to Ballard requesting an interview and he kindly agreed to answer me five questions by post on 13 April 2005.

Responses to my five questions duly came back written in longhand on two sheets of letter paper headed with Ballard's Shepperton address, still my most prized possession. My thank-you notes to Ballard were scribbled on a couple of Salvador Dalí postcards which my girlfriend at the time had brought me back from abroad, which annoyed her. This was to be my only personal contact with Ballard with the exception of a brief, mawkish and unanswered thank-you missive I dispatched to his address upon hearing of his fatal illness.

Ballard's response to being asked about "inner space" alludes to the central place of Surrealism and psychoanalysis in his creative methodology, but is more interesting for the way in which it negates any more solipsistic interest in the idea of "inner space" by emphasising that space as a space of mutual contamination between subjective and objective realities. As Ballard's reference to the projection of psychic contents into the external world makes clear, 'inner space' in his conception is an uncanny space in the Freudian sense, where distinctions between the real and the imagined break down; it is specifically associated with sites and experiences of trauma.

Ballard's representations of consciousness also open themselves up to other contexts than the theoretical-psychological, however. Notwithstanding Professor Roger Luckhurst's useful attempt to decentre previous trends in Ballard criticism which he saw as fusing a variety of distinct theoretical frameworks into a blurred quasi-religious haze, the element of mystical feeling in Ballard's work exists, being confirmed (if we're allowed recourse to the opinion of the author) quite explicitly by Ballard's allusion to his own paradoxical strand of "scientific mysticism" in his autobiography *Miracles of Life*. Ballard makes a similar confirmation here at a date between the publications of *Millennium People* and *Kingdom Come*, emphasising the importance of mystical self-dissolution in the same early novels which provoked the question's focus on death as transcendence.

Ballard's response to being quizzed about controversial psychiatrist R.D. Laing is interesting—indeed it almost seems disingenuous given the strong connections I felt I'd excavated between Laing, *Concrete Island*, and *High-Rise*, and given Ballard's persistent experimentation with his conception of 'psychopathology as freedom' and his creation of Byronic, charismatic maniacs from Vaughan in *Crash* to *Cocaine Nights'* Bobby Crawford. Is this something of a made-over Ballardian take on Laing the champion of schizophrenia as psychic breakthrough for the more neurophysiologically-minded noughties? Ballard himself elsewhere put his hands up to a similar tendency to mythologise himself to that which he here rightly attributes to Laing and Blair—indeed, one of the most insightful dimensions of his psychoanalytically-inspired project is the way he makes clear how we all routinely fantasise and mythologise ourselves into existence.

In a related sense, I was fascinated at this time by Ballard's ability to fuse inner and outer space, to show us how elements of psychic life (aggression, daydream, sexual fantasy), can leak into and give shape our external world, so that (in hyperbolic Ballardian mode) the machined concrete planes of motorway and airport landscapes might be considered manifestations of profound erotic longings or the metallic reality of a screaming police car be refigured as the mere reflection of a neural interval.

Ballard's Surrealist war-cry "Who needs real life?" continues his tendency to insist on what Jung called the psychoid nature of reality, the fundamental Moebian inter-permeability of mental and physical planes. His championing of imagination's power to re-enchant and sacralise the most quotidian realities remains an inspiration. However, the according of equal status to physical solidity and personal fantasy promulgated here is probably best done from a position of mature sanity I myself had yet to attain while immersing myself in these fascinating conceptualisations. There's probably a reason why our nervous system shows us our world as it does…

Ballard's response to my final question baffled me for ages. I still don't understand it. I think I came closer to understanding it as I read deeper in Freud and came across the idea of the screen memory or the psychotic hallucination as compromise-formations, illusory constructions thrown up to bridge intolerable fractures in the coherence of one's sense of identity.

In a similar way, here, Ballard's gloss on Nathan's comment links it back to the desperate rearrangements of reality by the protagonists of *The Atrocity Exhibition* on which Nathan comments throughout that book. Just as Travis, Travers *et al.* create tableaux of burning motorcades, bruised flesh and synthetic plastic to assuage their own nuclear-age traumas, so we all create compromise-formations, more or less physically real, which impose coherence for us upon experience, make us whole. Ballard's equation of image and reality becomes less paradoxical if one considers the sense in which an image of reality is literally all we have (neurological constructs, etc.)… This could lead us in a frightening direction, towards the sense that all life is an illusion, but equally it could lead us to a more empowering sense, hinted at by Ballard here, in which the fictive basis of our image of reality frees us up to make adjustments, to rearrange and reorganise our narratives of ourselves into something that makes sense to us. Across the body of Ballard's fiction and particularly in his more autobiographical writing, there's a sense that he's moving from one of these extremes to another, from the disorientation and loss of his youthful dispossessions (internment-camp prisoner, immigrant in his own mother-country…) to the assured self-definitions and narrative reorganisations of his masterful life-fictions.

Enough already. Let the great man speak. Enjoy.

J. G. BALLARD
36, OLD CHARLTON ROAD
SHEPPERTON
MIDDLESEX
TW17 8AT

TEL: WALTON-ON-THAMES
225692

13/4/05

Dear Mr Francis, Happy to answer your questions — I'll be fairly brief, since I don't want to walk too heavily on the green before your own print arrives on it, but I hope this helps.

1) Inner Space — I meant the invented space that you see in dreams and surrealist paintings in particular, but also in highly dislocated realities such as war zones, sites of plane crashes, earthquake aftermaths, derelict buildings, where the observer imposes his own fears, dreams, phobias — I think inner space so defined is present to some extent in my later novels.

2) Tendency towards mysticism? I hope so. There is a very strong quasi-mystical strand in my early fiction, from Drowned World to Unlimited Dream Co., but there are strands in Empire of the Sun. Probably it all goes

back to my wartime childhood. Part Stockholm syndrome (if you love your executioners they won't kill you) part attempt to make sense of the meaningless (to kill Kennedy again, but in a way that makes sense). I imagine this underpins all my writing. Of course, unconsciously we all fear death and devise strategies to deal with that fear. Needless to say, death doesn't wait any longer for us however much we learn to love him.

3) I have very mixed feelings about Laing. Like Freud, was he really a novelist? He saw mental breakdown and madness as romantic adventures, a very literary take on the human wrecks you find in real insane asylums, surrounded by desperate + exhausted relatives. Contemporary psychiatry tends to reject Laing's notion of family-generated illness, in favour of chemical imbalance explanations. "R.D. Laing" was his own greatest creation. Watching

his lecture, I felt that he was continually mythologising himself (rather like Tony Blair).

4) Who needs real life? I'm interested in the imagination, in enlarging our consciousness and awareness of the everyday so that the most mundane things become rich and strange. Existence is a complete mystery, probably an insoluble one, and a stone in the road has no greater claim to be real than my fantasy that Julius Caesar may have held it in his hand (he first crossed the Thames at Shepperton). Reality anyway is as much an artificial construct as anything else, constructed very convincingly by our central nervous system.

5) Yes. In his slightly pompous way,

Dr Nathan is usually right — I'm glad you cited Atrocity Exhibition, my forgotten book, though the Research group in San Francisco has helped to keep it alive. The point I tried to make there, and in much of my fiction as well, is that we can't accept the authority of the real and assume that the world will arrange itself for us in ways that will make sense. Quite the opposite. We need to reorganise and rearrange reality to reflect the inner meaning of our lives.

Best wishes,

JGBallard

Francis: To what degree do you feel that the preoccupation with 'inner space' which you stated at the beginning of your career as a writer has remained a constant theme throughout your work?

Ballard: Inner space—I meant the invented space that you see in dreams and surrealist paintings in particular, but also in highly dislocated realities such as war zones, sites of plane crashes, earthquake aftermaths, derelict buildings, where the observer imposes his own fears, dreams, phobias—I think inner space so defined is present to some extent in my later novels.

Francis: Many of your novels (particularly the early ones) seem to rehearse a paradoxical dynamic whereby the protagonist enacts a movement towards imaginary or imaginative fulfilment or transcendence which is simultaneously a movement towards death and dissolution. Freud's work on the interdependence of Eros and Thanatos seems an obvious point of reference here. Would it also be fair to associate this dynamic with what might be seen as a tendency towards mysticism in your work, in the sense that the mystic aspires to the dissolution of the self and unification with the one ultimate reality of the wider universe?

Ballard: Tendency towards mysticism? I hope so. There's a very-strong quasi-mystical strand in my early fiction, from *Drowned World* to *Unlimited Dream Co.*, but there are strains in *Empire of the Sun*. Probably it all goes back to my wartime childhood. Part Stockholm syndrome (if you love your executioners they won't kill you), part attempt to make sense of the meaningless (to kill Kennedy again, but in a way that makes sense). I imagine this underpins all my writing. Of course, unconsciously we all fear death and devise stratagems to deal with that fear. Needless to say, death doesn't wait any longer for us however much we learn to love him.

Francis: I have been very interested by the apparent sympathy between your work and that of RD Laing. In particular the characters in your novels of the early 1970s seem reminiscent of Laing's description of the schizoid individual, in that they enact withdrawals into private, solipsistic imaginative worlds. Would you care to comment on your encounter with RD Laing's work?

Ballard: I have very mixed feelings about Laing. Like Freud, was he really a novelist? He saw mental breakdown and madness as romantic adventures, a very literary take on the human wrecks you find in real insane asylums, surrounded by desperate and exhausted relatives. Contemporary psychiatry tends to reject Laing's notion of family-generated illness, in favour of chemical imbalance explanations. "RD Laing" was his own greatest creation. Watching him lecture, I felt that he was continually mythologising himself (rather like Tony Blair).

Francis: Your work tends to embrace a Freudian or surrealist sense of the irrational as in some way more deeply real and true than the rational. From a real-life perspective this seems a potentially harmful standpoint to take in many ways…

Ballard: Who needs real life? I'm interested in the imagination, in enlarging our consciousness and awareness of the everyday so that the most mundane things become rich and strange. Existence is a complete mystery, probably an insoluble one, and a stone in the road has no greater claim to be real than my fantasy that Julius Caesar once held it in his hand (he first crossed the Thames at Shepperton). Reality anyway is as much an artificial construct as anything else, constructed very convincingly by our central nervous systems.

Francis: Image—in the sense both of the visual image and of the imaginary—seems to be an absolutely fundamental keystone of your work (I'm thinking, of course, of your extensive use of art and other visual sources). At one point in *The Atrocity Exhibition* you even have Doctor Nathan assert that where images are born 'some kind of valid reality begins to assert itself'. Is this paradoxical equation of image and reality something you would stand by?

Ballard: Yes. In his slightly pompous way, Dr. Nathan is usually right—I'm glad you cited *Atrocity Exhibition*, my forgotten book, though the Re/Search firm in San Francisco has helped to keep it alive. The point I tried to make there, and in much of my fiction as well, is that we can't accept the authority of the real and assume that the world will arrange itself for us in ways which will make sense. Quite the opposite. We need to reorganise and rearrange reality to reflect the inner meaning of our lives.

The Impossibility Exhibition

by Paul A Green

ARTISTE

As Jacqueline Mayakovski deftly tacked up yet another rectangle of daubed sugar paper, Dr. Greenhaus speculated idly. Why was this mysterious girl in the paint-stained smock continually putting up these delinquents' paintings, day after day, as if to cover every surface in the building? Perhaps she found this display of motor skills compulsive, yet therapeutic. More likely she was an amnesiac performance artist, stranded

in the school long after the expiry of her corporate sponsorship, and now unable ever to face her journey home across the reptile-infested subways of the ruined city. She was smiling enigmatically, like the sun-faded clipping of Brigitte Bardot he'd found pasted inside a staff-room locker; and her lips flickered, as if in synchronisation with some fleeting subliminal impulse. But her comment was drowned in the roar of a Sea King landing in the playground outside, bringing in another contingent of exhausted riot police and bewildered behavioural dysfunction specialists. Everywhere, they were arriving too late. Their clients, an army of proletarian artistes manques, were fleeing the schools in their thousands. As the helicopter settled, whirling vortices of dust and litter were scattered against the chain-links of the playground perimeter fence.

EXHIBIT 2000

Every morning, after a night of uneasy dreams on the broken staffroom furniture, and token breakfast from a vandalised vending machine, he would try to decode the latent content of these infantile artefacts. Jacqueline Mayakovski continued her silent work throughout the night, like a spectral handmaiden of Delvaux gliding through the marble amphitheatres of sleep. Soon she would have decorated every floor of the nine storey building with the pupils' imagery. He wandered among their abstractions, crude spirals of cerise or magenta hanging like deranged miniature galaxies against the grey rectangular geometries of the dinner-room. Upstairs, the walls outside the biology lab were covered in watercolour surreal pastiches, cryptozoic vegetation sprouting a giant penis with a bow tie, an insect-headed woman with a flaming whip. The landscapes of such primal terrors were presumably beyond the reach of the cadres of psychotherapists and social workers who had once filled the school every day. Indeed, despite his own basic training in psychopathology (a hurried crash-course, before his enforced redeployment to the school) Greenhaus was unable to enter the mindscapes of these remedial-room Dalis and Ernsts. The once-prized doctorate in comparative literature that had hung over his desk at All Souls' was little use to him in his role as supply teacher. He should have taken up that option of Communications Consultant with the Mitsoguchi Corporation, but it was too late now.

MEDIA MASTER

In the English Department stockroom, among the piles of burned books, he found a working TV set. As bands of purple cloud darkened around the silhouettes of the gutted office buildings, Greenhaus watched the Headmaster guesting on an early-evening talkshow. "We are bringing them back into the school system," the Head told the studio audience, "and we shall restart the heart of our nation's classrooms with our pedagogic skills, our curriculum- mapping skills, our pastoral management skills. We are waiting to reclaim our youth any day now. It is not an impossible task..." Greenhaus had not seen a pupil for seventeen days and now only a handful of teachers managed to arrive for the staff meetings and case conferences that had once dominated their working day. Those who survived commuting by armoured bus left well before dusk. Many, like the melancholy Traven or the introverted Koestler, had been kidnapped (or killed) by their ex-pupils, who now owed their loyalties to rival groups of local militia, each flaunting its distinctive style of weaponry and sportswear. Greenhaus heard a footstep in the corridor and instinctively reached for his largactil  gun. Although its last dart had been discharged long ago, he found its presence reassuring. But the presence on the doorway was Jacqueline Mayakovski, who removed her dark glasses and produced a Luger from under her iridescent plastic raincoat. She held it in both hands, like a female investigator in a re-run of The Rockford Files. He could hear the distant throb of the helicopters. "You're always in the way, Dr Greenhaus. I've waited hours to get access to this room for the Exhibition. You're all making it impossible for us." Calmly she fired, into the heart of the TV set. The Headmaster's face imploded.

THE CATALOGUE OF APOCALYPSE

After their encounter in the English stockroom, Greenhaus saw little of Jacqueline Mayakovski in the days that followed. He imagined she held some private territory of her own, perhaps in the art studios on the fourth floor, where she nurtured edible fungi or cultivated luminous crystals. The security staff had finally withdrawn for the duration and there was no one else left to challenge their free movement around the building, or indeed question any aspect of their identity. Greenhaus was more preoccupied with the increasing difficulty of finding food in the roach-infested kitchens and with his ongoing attempt to devise a definitive collection of significant artefacts, his own response to the proliferating collage of pictures that covered the interior walls of the building, his uniquely private view. Patrolling the site and picking up litter had always been one of his regular academic duties. Now it was imperative for his psychic survival, a perverse archeology of the future. As he discovered the objects he assembled them in one of the English Department classrooms and spread them across the empty desks, visual aids for a object lesson in his own increasingly fissile consciousness. At the end of the day he itemised them in an old register:

• Fourth-year worksheets on AIDS with bar charts on the spread of HIV infection and comprehension passage on the symptomatic presentation of Kaposi's sarcoma.

• Video cassette of *The Slow Learning*, presumably a tape used in teacher training.
• Broken surveillance camera, torn from the lobby in a recent incident with intruders.
• Torn copy of *Sunday Sport*, headline: "Schoolgirls' six-in-a-bed sex romp with Sir!".
• Life-size papier-mâché effigy of Salman Rushdie, with pins protruding and extensive scorch-marks, made by Wahidur Ali.
• Star 'Vaders pocket electronic game— "Destroy Earth in order to save it!"
• Audio cassette—"Chaos Pathworking Tape—gives keys and formulae for tapping into Voidflow of Infinite Potential…"
• Polaroid snap of Jacqueline Mayakovski, in deep trance, scraping particles of clay off a potter's wheel, possibly a promotional photo for the school's creative arts course, more likely part of the documentation of a long-term time-based art activity.
• Broken twelve-inch single: *Style Assessment* by the Quantum Brothers—the Terminal (Death House) Mix.
• EEG records of staff alpha and theta rhythms in simulated stress situations.
• Tissue samples, in vitro, labelled "Left hemisphere, Wernicke's area, a typical fourteen-year-old."
• Designs for cosmetically effective "client-friendly" CS gasmasks, abandoned, for budgetary reasons, at the testing stage.
• Confidential minutes of a staff disciplinary hearing: "Dr. G's mood-swings giving rise to profound anxieties at the pastoral/pupil interface level."

RED ALERT

The classroom was empty, like a drained swimming-pool. However, although the effort of scouring the overturned filing-cabinets in the Headmaster's office had exhausted Greenhaus, he still stood for a full fifty-five minutes at the front of the darkening room, shouting at the overturned chairs and tables, as if trying to admonish a gang of escaping poltergeists. Despite himself, it was impossible to stop his anxiety ritual of teaching. The rigid templates of the timetable had been etched into his fragile spinal geometry over years, maybe decades, in the industry. His neural warning systems had been on full alert for so long that he could not remember a time when he hadn't spent most of his waking hours pre-empting hostile missile attacks or intervening in minor tribal conflicts. The blank cuboid geometry of the room, its insolent void of wired glass and grubby melamine, might , even now, conceal some vindictive prank learned from Ulster or Vietnam, a sticky membrane of Semtex under a pile of folders, a poisoned thumb-tack on the teacher's chair. He groped for the edge of the graffiti-gouged chalkboard, his pitted lips twitching, his arms waving in the familiar rhythms of exhortation and rebuke, his ears already roaring with the white noise of rioting adolescent mobs, his vision a reddish mist of primal fury. It was his responsibility to preserve world peace. But this was a crisis of the cerebellum, the deep brain, the saurian guardian of his most secret uterine territories, the Mezozoic realms of his Id. His adrenalin overload would rush him down the time-corridors to press the red button, to unleash the purifying radiation of his submerged megatons, those ultimate global peacemakers, which alone could bring him the primaeval silence he craved, the infinite silence of archeopsychic time. That would teach them a lesson.

MADONNA OF THE SUBURBS
When, hours later, he awoke from the sudden fugue, he found himself sprawled on the floor, hands around the charred throat of the Rushdie effigy, which was already crumbling into fragments like a ravaged mummy. The firedrill alarm was still buzzing, a high-pitched sine-wave undulating as monotonously as a line of man-made concrete dunes on a weapons-testing range. Jacqueline Mayakovski stood over him with a cup of black coffee and an apple. Her long iridescent coat hung from her shoulders like the plumage of an exotic bird. "You're getting carried away again, Dr. Greenhaus." She knelt and studied the sutures of his skull with clinical calm. "These fantasies of cosmic destruction and re-creation are all in your head." She had the bright but firm manner of a young mother confronting a wayward toddler in its first Freudian excesses. "You're suffering from iconic over-dose, Doctor. It's just one of the symptoms. If you'd had to study those children's pictures for months on end, as I have, you might begin to understand the whole syndrome. You'd better hurry up, before I start taking the exhibition down." She raised the coffee cup to his lips and glided away. He could imagine her now as a housewife in the lost paradises of the leafy suburbs, guiding anima of Botticellian garden-parties, an enigmatic madonna smiling down from the balconies of memory.

THE TERMINAL REPORTS

In the evenings, as he sat in the physics labs on the sixth floor, the signals from hundreds of orbiting TV satellites penetrating every tissue of his body, Greenhaus was sometimes tempted to pick up his infra-red binoculars and scan the tower blocks on the far side of the motorway. He hoped to see someone watching alien porn, some ghostly conjunction of limbs as distant and implausible as the docking of Iraqi and Iranian space modules. But tonight, as every night, he only glimpsed the dark outline of satellite dishes, tiny excrescent fungi sprouting above blank windows and empty walkways. Soon he was overcome by his other obsessive urge, to complete his terminal reports, a task as huge (and seemingly futile) as Jacqueline Mayakovski's exhibition, curated for pupils and parents who had long ago turned their backs on the static hand-made artefact to participate in the ever-shifting continuum of an exploding electronic universe. A few lights flickered in the towers, like cave-fires in a cliff-face of the night. He tried to ignore their allure as he thumbed through the interleaved carbons of the report forms and attempted to find convincing formulae to explain the increasing inability of the species to educate its offspring. "Lack of attention..violently disruptive behaviour... an habitual non-attender..."—the ready-made phrases in boxes, designed for faster ticking and a rationalised assessment procedure, no longer made sense, for clients whose hyper-fast senses were unsystematically deranged. They had long since taken the extra-mural option. The rumble of distant explosions and the distorted blare of sound systems on the night wind disturbed his concentration. The actual topology of the laboratory, its cage-like enclosure of space, was contracting around him, as if the gravity of his presence was warping the flickering fluorescent light. He had to move from this constricting spatio-temporal matrix. As he left, in search of Jacqueline Mayakovski and her Sybilline folios, he tossed the report forms into a wastebin and added a lighted match.

THE IMPOSSIBILITY EXHIBITION

"You see, Doctor, the pictures regress as the pupils get older." Jacqueline Mayakovski sat among the Rousseauesque jungle of her potted plants and sifted through the piles of pictures. "Here is a standard third-year fantasy." She pointed to one of the pseudo-surrealist gouaches that Greenhaus had noticed outside the Life Science room. In a burning desert, under orange skies, a squat, headless, earth-coloured hermaphrodite was being eaten by a robotic crustacean. The picture was entitled "Deathworld—James Tallis 3B." "That's just apocalyptic mannerism, I realise," she added, half-apologetically, "but compare it to what last year's fifth year were doing." The wall behind her was papered with torn sheets covered in wild scrawls, gestural spray-gun marks, a demented calligraphy that seemed compelled to cross a given space with as many savage loops and violent intersections as possible, as if that were the only way it could trace and affirm its actuality, in a polymorphous-perverse act of self-obliteration. "It's not just like the territorial death-tags on the subways," she said, with a faint shudder. Greenhaus recalled how travellers sometimes blundered into inner-city free-fire zones, often dying horribly, simply because they couldn't read such sinister tribal glyphs. "This is a unique collection of autographs, by a generation of autists. I'm not an intellectual, Doctor. I'll leave the rest of the explanations to you." She made for the door. He tried to follow, but her sure-footed agility had already taken her up the first turn of the darkened stairwell. His route also went upwards, through the smoke-filled corridors, where he lost her.

TERMINAL EXHIBITIONIST
"An electron," shouted Dr. Greenhaus, to the masses far below, "is a photonic system trapped in a space-time cavity..." Police searchlight beams stabbed the night sky. A rising wind was blowing bitterly up here on the roof of the school and he doubted if the young bodies pressed against the mesh of the playground fence could hear a word. The cheap megaphone was already filtering and processing his utterance, turning him into a mere transient sample in an acid-house mixdown. In any case, he was certain that the crowd had been drawn by huge tongues of flame, now licking the windows of the labs, under the impression this was the work of their peers. They were chanting unintelligibly and surging against the wire, as firemen began to run a hydraulic hoist up the sheer glass side of the building. Policemen with perspex shields glinting in the firelight formed a hollow square around the edge of the playground. A smaller group of officers—marksmen, trained negotiators?—were waving him down. He gripped the side of a ventilation duct and began to hurl textbooks into the darkness; but it was a futile display. It was only a matter of time as to who would get to him first, the kids or the Educational Security forces. Both extrapolations were negative. He had only minutes to finish his exposition.

TIME-WINDOWS (1)

Greenhaus threw away the megaphone and lifted a pocket cassette machine to his lips. Despite the increasing noise and smoke, he was determined to file his last report from the terminal zone. "The students' "paintings" are not merely the expression of anomie or socio-economic malaise. They are the semiotics of a mutant ontology, an autistic withdrawal from the physical constraints of Newtonian time and causality. Faced with the conflicting claims of "reality" and the "virtual reality" of the electronic media landscape, with the bewildering seductions of hyper-possibility, in which even the simplest of our actions creates an unpredictable wave-front of improbability, they are seeking relief in atavism." He crouched on the flat asphalt roof, shouting into the tiny microphone while the great rotors of the Sea King throbbed overhead. "For, as they accelerate along the time-gradient of adolescence towards adulthood, they feel increasingly trapped in the black hole of their own body- identities. The continuum folds back in on them, like the roof of a sabotaged aircraft. Matter itself is a time-trap."

TIME-WINDOWS (2)

As armed Ed Sec officers leaped from the hatch of the Sea King, Greenhaus wondered if Jacqueline Mayakovski had escaped the multi-storey inferno. He could not help feeling admiration and even affection for this serene self-possessed young woman, who had survived the horrors of the recent months with such grace and aplomb. He wished he'd paid greater attention during her earlier conversational gambits, about everyday hobbies like cycling or swimming or handicrafts. A gun barrel prodded his left pectoral. He didn't resist as two burly Australian Ed Sec orderlies grabbed his arms, while a thin lizard-faced medic searched for a vein in his scabbed flesh. As the needle sank in, the gannet-like screaming of the children slowly faded like a huge panoramic sweep of white noise; and the whine of the helicopter turbines sank to a diminuendo. He looked up. It was almost dawn. Light was breaking against the black towers, bursting through the terraced citadels of indigo cloud, and against the light he could perceive motion, avian movement, the beat of angelic wings. In her flimsy hand-made craft of paper and wood, the ornithoptric bird-woman of the art room was rising on the thermals of the burning school, far above the all-consuming flames of the Impossibility Exhibition, towards her reborn paradises in the forests of the South.

ANA BARRADO
Family Outing, Spaceport USA, 1991

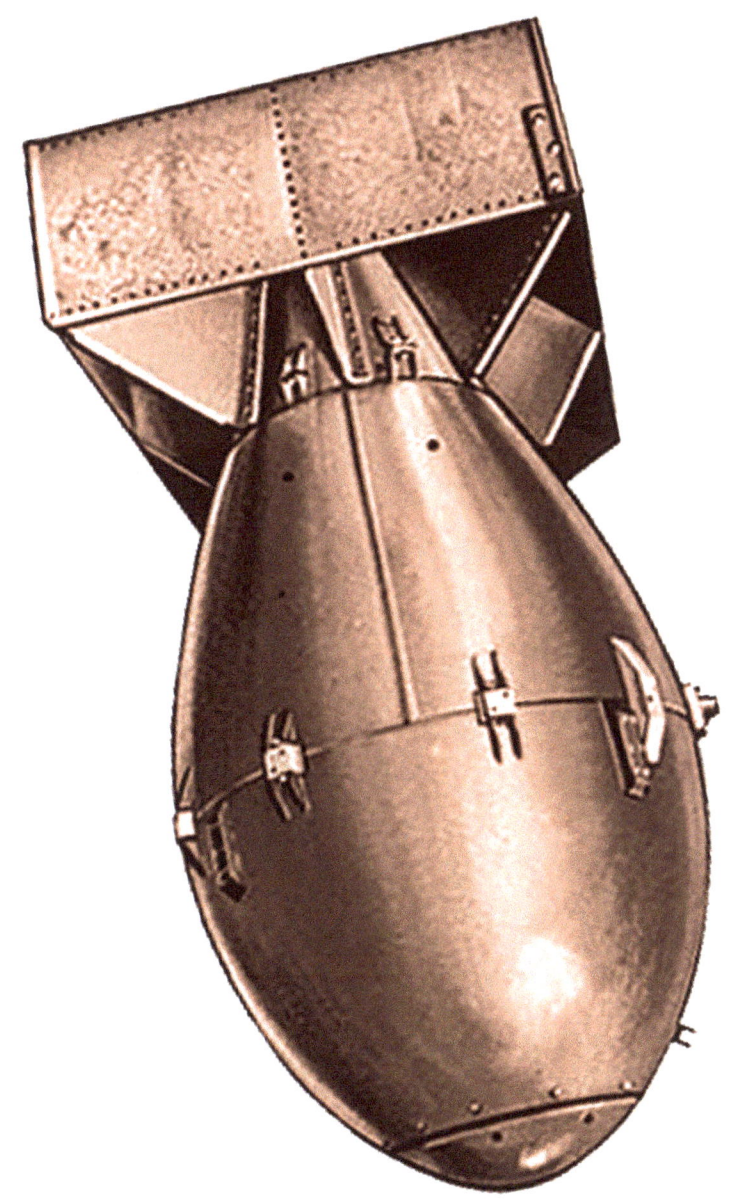

J.G.B. U.X.B.

by Toby Litt

A few years ago, in the Afterword to a collection of essays on Ballard's writing —produced after a two-day conference on his work—I proposed a thought experiment. "We have," I said, "got JG Ballard wrong. The whole lot of us." JG Ballard wasn't a writer at all. He was an obsessive, lifelong tunneller.

"Beneath the gloriously shabby house in Shepperton there exists a vast network of steel-lined passages, taking the form of a pyramid.

"Through this three-dimensional maze, for that is what it is, only Ballard knows his way.

"Only Ballard knows his way because, extravagant as it may seem, Ballard is the only human being ever to have entered these tunnels.

"The great pyramid-maze has been excavated single-handedly over the course of the past forty-seven years.

"Entered through a small padlocked trapdoor, located immediately beneath Ballard's desk, it is the reason Ballard moved to Shepperton in the first place; it is the reason—of course, there must be a reason—why he has never moved."

Ballard's books, I suggested, were written solely to fund (and to provide cover for) his tunnel-building mania.

But I have realised that this misexplanation for Ballard's work will no longer do.

The gloriously shabby house in Shepperton has been thoroughly gone over by estate agents, and no tunnel has been discovered.

But the problem of us—the lot of us—getting Ballard wrong still remains. We are becoming just a little too chummy with a fixed image of Jim. We think we know him so well, just as he (at times) seemed to think he knew himself.

I'm thinking, for example, of his 1983 interview with Charles Shaar Murray: *I would guess that a large part of the furniture of my fiction was provided ready-made from that landscape: all those barren hotels and deserted beaches, empty apartment blocks... the whole reality of a kind of stage set from which the cast has exited, leaving one with very little idea of what the actual play is about. All of that comes straight from the landscape of wartime Shanghai, and remember that the war there started in '37 when the Japanese invaded China and ringed the international settlement where I lived.*

I'm thinking, for example, of the disastrous final paragraph of his 1995 introduction to *Crash*: *Needless to say, the ultimate role of Crash is cautionary, a warning against that brutal, erotic and overlit realm that beckons more and more persuasively to us from the margins of the technological landscape.*

I want to go back, and plead with him, even in the form of a cliché—'Never apologise, never explain.'

Ballard was once a horribly explosive force; now he too often is presented as a defused bomb —something for the children to climb on, outside the Imperial War Museum. And so I'd like to propose another thought experiment. I'd like to tell an alternative story. I'd like to put my ear against the bomb and listen closely, just to see whether it might not still be ticking.

It is February 1945. We are in the Lunghua Civilian Assembly Center, eight miles southwest of the center of Shanghai, with a fourteen year-old boy named Jim. The concrete lowrises and close-packed khaki tents are Jim's domain, and he moves through the humid air with all the sheen and directness of a guided missile.

This Jim is an unusual boy—unusually mature

for his age, given what he's seen, but unusually naïve, given what's been kept from him.

Jim has been interned, along with his family, by the Japanese —and he is certainly aware that all across China the occupying Japanese forces are engaged in battles with the valiant soldiers of the Chinese Red Army.

Jim often overhears the grown-ups talking about "Communism," usually disparagingly.

But one of them, a young man of 25 who—for the sake of protecting his identity—we shall call Phillip... but Phillip speaks up for the bravery and idealism of the International anti-fascist struggle.

Phillip is neither handsome nor charismatic; he wears a pair of steel-rimmed glasses, although one of the lenses is cracked. He stammers, when put under pressure by his right-wing elders. Cambridge educated, Phillip is a very polite young English gentleman. But Phillip, beneath this, is full of passionate political commitment.

Jim has never seen this before, and it fascinates him. He starts to dog Phillip's heels, to try to get Phillip talking, to ask Phillip about this thing "Communism."

And, once Phillip realises Jim is serious—isn't just hoping to humiliate him—Phillip begins Jim's political education.

At great risk to himself, Phillip has managed to preserve a copy of Lenin's *What Is To Be Done?* and one of *The Communist Manifesto*.

He refuses to let Jim borrow them, but together—secretly— they go through each book, line by line.

Jim will later attempt to paint over his lifelong conversion to Marxist-Leninism with a thick gloss of pro-Americanism—and in this he will unwittingly be aided by the American film director Steven Spielberg ("P-51, the Cadillac of the Skies!").

However, following his early engagement with the absolute radicalism of Phillip, the rest of Jim's life will be dedicated to exposing the violent, perverse and repressive nature of Western Capitalist Imperialism.

Secretly, of course. It would not do for his ultimate motives to become known. Ballard must always keep his deadpan.

The adult Jim will write numerous essays, novels and short stories, will give almost countless interviews, all in a tireless attempt to weaken the foundations of Western Capitalist Imperialism.

Among the most notorious of these texts, and perhaps a step to far even for such a sophisticated subversive as Jim, will be *The Assassination of John Fitzgerald Kennedy Considered As a Downhill Motor Race*—a text explicitly intended to satirize and expose to ridicule the sacred position of the President of the United States of America.

In forwarding his secret mission, Jim will consort with other known anti-Imperialists— notably William S. Burroughs. But even to these intimates, he will give no hint of his true motivations, and make no mention of what he really learnt in the Lunghua Civilian Assembly Center in February 1945.

Thought experiment ends. Ridiculous—of course. Utterly ridiculous. Old Jim Ballard of Shepperton a bloody Commie? a fifth columnist?— get orft. Jim was sound as a pound —voted Thatcher — loved the Yanks. But put your ear closer to the bomb—the bomb packed with material as explosive as *The Atrocity Exhibition* and *Crash*... ...put your ear closer... tick, tick, tick. tick...

www.ingramcontent.com/pod-product-compliance
Lightning Source LLC
Chambersburg PA
CBHW041239240426
43661CB00071B/2919